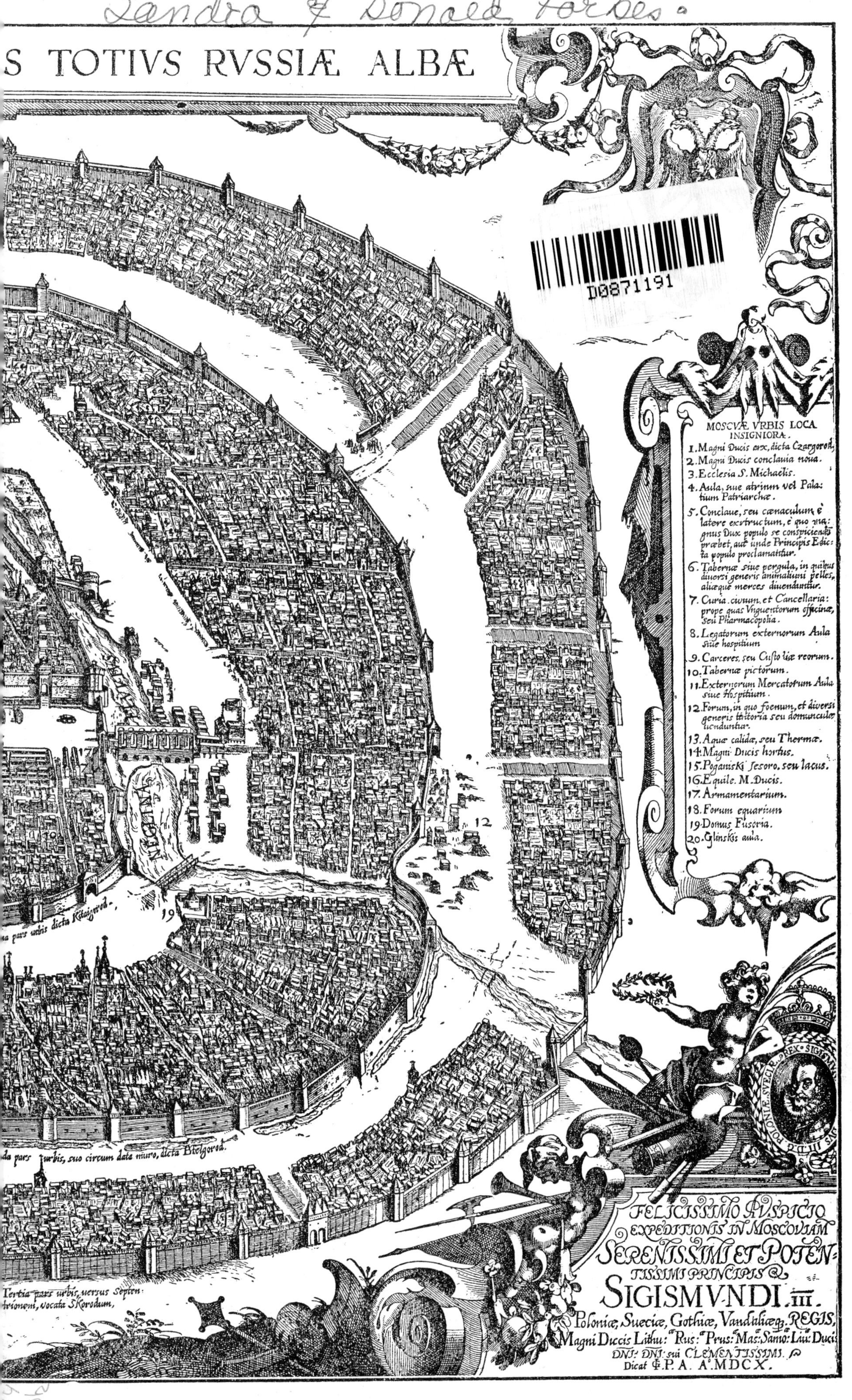
S TOTIVS RVSSIÆ ALBÆ
MOSCVÆ VRBIS LOCA INSIGNIORA.
1. Magni Ducis arx, dicta Czargorod.
2. Magni Ducis conclauia noua.
3. Ecclesia S. Michaelis.
4. Aula, siue atrium vel Palatium Patriarchæ.
5. Conclaue, seu cænaculum è latere extructum, è quo magnus Dux populo se conspiciendū præbet, aut unde Principis Edicta populo proclamatur.
6. Tabernæ siue pergula, in quibus diuersi generis animalium pelles, aliæque merces diuenduntur.
7. Curia ciuium et Cancellaria: prope quas Vnguentorum officinæ, seu Pharmacopolia.
8. Legatorum externorum Aula siue hospitium
9. Carceres, seu Custodiæ reorum.
10. Tabernæ pictorum.
11. Externorum Mercatorum Aula siue Hospitium.
12. Forum, in quo foenum, et diuersi generis tētoria seu domunculæ uenduntur.
13. Aquæ calidæ, seu Thermæ.
14. Magni Ducis hortus.
15. Poganiski Iesoro. seu lacus.
16. Equile. M. Ducis.
17. Armamentarium.
18. Forum equarium
19. Domus Fusoria.
20. Glinskis aula.
NEGLINA
12
19
pars urbis dicta Kitaigorod.
da pars urbis, suo circum data muro, dicta Btelgorod.
Tertia pars urbis, uersus Septentrionem, uocata Skorodum,
FELICISSIMO AVSPICIO EXPEDITIONIS IN MOSCOVIAM
SERENISSIMI ET POTENTISSIMI PRINCIPIS
SIGISMVNDI. III.
Poloniæ, Sueciæ, Gothiæ, Vandaliæq. REGIS,
Magni Duccis Lithu: Rus: Prus: Mas: Samo: Liu: Ducis
DNI: DNI: sui CLEMENTISSIMI.
Dicat Φ.P.A. A°. MDCX.

THE MOSCOW KREMLIN

1

THE ICONOSTASIS IN THE CATHEDRAL OF THE ASSUMPTION

THE MOSCOW KREMLIN

Its History, Architecture, and Art Treasures

by Arthur Voyce

UNIVERSITY OF CALIFORNIA PRESS
BERKELEY AND LOS ANGELES · 1954

UNIVERSITY OF CALIFORNIA PRESS
BERKELEY AND LOS ANGELES, CALIFORNIA

CAMBRIDGE UNIVERSITY PRESS
LONDON, ENGLAND

LIBRARY OF CONGRESS CATALOG CARD NUMBER 54–12167

PRINTED IN THE UNITED STATES OF AMERICA
DESIGNED BY JOHN B. GOETZ

TO RUTH AND DINA

PREFACE

This book is an outgrowth of an interest in Russian architecture and decorative arts that had its origin long ago, during my travels through Russian architectural and art centers and repeated visits to Moscow and the Kremlin. My purpose in this book is to acquaint the Western reader with some of the most notable aesthetic achievements of sixteenth- and seventeenth-century Russia, and to point out a number of little-known aspects of the Kremlin that have contributed to the expansion of political, religious, cultural, and artistic life of Russia.

To the best of my knowledge, the physical changes in the Kremlin within the last thirty-five years have been few and of relatively little architectural importance. A group of old buildings has been replaced by a large office building, a few monuments and the imperial eagles have been removed; but the walls, the towers, and 95 per cent of the churches and palaces remain as they were before the revolution, though they may function in a different capacity. Many of the structures have been repaired and restored to their original medieval state. Some of the cathedrals and churches and their sacristies have become religious museums; some of the palaces function as offices and meeting halls for the higher echelons of the governing party. Most of the collections in the Oruzheinaia Palata museum have been rearranged and enlarged, and some have been removed and placed in other museums. Largely, however, the more important buildings and art collections remain as witnesses of a rich but turbulent past.

The book is not intended to supplant the several voluminous works on the subject that appeared in Russia during the nineteenth and early twentieth centuries. Detailed references have therefore in many cases been omitted; the student is advised to turn to the larger studies mentioned in the bibliography. However, since most of my sources are Russian and not easily available in this country, an attempt has been made to present here the results of the more important research. Data and references to personalities, buildings, and art objects given in monographs or articles that have appeared since the publication of Rikhter's *Monuments of Ancient Russian Architecture,* Solntsev's *Antiquities of the Russian Empire,* and Zabelin's *History of the City of Moscow* have been included to provide access to the latest studies. In choosing the illustrations a similar attempt has been made to use the latest available; but a number of older, less familiar pictures have also been included because of their bearing on the history of the Kremlin as a whole.

Russian names, especially place and monument names, are at best unfamiliar to American readers. The names of the various members of the clergy, princes, and tsars have been transliterated in accordance with the system suggested by the Library of Congress, often including the English equivalent. Whenever a reference is made to a place name of the prerevolutionary period, the original form has been used and the modern form, where applicable, has been given in parentheses. Architectural and art monuments are given in English equivalents as translated from the Russian, and further identified by their Russian names in parentheses.

Much of the research for this volume was done and a large part of the material was collected while I was working on my study of *The Russian Decorative Arts and Crafts,* begun about five years ago on a Slavic Studies Fellowship at the Hoover Institute, Stanford University. During these years I have had many stimulating and helpful discussions with my colleagues at the Hoover Institute and visiting scholars from other universities, who, each in his own way, contributed valuable suggestions. I take this opportunity of expressing my sincere thanks to Professors Harold H. Fisher, Chairman, and Charles Easton Rothwell, Director, of the Hoover Institute; Professors Wallace Stegner and

Charles A. Allen of the English Department, Stanford University; and Professor John N. Hazard of Columbia University—for their advice and moral support.

My grateful acknowledgment for specific help is extended to the following:

The Rockefeller Foundation and the American Philosophical Society, for financial assistance during the years of my fellowship.

The Hoover Institute and Library, for the use of the institute's facilities; to Mr. Philip T. McLean, librarian, for placing the valuable Russian art collection at my disposal.

Mrs. Harold H. Fisher, who read the manuscript chapter by chapter in the draft stage, making many shrewd suggestions as to organization and style and greatly contributing to the final draft of the manuscript.

Mr. Adolph E. Anderson, who, with his keen feeling for essentials and language, exerted a strong influence on the compilation of the text.

Mrs. Inez G. Richardson and Mr. Ernest B. O'Byrne of the Hoover Institute, and Miss Verna F. White, for their coöperation in much detail work.

Mr. B. A. Dubensky of the Hoover Library staff, for assistance in checking the bibliography and transliteration.

Mrs. Ruth Robinson Perry, chief of the Hoover Library Reference Division, and her staff; Mrs. Maria Volkov, Mr. Joseph A. Belloi, Miss Jeannette M. Hitchcock, and Mr. Fred J. Priddle of the Stanford University Library—all of them coöperative participants in search of source material—for their unstinted and ever courteous help.

Miss Lucie E. N. Dobbie, Mr. John H. Jennings, and Mr. John B. Goetz of the University of California Press, for their wholehearted coöperation and sympathetic approach to the many problems involved in the editing and designing of this book.

A. V.

San Francisco

CONTENTS

ILLUSTRATIONS

ILLUSTRATIONS

I

INTRODUCTION

What the Acropolis was to Athens and the Capitolium was to Rome, the Kremlin was to Moscow—it was both the nucleus and citadel of the ancient Russian capital. Today it remains a living page from the distant past of the empire, and is still a word of magic that conjures up visions of the past. Around and about its walls, towers, churches, and palaces are woven innumerable legends and traditions, facts and fairy tales of Russian, Tartar, Lithuanian, Polish, French, and German origin—ballads of chivalry and nobility, treachery and cruelty, stories of heroism and self-sacrifice.

The Kremlin was the nucleus of old Muscovy, the core about which the scattered and feuding principalities were united and consolidated into a powerful state that was to become imperial Russia. Here were born both the concept of absolute monarchy and the desire for political independence; and here—when the Kremlin was nothing more than a rudely fortified village surrounded by a wooden stockade—the Grand Prince Dmitrii Donskoi defied the Tartar Khan Mamai. Within the Kremlin walls have taken place the main events of Russian history: the national disasters brought about by the Tartar invasions, the miseries of the Time of Troubles; the fires and destruction resulting from the French occupation, as well as the momentous events of the more fortunate years—the great deliberative assemblies of the boyars, the solemn convocations of the clergy, and the celebrations of the victories and triumphs over national enemies. The Kremlin was the scene of the wholesale butcheries of Ivan IV, the mutinies of the *strel'tsy*,[1] the struggle for power between young Peter I and his half sister Sophia—the plotting and counterplotting, the tortures and countless murders of the treacherous and treasonable, the faithful and innocent.

Situated in the center of Moscow, on top of a hill whose crown is about 125 feet above the level of the Moskva River, the Kremlin dominates the entire city, and holds within its walls all the memories and souvenirs of the city's past. Reminders of the restless, brooding spirits of its former occupants are everywhere. Within its walls were the cathedrals, the see of the Orthodox faith, the palaces of the tsar, the metropolitan, and the rich and powerful boyars. There also were the state, judicial, and executive offices (*prikazy*),[2] where foreign ambassadors were received, orders issued, and justice administered. The church, the throne, the military and the secular branches of the government—all were represented in the Kremlin by many remarkable edifices.

The Kremlin represented splendor and magnificence: buildings of white stone, rich marbles, varicolored tiles, and shining metals. Surrounded on all sides by walls, rivers, and a moat, it had the appearance of a powerful and picturesque fortress. A prodigious stage *décor,* with reds and golds predominating, painted against the background of the sky, the Kremlin remains an exuberant expression of polychrome decorative architecture, of essentially Russian elements: bulbous cupolas clad in gold and silver; octagonal or square towers giving rise to other towers surmounted by lanterns and slender, tent-shaped pinnacles; bright multicolored roofs producing the effect of enamel inlay; belfries and watchtowers, ramparts, and machicolated battlements; everywhere and above all, imposing on this decorative ensemble a sense of unity and domination, is the obstinate repetition of the Russian bulb motif scintillating in the air like so many balls of fire.

The entire Kremlin is one of the most impressive medieval citadels in the world. With its commanding situation on the banks of the Moskva River, its battlemented walls, varicolored towers and steeples, the variety of its palaces, cathedrals, churches, and belfries with their multitude of gilt or silvered domes—the whole panorama presents a diverse and astonishing unity of ancient and modern works.

Those who have seen it at the first flush of dawn, or have watched its colors fade with the setting sun, will long remember its moving beauty. To the art student the striking and most interesting feature of the Kremlin is the national character of its architecture—liberated from Byzantine traditions but not yet overpowered by Western influences. Here is a vivid illustration of two streams of world art—Eastern and Western infiltrating, modifying, complementing one another, and forming a complete synthesis of world architecture.

For more than two hundred years nothing of great architectural significance was added to the Kremlin. On the contrary, there was a constant process of destruction and vandalism. Additions were made in many styles, alterations and pious "restorations" in questionable taste. Precisely because of its long and colorful architectural history—the continuous participation of native and foreign, often anonymous masters—the Kremlin became the visual embodiment of medieval Russian architectural thought. This is a true product of the ageless creative spirit of the Russian people. It is not surprising that in the second half of the nineteenth century, when the trend toward the Russian Renaissance was at its height, the Moscow Kremlin was an inexhaustible source of architectural inspiration.

II

SITE, PLAN, AND CONSTRUCTION FEATURES

The Kremlin, the architectural core of Moscow, is almost the exact center of the city. On the south is the Moskva River; on the east, the Red Square; on the west, the Alexander Park and a new, wide boulevard. From it radiate, in practically all directions, the great arterial thoroughfares of the capital. Location and historical significance make the Kremlin the very heart of Moscow.

Strictly speaking, the outline of the Kremlin is an irregular pentagon; its sides curve slightly—concavely on the south and convexly on the east and west—and its perimeter is about a mile and a half. More broadly, except for slight irregularities, the outline of the Kremlin can be thought of as an almost equilateral triangle whose southwest angle is obtuse. The topography of its site—at the confluence of the Neglinnaia and Moskva rivers, forming the southwest vertex of the Kremlin triangle—predetermined the development of its plan.

The walls, flanked by towers, are arranged in straight, short lines with definite breaks. Only on the south side, which faces the Moskva River, are the breaks somewhat softened. Here the wall forms a curve that is parallel to the almost crescent-shaped river bend. The top of the south wall is about sixty-five feet above the level of the river. Again and again, under successive shocks of war, the walls and towers have been damaged and rebuilt, but they have remained substantially unchanged in form. Moscow was burned by the Russians to resist Napoleon; yet most of the Kremlin remained unharmed, for the devouring fires did little else than scorch the towers.

The present surrounding high wall is studded with nineteen towers: three massive circular towers—one at each angle of the triangle; five steepled gate towers; and eleven watch towers and barbicans of various shapes. The interior faces of the Kremlin walls are marked by many shallow-arched niches; and there is strong reason to believe that within these thick walls are many passages, corridors, stairways, and secret chambers of which only a few are known.

The Kremlin fortifications were designed in accordance with theories of military defense that were revolutionized by the invention of gunpowder. The walls are from twelve to sixteen feet thick. The ramparts, about eight feet wide with battlements on the outer side and a low parapet on the inner, are supported on filled-in arches. These ramparts served as battle stations from which showers of arrows were discharged through the embrasures; later they were mounted by the musketeers, riflemen, cannoneers, and their ordnance. Now these ramparts form a pleasant walk around the Kremlin and, at some points, reveal a breath-taking view of the city across the river as well as of the Kremlin plazas and gardens.

For military defense, the walls at certain places were built, not in a straight line, but with slight angular breaks or zigzags. The towers were somewhat advanced beyond the wall line, so that each one of them could be seen from the neighboring towers and all enemy activities could be closely observed. At places most likely to be attacked, the towers were closer together, the distances being calculated so that the attacker could be repulsed by cross fire from the flanking towers. Each tower was designed as a small fortress, independent and self-sufficient. The corner and entrance towers were considered impregnable—the enemy could penetrate them only through a narrow aperture in the roof. All the entrance towers had the additional protection of their barbicans, fronting ing the main gates and connected with them by drawbridges.

The fortifications' firing stations were arranged for three levels of combat fire: upper, middle, and lower. The ground level at the walls and towers was always higher on the inside than on the outside of the walls. The walls, towers, cathedrals, and other structures had underground passages, waterpipes, large vaulted cellars, and storage places for supplies of food, ammunition, and arms.

Fabritsius[1] cites the chronicles of Krekshin (a contemporary of Peter I): "Peter Friazin [Pietro Solario] constructed two barbicans or secret

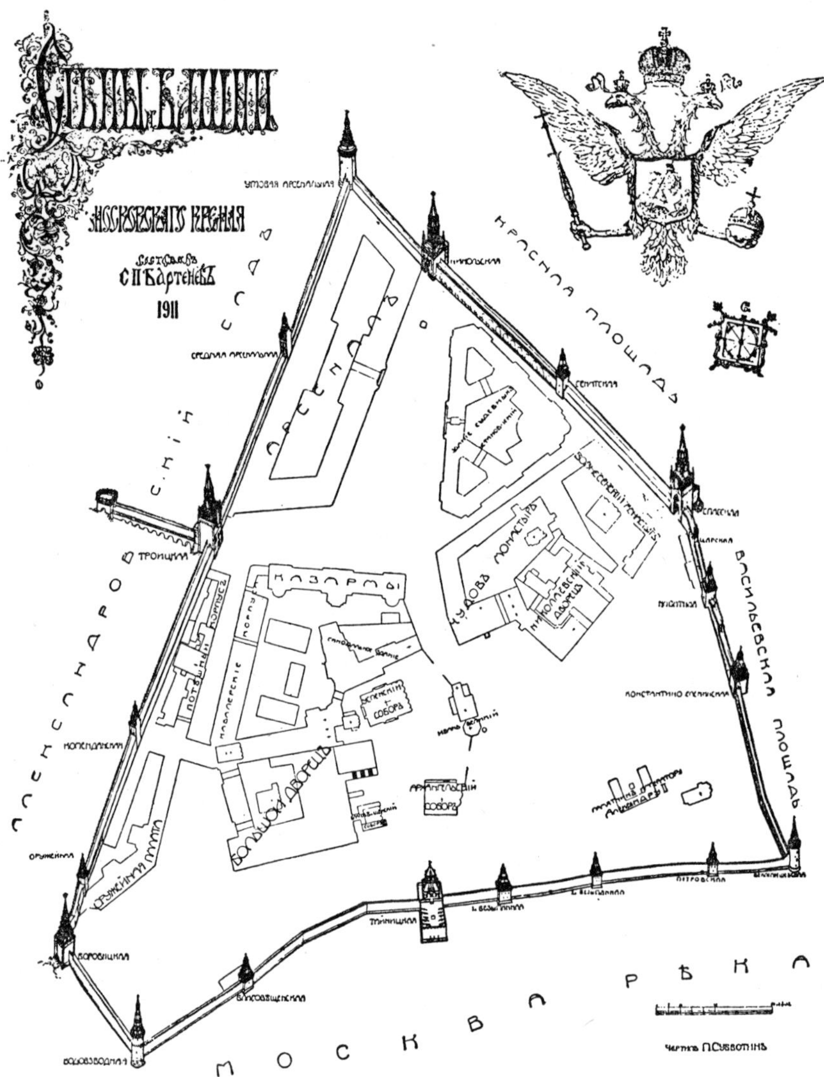

Figure 1. Plan of the Kremlin walls and towers, 1911.

towers and many houses, and he built roads branching off underground. He built an underground water system of masonry conduits, with a water flow like unto rivers through the entire Kreml'-city, to be used during siege." One of the secret passages of Pietro Solario was discovered at the end of the nineteenth century. Starting near the Tainitskaia Tower, it extends throughout the entire Kremlin; leaving the Kremlin walls, in the neighborhood of the Nikol'skaia Tower, it continues under the Alevisian Moat, where it was formerly adjoined by a large mansion; it then turns in the direction of the present 25th of October Street (formerly Nikol'skaia Street). There are indications that another underground passage once extended from the Tainitskaia Tower to Razin Street (formerly Varvarka), passing under St. Basil's Church. These underground passages were used by the embattled and besieged garrison to make their surprise sorties and attacks or to spy on the enemy activities.

The walls follow the topographical contours of the ground and therefore at some places wander up and down the hill, adding to the uniqueness and picturesqueness of the fortress. The rigid, strictly geometrical plans of Western fortresses are absent here. Instead of adapting and shaping the ground to some preconceived rectangular or octagonal plan, the Russian planners of the Kremlin visualized and designed its ensemble as an integral part of the location. They blended it with the hill and the curves and bluffs of the Moskva and Neglinnaia rivers.

Within the walls the plan is extremely interesting. The elevated plateau, reaching the line that extends from the Borovitskiia and Spaskiia gates, breaks and forms a sharp escarpment visible from across the river and from the bridges. On the brow of this hill a great esplanade and the best architectural monuments of the Kremlin were developed. The Arkhangel'skii, Blagoveshchenskii, and the Uspenskii cathedrals, the Belfry of Ivan the Great, the white buildings with their gilt cupolas, the green declivity with the walls at the very edge of the river—all together they create an unforgettable sight.

III

HISTORICAL BACKGROUND

At the beginning of the twelfth century the political center of Russia began to shift toward the east. Under pressure by the nomads of the steppes, the Russians began to migrate from the lands of the Dnieper basin to the forest regions of the upper Volga.

The Russian colonization of the Volga began in the eleventh century. Rostov, Suzdal', Iaroslavl' on the Volga, and Vladimir on the Kliazma were all founded in this epoch. The greatest colonizing activity, however, dates from the middle of the twelfth century, when the various settlements coalesced into the principality of Vladimir-Suzdal', opening the Moscow era.

On the wrecks of the Kievan state a new Russia was born, and perhaps it is significant that the largest cities of this new Russia carry the names of the cities of southern Russia: Vladimir, Iaroslavl', Pereiaslavl'. The settlers from the Dnieper region brought with them their cultural traditions, popular songs, and epic poems (*byliny*).[1]

The ethnic, social, and political structure of the Vladimir-Suzdal' region was quite different from that of Kiev, and this divergence became

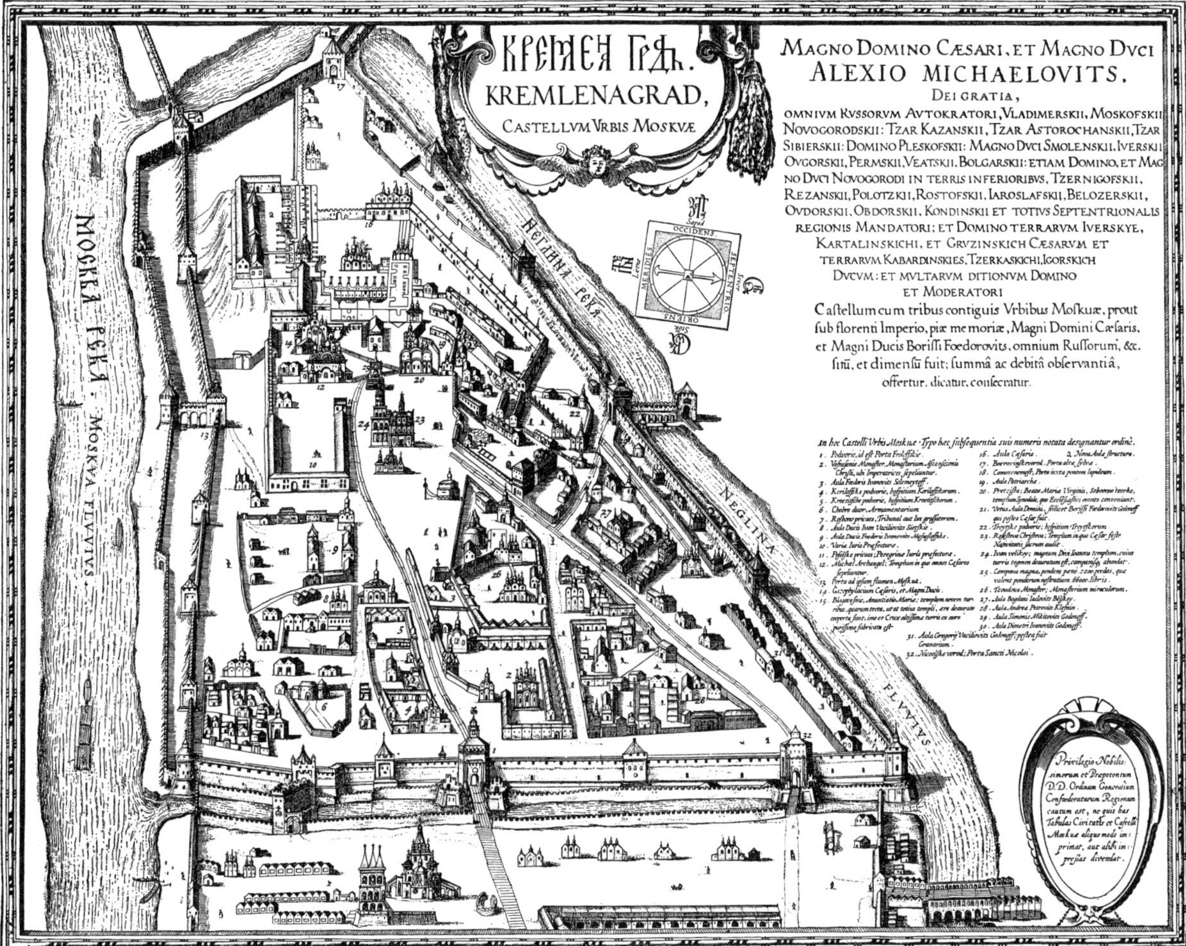

2

PLAN OF THE KREMLIN IN THE REIGN OF BORIS GODUNOV

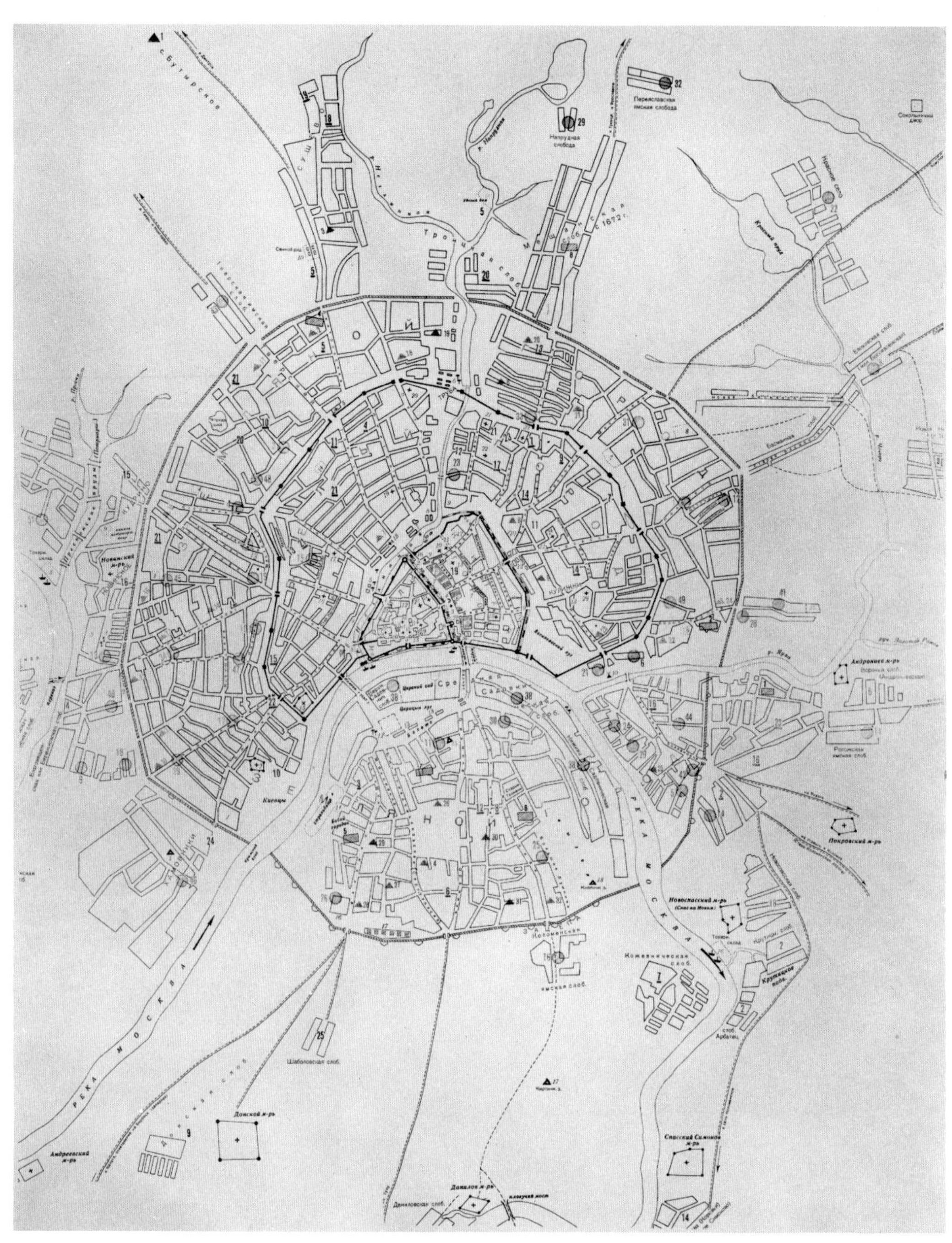

3

MOSCOW IN THE MIDDLE OF THE SEVENTEENTH CENTURY

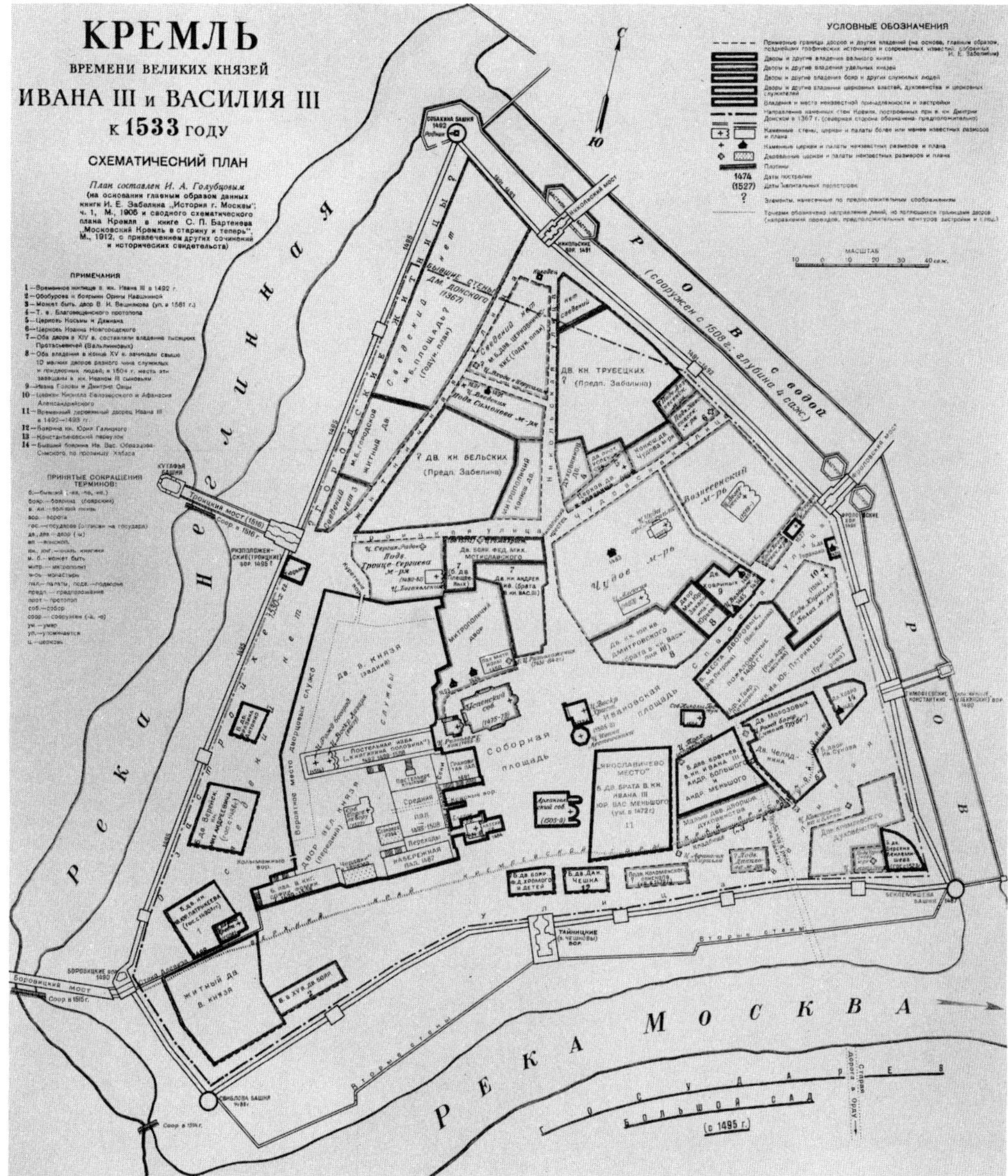

4

THE KREMLIN ABOUT 1533

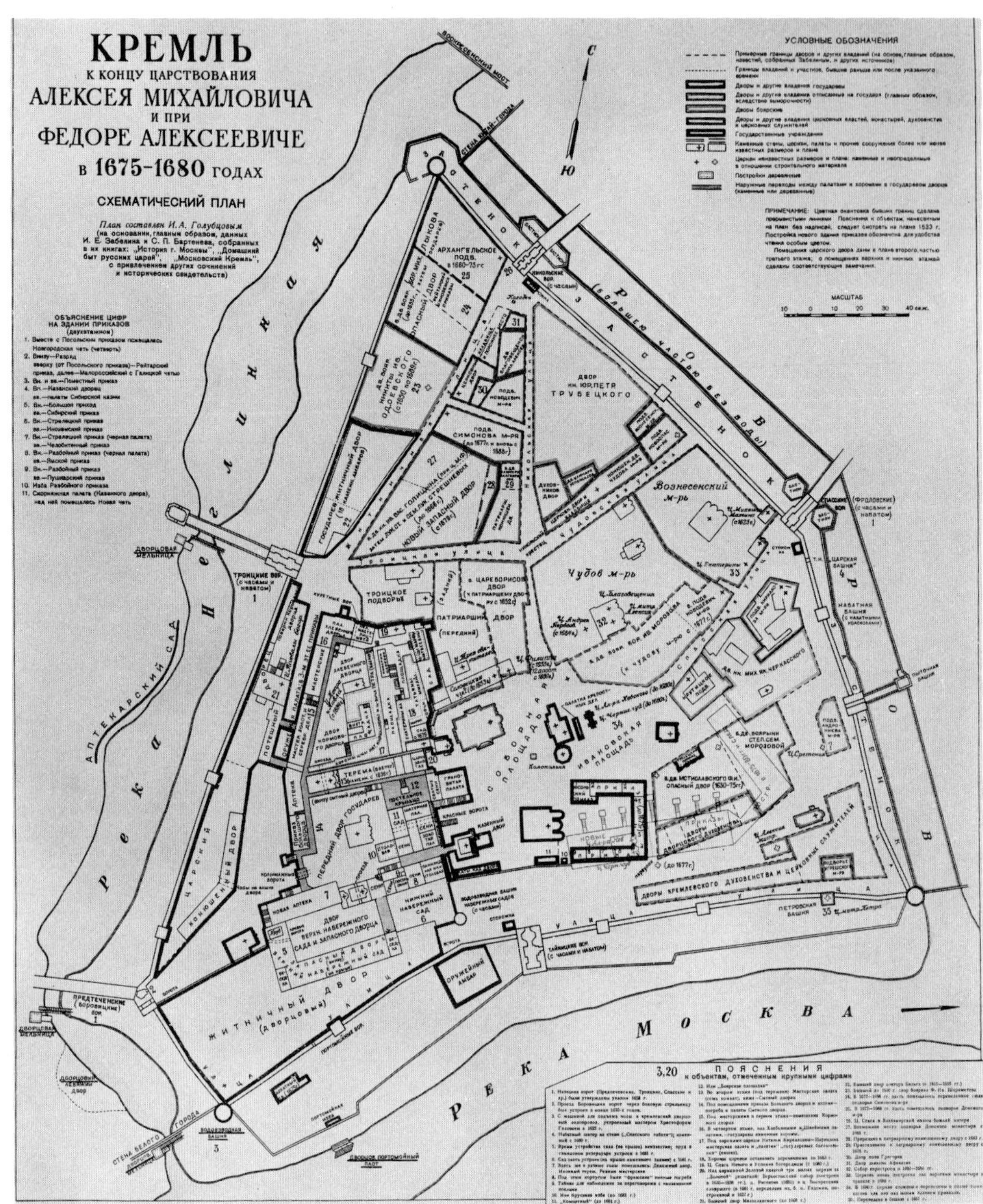

5

THE KREMLIN NEAR THE END OF THE SEVENTEENTH CENTURY

6

THE KREMLIN FROM THE MOSKVORETSKII BRIDGE

7

MODEL OF THE SEVENTEENTH-CENTURY KREMLIN

8

DMITRII IVANOVICH DONSKOI

9

IVAN THE TERRIBLE

10

IVAN III

even more marked through the economic and cultural influences upon Suzdal'. Commercial activity was carried on by entirely new routes. Relations with Constantinople were limited, and contacts with the Germanic Hansa or with Scandinavia were difficult.

In contrast, there were established, via the Volga and its tributaries, active exchanges with central Asia and the Caucasus. The Volga, on which the Suzdalian princes maintained a fleet, became the great commercial and civilizing route of the new Russia; and as Kiev was naturally drawn by the Dnieper toward Byzantium, Suzdal' was carried by the Volga's course toward Asia.

Moscow was not the first capital of this new Russian state. Until the time of the Tartar invasion Vladimir, on the Kliazma River, was the political, intellectual, and artistic center of the Suzdal' principality. The name of Moscow appears in the Russian chronicles for the first time in 1147. A number of tales speak of the founding of the city. One legend, cited by sixteenth-century Russian chroniclers,[2] says that Moscow was founded by Mosokh, the sixth son of Japhet, and husband of Kva—hence Mos-Kva; Mosokh and Kva had a son named Ia and a daughter named Vuza—hence the name of the Iauza River, which joins the Moskva River a short distance downstream from the Kremlin.

Another curious tale, from the middle of the seventeenth century, repeats the thesis propounded by the Pskov monk Filofei (Philotheus, *circa* 1480) declaring Moscow as the "Third Rome"; one of the monk's premises was that, like the first Rome and the second (Constantinople), Moscow had been built upon blood. This story says that the founder of Moscow, Grand Prince Iurii Dolgorukii, on a visit to the domain of the boyar Kuchko, killed the owner for not showing him proper respect; the grand prince then sent the boyar's sons and beautiful but evil daughter Ulita to Vladimir to his virtuous son Andrei, who married Ulita. Irked by the unresponsiveness of her ascetic husband, Ulita plotted with her brothers and killed Andrei. The murder was avenged, and the evil woman was executed in a horrible manner. The Kuchko brothers, who fled to their father's estate, were seized and executed, and their villages were confiscated. The tale concludes that "God put it in his [Iurii's] heart" to build a city on the site of one of the Kuchko villages on the Moskva River bluff, the very spot where the Kremlin now stands, and thus the city of Moscow was founded.[3]

For more than a century Moscow remained an obscure town of the Suzdal' province. The chroniclers do not allude to it except to mention that it was attacked and burned by the Tartars under Batu in 1237. The real founder of the principality and the dynasty of the Moscow princes was Daniel, a son of Alexander Nevskii, who had received this small town and a few villages as his *udel*[4] (appanage).

The city of Moscow (*Gorod* or *Grad Moskva*)[5] was formed around the fortified triangle—the estate of the reigning prince. The settlement was a nodal point at the crossing of the south-north and east-west trade routes, and its location was ideally suited for defense from attacks. Special fortifications were extended later from a point upstream on the Neglinnaia River to the Moskva River, thus forming the east side of the triangle and guarding the fortress at its most vulnerable point. The Kremlin of Pskov was built on a similar location between the Velikaia and Pskova rivers, as was the Kremlin of Iaroslavl' between the Volga and Kotorosl' rivers.

The expansion of ancient Russian cities was often effected by extending the walls along the rivers and building successive, concentric walls around the new quarters. Pskov and Moscow both grew in this manner. In the reign of Prince Ivan Kalita[6] (1327-1341) most of the buildings, surrounding walls, and defense towers of Moscow were constructed of heavy oak timbers—thus the city became an oak city (*grad dubovyi*). The existence of ditches in 1156 and the remnants of the oaken stockades of 1339, discovered in the nineteenth century, point to the extension of the city precisely in the direction of the future Red Square—toward the east.

The word Kremlin—or, to be exact, *Kreml'*—appears for the first time in 1331 in connection with the report of the Moscow fire. Then for nearly two hundred years the word disappeared from the chronicles and historical documents. Until 1367, when the walls were still wooden, the settlement was called *gorod* (fenced-in town). When a wall was built around the adjoining settlement of Belgorod (White City) in 1589, the name *Kreml'*[7] was reëstablished and became permanent.

During the past six centuries the appearance of the Kremlin has changed many times. All the epochs of Russian history have left their imprint on this congregation of heterogeneous buildings, in the construction of which Ivan Kalita, Ivan III, Catherine II, and Nicholas I all collaborated.

The history of the Kremlin can be divided into three principal stages: the primitive wooden Kremlin; the "Italian" Kremlin of the times of the Renaissance; and the modern Kremlin, to which Catherine II added buildings in the pseudoclassic style (notably the Senate Building) and which Nicholas I further muddled by the construction of the huge mass of the Grand Palace (Bol'shoi Kremlevskii Dvorets) in pseudo-Russian style.

Of the Kremlin of the fourteenth century nothing remains except the small Church of the Saviour in the Forest *(Spas na Boru)*, encased as a relic within the court of the Grand Palace. The other churches, built in the reign of Ivan Kalita, were all reconstructed by Ivan III.

Though by no means the oldest of medieval Russian fortresses (*detintsy*),[8] the Moscow Kremlin is one of the outstanding and most colorful. Its construction was a new and important page in the history of Russian fortification architecture, and its influence on the civil as well as ecclesiastical architecture of Russia was far-reaching. All the succeeding fortification structures of the various cities and monasteries imitated the Kremlin in one way or another—for example, the Kremlins of Tula, Kolomna, Gorkii, Zaraisk, Smolensk, Iaroslavl', and a few others that have not survived (Mozhaisk, Kozal'sk).

The history of the Kremlin and of Moscow is closely interwoven with the engrossing story of the steady growth of the principality's power under the domination of the Mongol horde.[9] Around the Moscow principality a new state was organized. A dynasty of rival princes grew up—hard, cunning, and persevering—who continued their personal feuds, brother fighting brother, hoarding wealth in their treasuries, and administering their states as private possessions. A few giant figures among them were destined to become the founders and builders of the Moscow state, the future Russian Empire.

It is not the purpose of this book to follow the political history of Moscow. However, a few of the more important events and significant personalities, insofar as they influenced the construction and growth of the Kremlin, must be singled out.

Ivan Danilovich Kalita, Grand Prince of Moscow (1327-1341), obtained from the Mongol horde (*circa* 1328) the title of *Velikii Kniaz* (Grand Prince). Later he also managed to wheedle out an appointment, as general tax collector for the Tartars, thus rapidly increasing his wealth as well as his power. Kalita, whom Karamzin called the "Consolidator of Russia,"[10] extended the territory of the principality of Moscow by constant and well-considered purchases and other acquisitions, a policy continued by his successors. The city of Vladimir was still the legal capital of Russia; but Moscow had become the real capital, and Kalita was endeavoring to obtain legal recognition of the fact. The Metropolitan of Vladimir, Peter[11] (1305-1326), who had an affection for Moscow, often resided there. His successor, Feognost (Theognostus), established himself there completely. Then the Holy See, and with it the religious supremacy that had first belonged to Kiev and later to Vladimir, moved to Moscow. The rise of Moscow to the position of a political center, as well as the enhanced importance of the Kremlin, is largely the result of its becoming the center of religious life.

Kalita did all in his power to give Moscow the prestige of a great metropolis. He built the first masonry churches in the Kremlin— the Cathedral of the Assumption, the Cathedral of Archangel Michael, the Church of Ioann Lestvichnik,[12] and finally the Church of the Saviour in the Forest—and also rebuilt the Kremlin walls. In place of the aging and flimsy pine stockade, he erected massive walls and towers of huge oak timbers.[13]

Kalita's grandson, Dmitrii Ivanovich Donskoi (1363-1389), was the first Russian prince who had the audacity and the organizing ability to defy and defeat the Tartars. The memorable battle of Kulikovo[14] (the Field of Woodcocks) on the Don (1380), which gained for Dmitrii his surname of Donskoi, proved to the Russians that the dreaded enemy was not invincible.

In 1367 Prince Donskoi laid the foundation for the stone walls of the "city" of Moscow, (that is, the Kremlin) and proceeded to push the building operations with great vigor. The new stone walls were erected at an average distance of 220 feet beyond the old wooden walls, thus considerably enlarging the area of the city.

The new walls and towers of Moscow were built of white cut stone, following the building techniques prevailing in the Suzdal' principality (two revetments filled with rubble). A moat was dug around the walls; the gates were iron-clad, and battlements were erected on the walls, their embrasures protected by heavy wooden shields (*zaboroly*); artillery was soon installed on the Kremlin ramparts.

The stone Kremlin, even more than the wooden, reflected the growing political importance of Moscow. The strength of the walls and the security offered within them were a very potent factor in the rise of the grand prince's authority over the lesser princes and boyars[15] and the various lower classes of the populace. The Nikonian chronicles remark that after the construction of the Kremlin was completed, the grand prince of Moscow proceeded "to impose his will upon all the Russian princes."

The Kremlin soon proved its worth as a defensive fortress. When Ol'gerd, Prince of Lithuania—goaded by his brother-in-law Prince Mikhail of Tver'—marched to the very walls of the Kremlin with a large army in 1368, he did not even attempt to storm the new fortress. Two years later he returned; this time, after having spent eight days in futile attempts to penetrate the defenses, he sued for peace. Dmitrii Donskoi granted him only an armistice. "It would be quite right to say," remarks

Zabelin, "that the stone walls of Moscow became the glorious buttresses which very soon inspired a sharp and direct turn to the idea of state unity. This idea of unity found its practical expression, some ten years later, in the gathering within the walls of 'Whitestone' Moscow of regiments from all over Russia for their march to the field of Kulikovo."[16]

In 1382 the Tartar Khan Tokhtamysh succeeded in penetrating the defenses of the Kremlin. The Tartars burned the Kremlin and destroyed everything around it, including the most precious documents and the oldest archives of the principality; they massacred about 24,000 persons of all ages—this was Tokhtamysh's revenge for the defeat the Mongols suffered at Kulikovo.

The city was quickly rebuilt. New large mansions of wood and stone made their appearance. The contemporary chronicles and other documents speak of the stone palace of Prince Vladimir Andreevich (a cousin of Dmitrii Donskoi) decorated with a mural panorama of Moscow by Theophanos the Greek.[17] Prince Donskoi's "golden-roofed" Palace-on-the-Quai (Zlatoverkhii Naberezhnyi Terem), which was gutted and sacked by Tokhtamysh, was rebuilt and luxuriously refurnished by Vasilii I, the son of Donskoi. The newly erected Cathedral of the Annunciation (in the Kremlin) was decorated with frescoes by Theophanos and the Russian painters Prokhor and Andrei Rublev.[18]

At the end of the fourteenth century Moscow consisted of several large districts: the Gorod (city) proper—that is, the walled-in Kremlin; the adjoining Posad, a tradesmen's and artisans' quarter east of the Kremlin walls (surrounded by a masonry wall in 1534-1538, when it became known as Kitai-Gorod);[19] the "Zagorodie," the settlements beyond the city; and the "Zarechie," the settlement on the south side of the Moskva River. As in most medieval Russian cities these settlements were grouped around the Detinets, the citadel of the reigning prince—that is, the Kremlin—forming a series of concentric belts. A number of arterial roads led toward the center from neighboring cities, provinces, and principalities. With the growth of the city these old roads became the principal city streets. Thus in present-day Moscow, Gertsen Street (Herzen, formerly Nikitskaia) was originally the main highway to Novgorod; Gorkii Street (formerly Tver'skaia) was the highway to Tver'; Sretenka led to Iaroslavl'; and Prechistenka was the old road to Smolensk.

In 1366-1367, during the reign of Dmitrii Donskoi, the area of the Kremlin was almost the same as it is today, except that the northeastern corner was somewhat blunted. At the end of the fifteenth century, when the present Kremlin was being built, the Nikol'skaia Tower was moved some distance forward, and a new corner tower, presently known as the

Uglovaia-Arsenal'naia (Corner Arsenal Tower), facing Mokhovaia Street and the Historical Museum, was erected.

When Dmitrii died, the principality of Moscow was by far the largest of the northeastern states. Vladimir, the former capital, had receded into the background, and the importance of Moscow as the national capital was firmly established. A primary cause of the increasing importance of Moscow was its exceptionally favorable geographical position, at a junction of several highways leading from south Russia to the north and from the territories of Novgorod to those of Riazan'. The Moskva River, a tributary of the Oka, gave Moscow access to the great Russian artery, the Volga. The trade route down the Volga to Astrakhan', on the Caspian Sea, was developed, and Russia's relations with the West were maintained through the intermediary of the Genoese colonies of Kaffa and Azov. Moscow soon became the center of international commerce.

The authority of the Golden Horde over the Moscow principality continued for many years after the death of Dmitrii. Dmitrii's successors were sometimes in open rebellion, but more often submitted humbly to the Tartar khans. Submission and a transient acquiescence paid in some ways, for the Tartars undertook to protect Moscow from conquest by her Western neighbors. While Russia, under the Tartar rule, was working out her unity, the Golden Horde, after the death of Tamerlane in 1405, was torn by internal dissensions and dismembered into three khanates, which were soon to disappear from the political scene.

Of the fourteenth-century stone Kremlin, nothing remains. The numerous fires and enemy sieges and sackings destroyed its walls, which had been made of white sandstone—not a very durable building material. Another reason for its short life was the fact that the damaged walls were usually repaired in wood; this was done to such an extent that to one Western visitor, in 1475, the entire Kremlin seemed to be constructed of wood. In 1460 the builder V. D. Ermolin restored a part of the wall extending from the Borovitskiia Gates down to the Moskva River; he also rebuilt the Spas (Saviour's) Tower in white sandstone. This tower, in its 1460 version, has not survived; a poorly preserved stone panel with a carved relief of St. George is the sole remnant.

In the second half of the fifteenth century Russia was still surrounded by the hostile Lithuanian empire on the west, the lands ruled by the Tartars on the east, and the Swedes and the Teutonic knights on the shores of the Baltic. In spite of the century and a half of efforts by the Moscow princes to extend their domains, to unite and consolidate the various principalities into one state, there was still much dissension and strife. Novgorod and Pskov were independent and troublesome. Moscow, with no direct access to the sea, had only intermittent relations with the centers of European civilization. Thus, at the beginning of the Renaissance in Western Europe—the crumbling of feudalism and the rise of powerful states—Russia, just emerging from the Tartar domination, waking up from the long nightmare, found herself still in the Middle Ages. The man who was to liberate his country from the Mongol yoke and bring it closer to the culture of the West was the resourceful and crafty prince Ivan III, the precursor of Ivan the Terrible and Peter the Great.

Ivan succeeded in annexing almost all the hitherto independent principalities and cities of northern Russia—Novgorod, Tver', and the minor appanages on the upper Oka. He was victorious in Lithuania and Livonia, and he acquired territories that had not been included within the boundaries of the old Russia, pushing the frontiers of the new Russia as far as Finland, the White Sea, and the frozen seas of the north, and toward the Ural Mountains on the east.

Ivan III also instituted systematic building operations, developed the mineral riches of his country, and patronized the arts. In addition to his surname, "The Great Gatherer of the Russian Land," *(Velikii Sobiratel' Zemli Russkoi);* he acquired the added "dread" or "terrible" *(grozny).*

An event of the greatest importance, in its influence on Russian social life, art, and architecture, was Ivan's marriage to the Byzantine Princess Zoe, daughter of Thomas Palaeologue (a brother of the last Byzantine emperor), who had, after the fall of Constantinople, taken refuge in Rome at the court of Pope Sixtus IV. The marriage was consecrated in 1472, and Zoe took the name of Sophia Fominichna. With her a multitude of priests, artists, architects, and all kinds of professional people came to Moscow, not only from Rome, but from Constantinople and other cities. They brought with them Greek and Latin books, priceless ancient manuscripts, icons, and ecclesiastical art objects, thus laying the foundation for the great Library and Vestry of the Patriarchs (Patriarshaia Riznitsa). Thus the princely court of Ivan III was introduced to Byzantine court etiquette and the pomp and glitter of a formerly powerful imperial dynasty.

Moscow came to regard itself, not only as an Orthodox kingdom, but as the exclusive Orthodox state and as the depository of the true faith in the world. A number of events outside Russia, coinciding as they did with the consolidation of Russia, made the rulers of Moscow consider themselves the successors of the Byzantine emperors. The first of these events was the Council of Florence[20] (1439), at which the Greeks, hoping to obtain papal help against the Turks, agreed to a union with Rome and recognized the primacy of the pope. The metropolitan of Moscow, the Greek Isidor, gave his assent to the union; but he was deposed by the authorities in Moscow, where no need was felt of seeking favors from the Latins. Somewhat later (1446) the Russian Church was declared autocephalous and independent of the Greek patriarch. This was a decisive step toward national independence and a place at the head of the Orthodox world.

When Constantinople fell to the Turks in 1453, the Russians preferred to regard this catastrophe as God's punishment for the sins committed by Byzantium in having compromised with the Roman Catholic Church at the Council of Florence. Byzantium fell, it was said, because it had broken away from the true faith and had embraced Latinity, leaving the Russian Church the only independent Orthodox Church. Moscow felt itself stronger than ever, proud of its unshakable fidelity to a faith it held unquestionable.

Now that Constantinople (Tsargrad) and all the Eastern states and churches were in the hands of the infidels, Moscow was looked upon by the Russians as the successor to both ancient Israel and Rome. The concept of Moscow as the heir to the Roman and Byzantine empires was first formulated by the Elder (*starets*) Filofei (Philotheus) of the Pskov Monastery of Elezar in his epistle to Grand Prince Vasilii III: "Two Romes have fallen, and the third stands, while a fourth is not to be." ("*Dva Rima padosha, a tretii stoit, a chetvertomu ne byti.*") Relevant legends were revived, and an imperial genealogy was later officially devised, according to which the Rurik dynasty was shown to be descended from Prus, the brother of Augustus Caesar; consequently the ruling dynasty of Russia was of imperial Roman origin. Ivan III's marriage to Zoe added no little to the transfer of primacy from the second Rome to the third. The ruler of Moscow took up the role of successor to the Byzantine emperors and the Roman Caesars, and became the head and protector of the Orthodox faith. For the new arms of Russia he adopted the double-headed eagle of Byzantium, and for dealing with foreign courts the title of tsar was assumed; in internal acts this title was accompanied by the word "*Samoderzhets*" (the counterpart of the Byzantine "*Autokratos*"). The concept of Russia as the new Israel found its final expression in the Book of Degrees of the Imperial Genealogy (*Stepennaia Kniga*) about 1563.[21] In 1589 the idea of Moscow as center of one true faith received its final affirmation when the metropolitan of Moscow was raised to the rank of patriarch with the sanction of the four Eastern patriarchs, who now looked to Moscow and her mighty tsar to protect Eastern Christendom.

As was perhaps to be expected, this period of enthusiasm and quickened spirit was also an inspiring period for Russian architecture. Moscow, having become the metropolis of orthodoxy, the new city of Constantine (a new Tsargrad), and aspiring to rival the older centers of culture, launched a program of building new and magnificent cathedrals, great palaces, and residences commensurate with her international importance.

IV

THE ITALIAN KREMLIN

In the second half of the fifteenth century the "Whitestone" Kremlin (*Kreml' Belokamennyi*), from the days of Prince Donskoi, was aging rapidly and getting a bit shabby. The cathedrals, the prince's palace, and the various mansions were becoming old, dilapidated, crowded, and unfit for the new ceremonial pomp and court functions; they were certainly not worthy of the dignity, the international position, and the wealth of the lord of Moscow.

In 1474, spurred on by his wife, Ivan III sent a mission to Italy headed by one of his boyars,[1] Simeon Tolbuzin, to find the best architectural and engineering talent available. Tolbuzin was able to bring back with him Ridolfo Fieravanti Aristotele of Bologna.[2] Like Leonardo da Vinci, Fieravanti was at once an architect, an engineer, an expert in hydraulics, military fortifications, pyrotechnics, and metal casting. His fame had spread beyond the boundaries of his native land, and many municipalities and reigning dukes were clamoring and competing for his services. Fieravanti declined all invitations in favor of going to Moscow, where, he felt instinctively, were greater opportunities for a full expression of his many and varied talents.

Sixty years of age, in good health, full of energy, and at the very height of his creative talents, in January, 1475, Fieravanti set out for Russia together with the Russian ambassador Tolbuzin. According to the Russian chronicles, he took along with him his son Andrei and his pupil and helper Pietro. The salary agreed upon was ten rubles[3] per month (approximately two silver pounds).

In 1488 Ivan again sent to Italy, this time the Greek brothers Demetrios and Manuel Rhalev, to find architects, jewelers, metalsmiths, and arms manufacturers. These brothers deserve credit for securing the services of another great Italian architect (one of the principal builders of the Kremlin), Pietro Antonio Solario (or Solari) of Milan.

In 1493 another mission, headed by Manuel Doxa Angelov and Daniel Mamyrev, was sent to the court of Ludovico il Moro of Milan. There they persuaded the Milanese architect Alevisio, "Maestro da muro," to work in Moscow. In 1499 Demetrios Rhalev was sent on a second mission to Venice, Rome, and Naples to interview and procure the services of various artists. He came back to Moscow in 1504 at the head of a large group.

Most of the architects rounded up by the various embassies of the Moscow grand prince were northern Italians, hailing mainly from Milan (Marco Ruffo, Solario, Alevisio Novyi). This fact may explain the resemblance of the early sixteenth-century Kremlin walls and towers to those of the castles of northern Italy. The construction of the Kremlin cathedrals and churches was quite a different matter. There, instead of building in the Renaissance style, which, in Western Europe, they masterfully imposed everywhere, these Italians had to follow Russian models and to build as their Russian patrons ordered. The appearance of the Italians in Moscow served only as an incentive and a stimulus that inspired a reaction against the traditions of Byzantine art, and thus served to make Russian art and architecture independent

The son of Ivan III (by his second wife, Sophia), Vasilii (1505–1533), continued his father's traditions and dispatched a mission to Pope Clement VII, asking for coöperation in selecting and hiring architects, technicians, and skilled craftsmen. However, the pope was in no position to give technical help to Moscow at that time, and the mission returned home with only a small number of architects and craftsmen.

Early in the sixteenth century, Italian architects, artists, and artisans began to lose favor with the Russians. Perhaps the main reason for this was the fear of "Latinity," fear of the persistent efforts of the popes to effect a union between the Roman and the Orthodox churches. The Italians were naturally suspected of aiding the pope, and so they were replaced by Germans, English, and Dutch. Not until the eighteenth century, under Peter the Great, was an Italian architect again invited to Russia.

The Italian architects and engineers were put in charge of the Kremlin reconstruction. There are no definite records that Fieravanti participated in the building of the fortifications of the Kremlin; but the facts that he was famed in his day as a specialist in military engineering and that the construction of the new Kremlin was begun during his stay in Russia justify the supposition that he took part in its construction or at least acted as consultant in design. The undertaking of such a large group of masonry structures in the Moscow of that day became possible only after Fieravanti organized a plant for brick manufacturing, taught the Russian builders how to prepare good mortar, and introduced a number of technical building processes.

The principal architects of the Kremlin fortifications as they existed until the seventeenth century were Marco Ruffo (Marco Friazin), who arrived in Moscow about 1480; Pietro Antonio Solario, 1490; Antonio Friazin,[4] 1485; and Alevisio the Milanese, who arrived in 1494. There were other architects, but very little information about them exists. The Italians who worked in Moscow under Ivan III and his successors left a profound impression on Russian civil architecture; the walls and towers of the Kremlin (but not their superstructures) are their work, as is the Granovitaia Palata (the Palace of Facets).

Stonecutting and the manufacturing of brick[5] and mortar were organized on a large scale, and building operations began in earnest. In the spring of 1485 Antonio Friazin started work on the Tainitskaia Tower[6] near the Moskva River. The towers and walls of the south side of the triangle were erected first, because this side seemed most likely to be attacked by the Tartars. In 1487 Marco Friazin (Marco Ruffo) laid the foundation for the southeast circular corner tower, the Beklemishevskaia;[7] one year later Antonio Friazin built a similar corner tower, the Vodovzvodnaia,[8] on the southwest, equipped with a secret underground passage.

In 1490 Pietro Antonio Solario—"architecton," as he is called in the chronicles—erected two towers: one on the west side of the Kremlin near the Borovitskaia, another on the east side near the Konstantinovskaia Tower—and built a wall between the Vodovzvodnaia and Borovitskaia towers. In 1491 he and Marco Ruffo erected two gate towers on the east side of the Kremlin: the Spasskaia (formerly known as the Frolovskaia) and the Nikol'skaia.

In the same year Solario built the wall from the Nikol'skaia Tower to the Neglinnaia River, where in 1492 he erected a circular tower: the Uglovaia-Arsenal'naia (the Corner Arsenal Tower, formerly known as the Sobakina).

This strategically important tower—the last work of Solario—is distinguished by its monumentality and is outstanding as a fortification. In its base the architect included a water reservoir supplied by a seemingly inexhaustible spring that is still active. It is quite possible that Solario's death (*circa* 1492) was the result of a cold he contracted during the construction of this underground water reservoir. Solario's activities in Russia lasted only a short time but were very fruitful. There is good reason to believe that before his death Solario recommended to Ivan III that Alevisio the Milanese should be appointed as his successor in charge of building operations. The fact that negotiations for Alevisio's services were begun in 1493 would seem to substantiate the supposition.

The death of Solario did not put a stop to the construction of the Kremlin. When the fortifications of the east side were finished, work was begun on those along the Neglinnaia River. Before these walls and towers could be erected, some complex preliminary hydraulic work in connection with ground preparation was necessary. The banks of the Neglinnaia had to be shored up and strengthened so that they could withstand the pressure of the proposed huge structures. At the same time it became evident that, for strategic and fire control purposes, it was necessary to clear all existing buildings from a large strip of land along the Kremlin wall. Ivan III issued an order to the effect that the entire area along the proposed wall to the width of some 760 feet should be cleared of the existing graveyard, churches, mansions, and their appurtenances. The clergy and the gentry, naturally, did not relish this order and there was much grumbling and complaining. The Archbishop Gennadii wrote that the removal of existing churches and graveyards was an act of sacrilege. The news and magnified rumors about this "godless" act spread far and wide, causing much trouble for Ivan III.

Before construction of the new fortifications was begun, many fires broke out; these were interpreted by the populace as a sign of God's wrath, as punishment for removing the holy edifices and disturbing the bones of the dead. Ivan III, however, continued the building operations with great vigor. Alevisio the Milanese was in charge of preparing the ground work—excavating, draining, and strengthening the foundations for the proposed towers and walls, as he later supervised the building of the walls and towers. In 1495 the foundations for the last wall were laid; but not until 1499 were the wall itself and the Troitskii Gates and Tower—the last link in the chain of defenses—completed. The stone triangle of the Kremlin's battlemented enclosure became a reality. The area of the Kremlin had expanded to its present size: sixty-five and a half acres.

At the same time extensive construction had been going on inside the walls. The Pskov architects (unfortunately anonymous to us) were working on the Cathedral of the Annunciation (Blagoveshchenskii Sobor) from 1483 to 1489. In 1487 Marco Ruffo laid the foundation for the Palace on the Quay (Naberezhnaia Palata); in 1491, in association with Pietro Solario, Ruffo finished the construction of the Palace of the Facets (Granovitaia Palata).

In 1493, after having finished the series of buildings intended for formal court functions, the architects of Ivan III began work on the private living quarters of the prince. In July, 1493, a large fire broke out. In a few hours the entire capital became an ash heap, and Ivan had to seek shelter in the village of Podkopaevo. The devastation was so great that the building of the palace was postponed until the spring of 1499. For protection from possible future fires, Alevisio the Milanese built the inner Kremlin wall extending from the Borovitskiia Gates to the court of the grand prince (abutting the apartments of Grand Princess Sophia), thus separating the palace proper and its many service and storage buildings from the rest of the Kremlin.

The construction of the palace took several years. During this time the foundation for the new Cathedral of Archangel Michael (Arkhangel'skii Sobor) was laid, under the supervision of another newly arrived architect, Alevisio Novyi.

At the same time many other masonry buildings were being erected in the Kremlin by the higher dignitaries of the church, wealthy boyars, and merchants. Ivan III witnessed with great satisfaction the removal of the old crumbling *khoromy* (mansions) of his forefathers and predecessors—buildings identified with the unhappy years of servitude and degradation. The Court of the Tartar Khans—the building used to house the ambassadors of the "Golden Horde," identified with so many humiliating experiences—was torn down. With the elimination of these material symbols of servility Ivan could look forward to a united Russia, a sovereign state free to make contacts with the West, to establish treaties on an equal footing, to exchange ambassadors with the centers of Western culture, and to invite the badly needed artists, architects, engineers, and technicians.

Thus at the beginning of the sixteenth century the Kremlin was growing rapidly in strength, grandeur, and beauty. Ivan III died in 1505; and the reconstruction of the Kremlin was completed in the reign of his son, Vasilii III.

In 1508 Vasilii III moved into the recently completed palace. At the same time, according to the Nikonian chronicle, "he instructed Alevisio to dig a ditch along the east side of the Kremlin wall, face its banks with stone and brick, dam up the Neglinnaia River, and build reservoirs around the town" (that is, the Kremlin). And so along the Red Square, known until the middle of the seventeenth century as the *Pozhar*,[9] a deep moat was built, extending from the Neglinnaia River to the Moskva River. Several dams were constructed along the Neglinnaia, and a number of extensive reservoirs were dug in the vicinity. Thus it became possible to fill the moat with water and connect the Neglinnaia River, from a point above its mouth, with the Moskva River. During the recent excavations made in connection with the construction of the Moscow subway, it was discovered that the water was diverted to the moat from the reservoirs through an underground canal located underneath the present Revolution Square. Somewhat later the remnants of the ancient dam were discovered at a point below the Corner Arsenal Tower of the Kremlin. Extending from this dam some old brick-and-white-stone work was found facing the old water reservoirs and canal. An indication of the magnitude of the works can be gained from the size of those ancient bricks—each one of them weighing 40 kilograms, as much as nine modern bricks.[10] The moat was from thirty-one to forty-two feet deep and from one hundred to 120 feet wide. Low battlemented walls extended along both sides of the moat which was spanned by drawbridges at the Spasskiia and Nikol'skiia gates. The Kremlin thus became an island fortress.

At the same time other defensive elements were added. An additional brick wall of a lesser height was constructed along the Moskva River, and two walls were built along the Alevisian moat. Additional towers were erected opposite the Secret Tower (Tainitskaia), Trinity Tower (Troitskaia) and the Konstantinovskaia—each connected with its opposite by bridges. Alongside the Saviour's (Spasskaia) Tower there were two bastions. All these additional defensive elements were removed in 1801, with the exception of the Kutaf'ia Tower and the bridge that connects it with the Trinity Tower.

The Italians introduced a new concept of the fortress wall, quite different in character from that of the old Russian white-stone Kremlins or *Detintsy*. The very fact that stone was given up in favor of brick indicated a revolution in Russian building technique. Henceforth stone was to be used for wall bases, decorative bands, cornices, and various ornamental features. The brick walls were laid straight up, and in the seventeenth century, by order of Tsar Feodor Alekseevich, were heavily whitewashed (the present red hue of the Kremlin walls is not in keeping with the original color scheme). The graceful rise of the walls and towers is the result, not only of the fine proportions and slenderness of their architectural elements, but also of the special bricklaying technique employed.

In 1625 the English builder and clockmaker Christopher Halloway[11] built the upper stories and tent-shaped roof of the Spasskaia Tower; in 1636 the upper stories of the Kolymazhnaia Tower[12] (over the entrance gates to the front court of the Terem Palaces) were constructed; and between 1672 and 1686 all the other towers, with the exception of the Nikol'skaia, received their decorative roofs. In 1680 the small Tsar's Tower (Tsarskaia Bashnia) was built over the wall between the Petrovskaia and Blagoveshchenskaia towers. The stately but stern-looking Kremlin fortress, as depicted on the Godunov Plan (*circa* 1600), became the very decorative and picturesque ensemble of buildings shown on the engravings and drawings of the eighteenth and nineteenth centuries.[13]

11

THE SAVIOUR'S TOWER

12

THE ARMORY TOWER

13

THE FOREST TOWER

14

THE TRINITY TOWER

15

THE WATER-PUMPING TOWER

16

THE BEKLEMISHEV TOWER

V

TOWERS AND GATES

The sixteenth-century Kremlin had, on certain of its more vulnerable sides, double and triple walls battlemented and studded with towers, barbicans, drawbridges, and all the appurtenances of a medieval fortress. As a military stronghold it was fully as powerful as the fortified castles of Milan and Metz, and was as much larger, without the dour, forbidding appearance of the latter. The newly erected cathedrals with their shining cupolas, the elegant palaces, picturesque *terema* with their observation platforms, lanterns, and varicolored roofs gave the fortress the appearance of a fairy-tale town long before the storied superstructure—the "tents," spires, and lucarns—were added to the towers in the seventeenth century.

Each tower is composed of two principal parts: a massive square or circular base erected in the reign of Ivan III and a superstructure added to it at the end of the seventeenth century.

The bases differ in size and proportions; but in all them, especially in the square towers, there are certain similarities of exterior appearance as well as of their inner structure.

The differences are more apparent in the superstructures, whose forms and architectural treatment are quite varied. Some of the superstructures are especially notable—for example, that of the Petrovskaia Tower among its sister gateless towers, and the terraced one of the Borovitskaia Tower among the gate towers. The remaining towers differ greatly, but close examination reveals a definite interrelationship and a well-studied, systematic orderliness in their architectural concept.

All the five Kremlin gate towers—the Saviour's (Spasskaia), Trinity (Troitskaia), Nikol'skaia, Borovitskaia, and the Secret (Tainitskaia)[1]—are composed of two elements: the main tower with its superstructure, and a barbican tower in front covering and protecting the entrance gates.

The base elements of the main towers (erected during the reign of Ivan III), in their exterior appearance and inner layout, are designed in accordance with a scheme common to all the towers except the Secret (Tainitskaia) and the Borovitskaia in part. Their superstructures, which constitute a later addition to all the towers except the Trinity, differ from each other to such an extent that it is difficult to find any definite similarity. The same can be said of the barbican towers—all five, without exception, differ sharply from each other.

The most remarkable of the entrance gate towers is the Saviour's Tower (Spasskaia Bashnia)[2] rising above the main entrance to the Kremlin. A small two-story barbican annex tower at the front of the structure formerly served as vanguard blockhouse. The Saviour's Tower is marked by Russian and Latin inscriptions, indicating the name of the architect and date of construction: "Built by Pietro Antonio Solario, the *Mediolanets* (the Milanese) in 1491." The first story of the barbican tower serves as a porte-cochere. The second houses a covered gallery, encircling the open passageway. Over this gallery, at the third-story level of the main tower, is an open terrace protected by a battlemented parapet.

The Saviour's Gates (Spasskiia Vorota), across from St. Basil's Church, are so named because of the image of Christ painted on the wall over the entrance. A handsome lantern formerly hung in front of the gilded frame around the image, and candles were zealously kept burning in it day and night.

Over the gates rise the ten-story main tower and steeple. The long, vaulted entrance, passing through the barbican tower and through the substructure of the main tower, is decorated with seventeenth-century frescoes that are a mixture of Italian Renaissance ornamental elements and Oriental motifs. The tower's foundation, rectangular in plan, is massive at its base and double-walled; the space between the walls houses a stone stairway supported on Gothic vaulting. The tower, the original part of which was built in 1491, is the tallest (238 feet) and the handsomest of the Kremlin's nineteen towers. In 1625, in place of the original battlements, a superstructure of storied galleries, balconies, and decorative parapets, a slender octagonal belfry rising out of a square base, and an open arcaded lantern topped by a graceful spire were added to the tower. The Englishman Christopher Halloway decorated the superstructure's architectural elements in a remarkable manner. The ogee gables and pointed arches are richly embellished with flamboyant Gothic ornamentation. Flying buttresses support the tall superstructure; turrets, pinnacles, clustered columns, carved pilasters decorate the various receding stories—all the wealth and variety of the florid decorative features of the dying flamboyant Gothic were combined with the elegance and grace of the Renaissance. The balusters, crockets, corbels, and finials, combined with the delicate white-stone open-work carved gables, create a most effective play of light and shade. Originally too, monsters and grotesque beasts peered through the tower ballustrades; niches housed allegorical and symbolical sculptured figures *(bolvany)* that, owing to a peculiar sense of modesty in the seventeenth century, were clothed in colorful costumes. All this wealth and variety of architectural and decorative features conditioned the pattern of Russian architectural thought of the seventeenth and eighteenth centuries and greatly influenced the work of Bazhenov and Kazakov.[3]

The Spasskaia Tower has a complicated inner arrangement. Large chambers rise to a great height; passages are built within the thickness of the walls. The clocks, chimes,[4] and their mechanisms, which were formerly at a lower level, are now on the eighth, ninth, and tenth floors.

The history of the Spasskaia Tower is most intimately connected with the history of the Kremlin—that is, with the history of the consolidation and growth of the Moscow Empire. As the main entrance to the Kremlin—the religious and secular center of the state—the Spasskaia Tower occupied a spot of great significance.

Through these gates the varied spectacle of the multitudinous activities of the Kremlin ebbed and flowed. All the solemn rituals and the pageantry of the great ceremonial processions of Church and State were closely associated with these gates: all the coronation and triumphal parades, the troops departing for war, the funeral corteges had to pass through. Especially notable were the traditional Palm Sunday processions from the Kremlin to St. Basil's and the Lobnoe Mesto.[5]

North of the Saviour's Tower, behind the present Lenin Mausoleum, is the Senate Tower, so named because of its proximity to the former

Senate Building that is now the seat of the Soviet government. In 1918, on the first anniversary of the revolution, a symbolic bas-relief by the sculptor Konenkov was placed on the tower wall as a monument to honor the fallen revolutionists buried in the "Brothers Grave" at the foot of the wall.

North of the Saviour's Gates and Tower, opposite the Historical Museum, are the Nikol'skiia Gates and Tower, erected by Solario at the same time as the Saviour's Gates. The gates are named for St. Nicholas,[6] whose picture was formerly above the entrance. Over the old square base of the tower is a balcony surrounded by a parapet and adorned with a Gothic turret at each corner. From the middle of this balcony rises the central octagonal part of the tower with two rows of arches for the suspension of bells. The upper row of arches is surmounted by a green pyramid on which the Russian imperial arms were mounted. The superstructure, built by K. I. Rossi[7] early in the nineteenth century, was destroyed by the French in 1812 and rebuilt by Beauvais in 1820.

The Kremlin wall grows lower near the bulwark at the northern corner where the massive Corner Arsenal Tower stands. At this point the wall turns to the southwest along the now invisible Neglinnaia River.

The Trinity Tower and Gates[8] are in the west wall of the Kremlin. This tower closely resembles the Saviour's Tower, but the proportions are not so attractive.

The road from these gates leads across the Trinity Bridge (Troitskii Most), the parapets of which are furnished with battlements and embrasures similar to the walls of the Kremlin. This bridge crosses the Neglinnaia River, which formerly played an important role in the defense of the Kremlin. In 1817-1819 the river was arched over with brick, on which Beauvais laid out the Aleksandrovskii Park, in 1826. At the west end of the Trinity Bridge is the Kutaf'ia Tower,[9] a picturesque, two-story massive structure surmounted with battlements and embrasures.

The architecture and the decorative elements of the Trinity Tower have a pseudo Gothic flavor; but this tower lacks the flying buttresses and the exuberance of ornamentation found in the Saviour's Tower. The interior of the Trinity Tower and its front-protecting barbican (the Kutaf'ia Tower) were considerably altered and disfigured in the nineteenth century. The upper decorative elements of the Kutaf'ia Tower were done in the so-called "Naryshkin" style, very much in vogue in the late seventeenth century. Its ornamental motifs, which have a touch of the pseudo Gothic, influenced the Moscow architects of the second half of the eighteenth century.

The Borovitskiia Vorota[10] (gates) are near the southwest angle of the

Kremlin at the mouth of the Neglinnaia River, the site of the first settlement on the Kremlin hill and once a dense forest. The wall of the Kremlin, thicker here than elsewhere, is penetrated by the arched gate. Unlike the others, this gate is surmounted by no tower. Slightly to the south stands the Borovitskaia Tower, which is different from all the other towers of the Kremlin in style of architecture. The proportions of this tower are particularly impressive, the most striking feature being the superstructure. Above a large and tall base four successive square, terraced elements rise, one out of the other, gradually diminishing in size. A circle of handsome arches and an octagonal green-tiled spire top this tower, which forms a beautiful pyramid. Opinions differ as to the origin of its style. An Oriental derivation has been suggested—it does have a certain resemblance to the Sumbeka Tower[11] in Kazan'; but careful analysis reveals a similarity to the Kremlin *terema* and the seventeenth-century *khoromy*[12] at Kolomenskoe. The forms of its architectural elements have undoubtedly been influenced by the spirit of medieval Russian wooden structures, as its decoration seems to have been derived from old Russian sources. To this gate belongs the dubious distinction that Napoleon chose it for his entrance into the Kremlin in 1812.

All the tall, square gate towers—Spasskaia, Troitskaia, Nikol'skaia, and Borovitskaia—have octagonal "tents" *(shatry)*. The other square towers—the Second Bezymiannaia (Nameless), the Middle Arsenal'naia, the Komendantskaia, and Oruzheinaia—have rectangular tents resembling a truncated square pyramid; only the top spire is in the shape of a small octagonal pyramid. The First Bezymiannaia, Tainitskaia, Blagoveshchenskaia, and Konstantinovskaia towers maintain their simple and austere form of a rectangle into the upper tent—that is, throughout all their tiers.

Although the tower superstructures have certain similarities in their forms, they are dissimilar in the proportions of their parts. Moreover, the ratios of the base to the superstructure differ considerably in the various towers. The result is that each tower is an independent work of architecture with distinct individual characteristics.

The so-called "blank" towers (containing no gates)—the Konstantino-Eleninskaia and the Nabatnaia (between the Beklemishevskaia and the Spasskaia) the Senatskaia, Sredniaia-Arsenal'naia, Komendantskaia, and Oruzheinaia (between the Troitskaia and the Borovitskaia), the Blagoveshchenskaia (between the Vodovzodnaia and Tainitskaia)— are all similar in type of architecture. Their basic composition is a massive rectangular battlemented block, serving as a base and terrace for a smaller fenestrated cube that in turn supports a truncated pyramidal element with a tent on top. The Nabatnaia (Alarm Tower) is one of the best-proportioned of the blank towers. Between the Nabatnaia and the Spas towers, hemmed in between the merlons and the parapet and resting directly on the wall ramparts, is the Tsarskaia Bashnia (Tsar Tower). Before the Tsar Tower was built in 1680, a wooden pavilion occupied the site. According to tradition, Ivan IV (the Terrible) sat in this pavilion and watched the gruesome executions in the Red Square below. The lower tier of the Tsar Tower is supported on Gothic arches; the superstructure is carried by four balusterlike columns. This decorative column motif became very popular in the seventeenth century and later was reintroduced to eighteenth-century architecture by Kazakov, who used the motif extensively in the Petrovskii Palace in Moscow in 1775-1782. The four columns support an octagonal tent with four corner finials.

The corner towers—the Beklemishevskaia, Vodovzvodnaia, and the Arsenal'naia—consist of a substructure, a two-tiered base for the superstructure, a truncated tent-shaped story, an observation platform and lantern, and a small tentlike spire.

The substructure of these towers is cylindrical in form (the Arsenal'naia substructure is a sixteen-sided polyhedron) with a white-stone base and decorative band. The parapet consists of machicolated battlements. The walls are smooth, with the exception of those of the Vodovzvodnaia Tower, which are rusticated and decorated with an arcature at about mid-height. The windows are semicircular; the Beklemishevskaia Tower has also two rows of narrow loopholes, and the Vodovzvodnaia Tower has a row of circular windows at the bottom.

The base for the superstructure consists of two tiers—the lower circular, the upper octagonal—the decorative treatment of which varies with each tower.

The truncated tent-shaped story is octagonal, each side having two rows of windows, their architraves embellished with columns and pediments.

The observation lantern is also octagonal, each side having a single pedimented window in the Vodovzvodnaia and Arsenal'naia towers. The windows in the Beklemishevskaia Tower lantern have only a cornice.

The spires are likewise octagonal and are terminated by five-pointed stars[13] that revolve at the slightest air movement, shine and sparkle with gold and rubies in daylight, and can be seen for miles at night.

The superstructures of all the circular towers spring from a two-tiered round base and pass at a certain height into a truncated pyramidal form surmounted by an octagonal drum and a tent.[14]

In 1707, Peter the Great, anticipating an attack on Moscow by the Swedish King Charles XII, and realizing that the aging fortifications of the Kremlin and Kitai-Gorod were no match for the might of the Swedish army, ordered the erection of a series of earthen bastions around the entire fortress. These bastions enclosed the areas occupied at present by the Alexander Gardens, the Revolution Square, the southern end of the Sverdlov Square, the approaches to the Theater Square, and the Moskvoretsk and Kremlin quays. These fortifications were not removed until 1817–1823; their remnants can still be seen in the Kremlin wall embankments of the Alexander Gardens.

In 1802 the architect Rossi added the present upper stories and decorative pyramidal roof of the Nikol'skaia Tower. In 1805 the aging and crumbling Vodovzvodnaia Tower was torn down and rebuilt. The rebuilt Vodovzvodnaia, the Petrovskaia, and the First Bezymiannaia (Nameless) towers, as well as the wall between the Nikol'skaia and the Uglovaia-Arsenal'naia, were destroyed in 1812 by order of Napoleon, but were rebuilt in 1817–1819 by the architect Beauvais in collaboration with Gilardi. This "restoration" was unfortunately not a very happy one: the "Empire" treatment of the superstructure, the pyramidlike roof, the half-engaged corner columns, the paneling, and the door pediments of the Petrovskaia are not in harmony with the rest of the Kremlin.

Since the earliest times the gaping holes in roofs, the crumbling wall facing, the chipped battlements, the damaged decorative details—all these and other minor mutilations of the Kremlin were neglected. During the eighteenth century some of the arched openings were filled, and passageways and stairways were blocked on the mere whim of caretakers. On the other hand, the supernationalistic spirit, rampant in the second half of the nineteenth century, overreached itself in the effort to restore the Kremlin to its ancient self. Those "restorations" were not always based on scientific research, nor were they done in good taste.

From the indicated various episodes in the life of the Kremlin it is quite clear that the least authentically preserved part is the side facing the Moskva River. Here only two towers are original—the Beklemishevskaia and the Blagoveshchenskaia. However, this side is not of essential importance in establishing the picturesqueness of the Kremlin. The most striking view is from the west, especially from the Kamennyi Most (Stone Bridge). This view has been recently further enhanced by the removal of the many unsightly huts that formerly clustered along the Moskva River.

VI

CATHEDRALS, CHURCHES, AND MONASTERIES

The triangular enclosure of the Kremlin contains within its relatively small area the Russian counterparts of Reims, Saint-Denis, and Sainte-Chapelle of France. Few places, except the Athenian Acropolis and the Roman Capitolium, contain within a small area all the significant monuments of a nation's past.

The cathedrals are grouped around Cathedral Square (Sobornaia Ploshchad'), which has since the end of the fifteenth century been the heart of the Kremlin and its most picturesque spot. East of the main façade of the Grand Palace stands the Cathedral of the Annunciation (Blagoveshchenskii Sobor[1]), and opposite this is the Archangel Cathedral (Arkhangel'skii Sobor). Behind the Palace of Facets (Granovitaia Palata) the great dome of the Cathedral of the Assumption (Uspenskii Sobor) rises from among the cupolas and crosses of surrounding churches. The Palace of the Patriarchs stands on the north side of the square; on the east rises the Bell Tower of Ivan Velikii, built by Boris Godunov in 1600. Near by are two other bell towers, one of which was built in 1532–1542 by the Italian architect Bono.

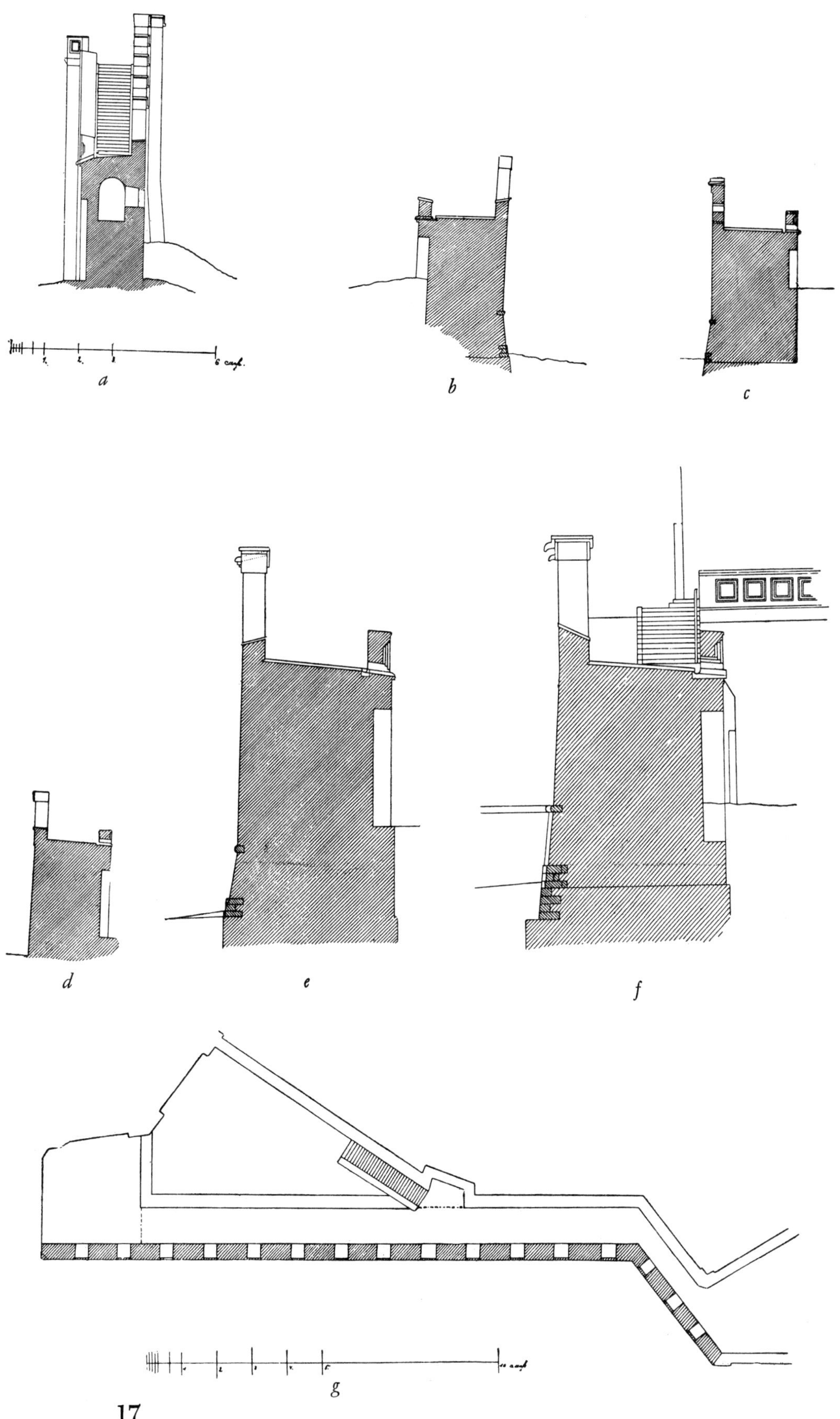

17

SECTIONS OF THE KREMLIN WALL

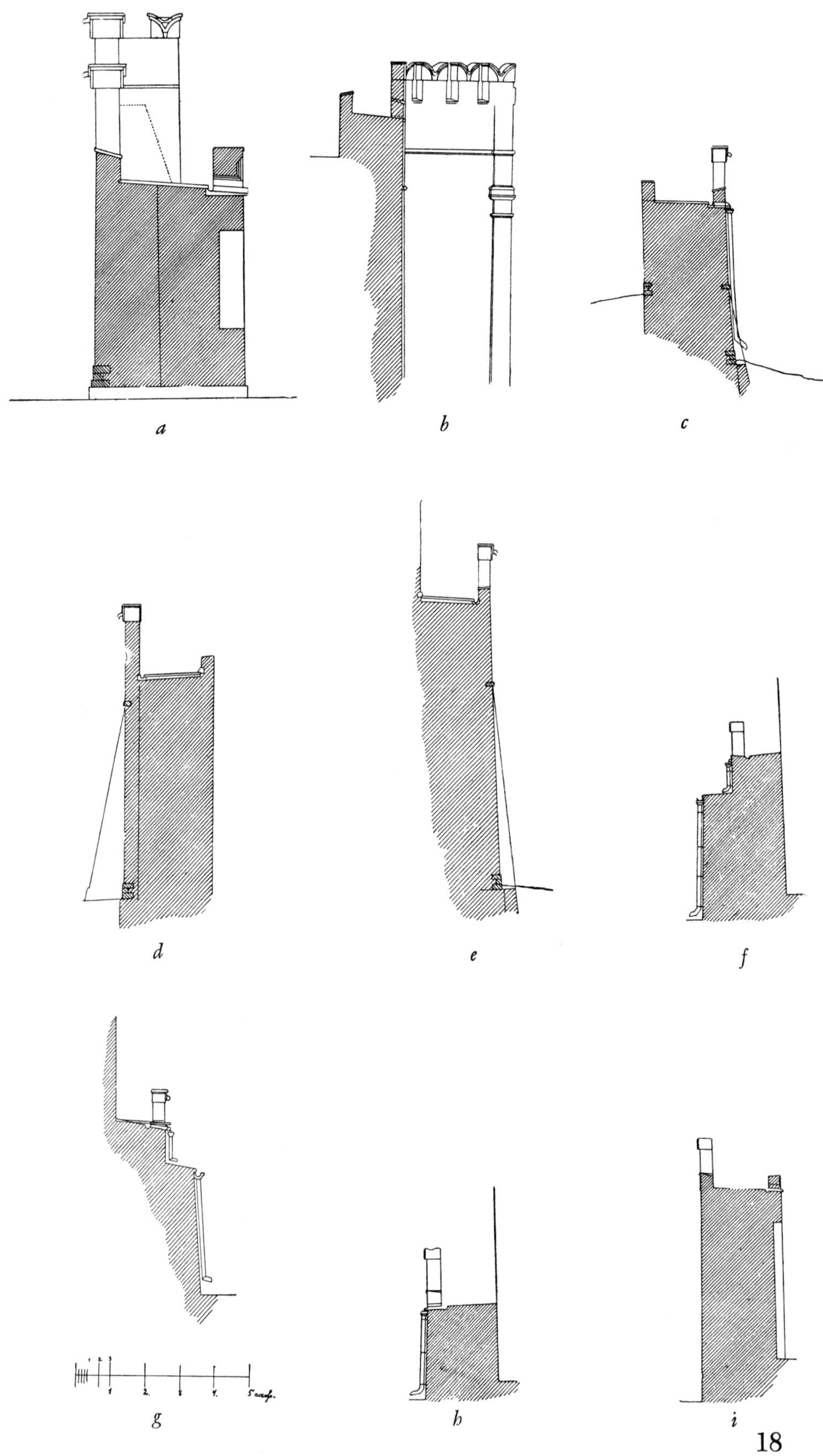

18

SECTIONS OF THE KREMLIN WALL

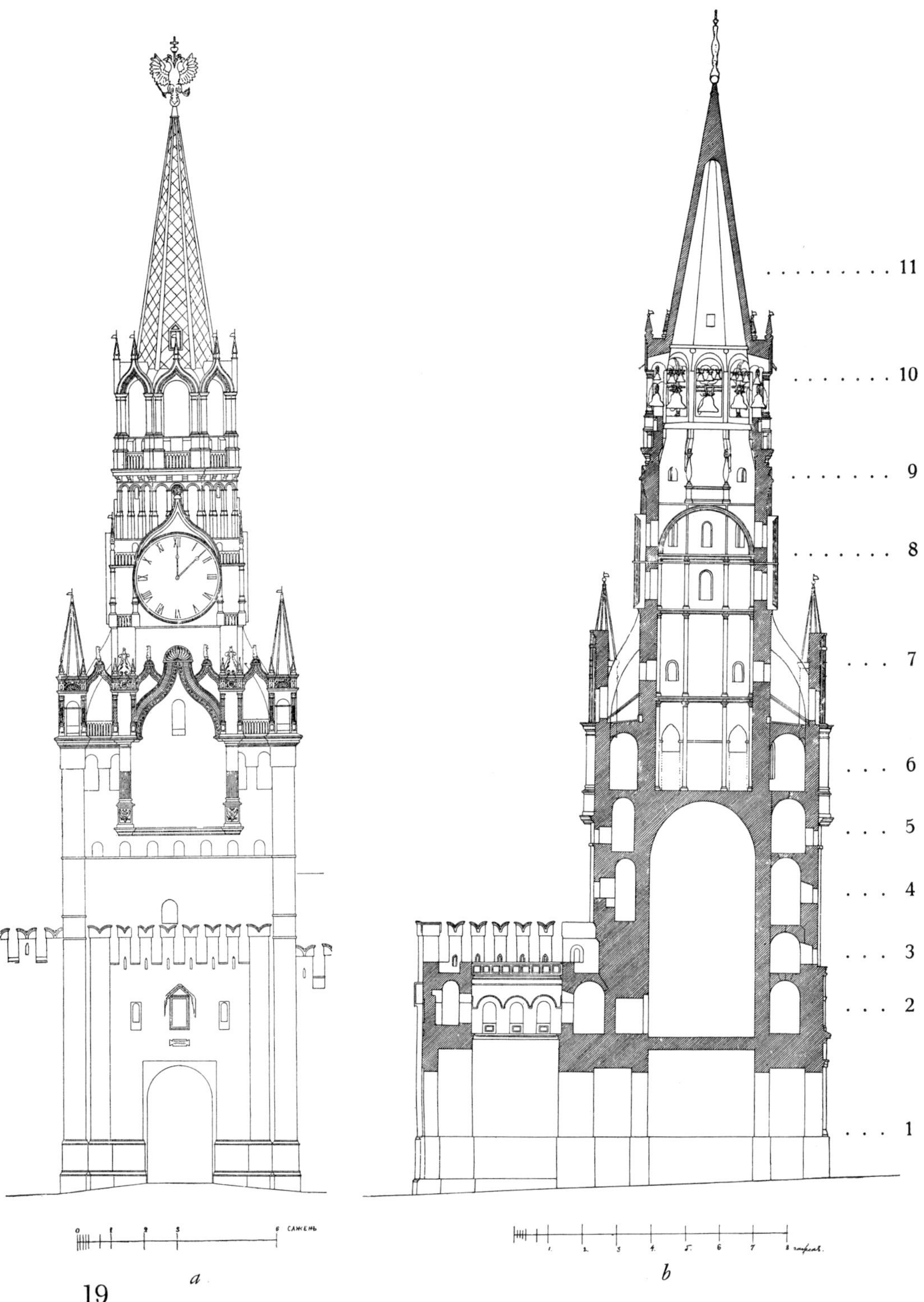

19

ELEVATION AND SECTION OF THE SAVIOUR'S TOWER

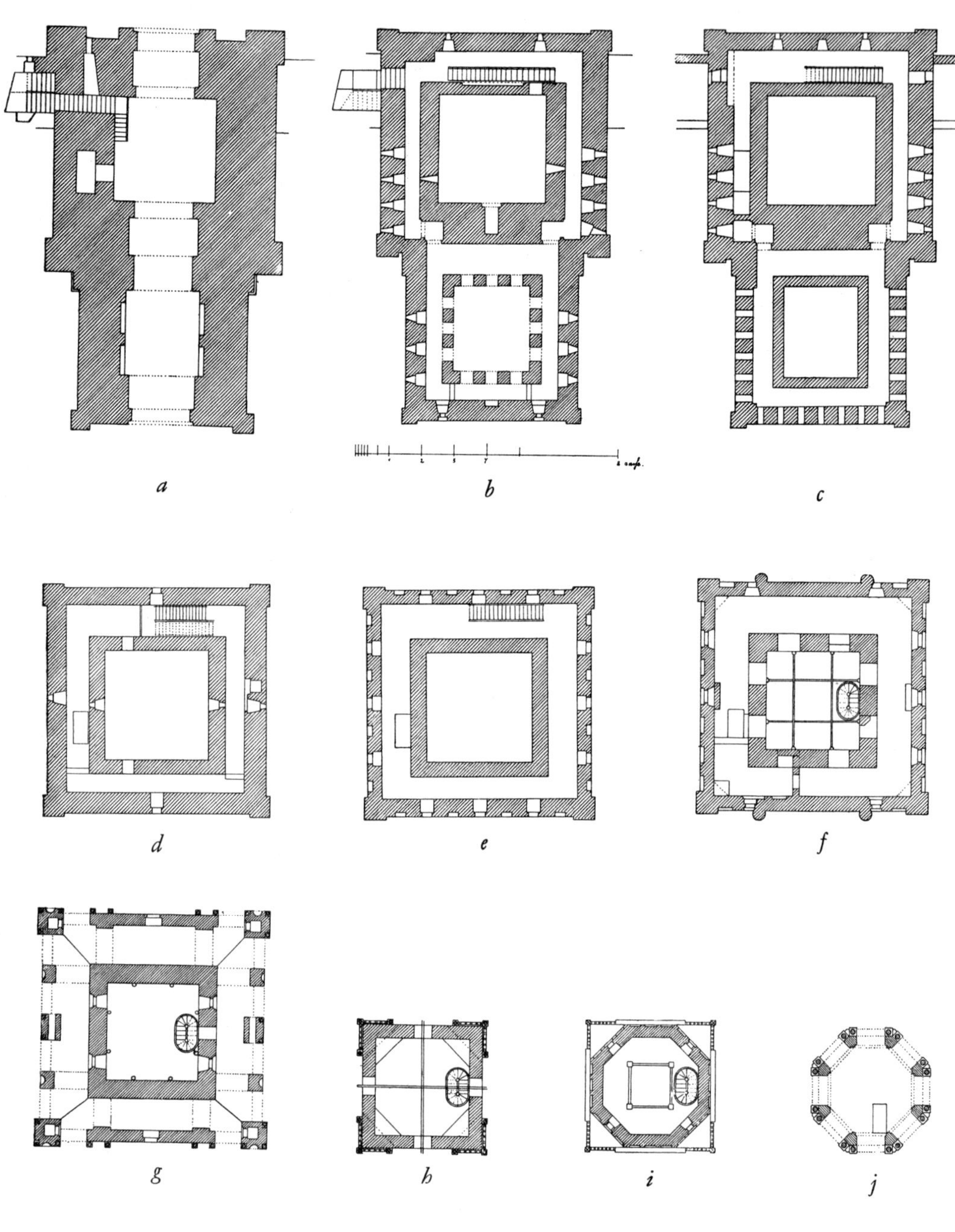

20

FLOOR PLANS OF THE SAVIOUR'S TOWER

21

DECORATIVE DETAILS OF THE SAVIOUR'S TOWER

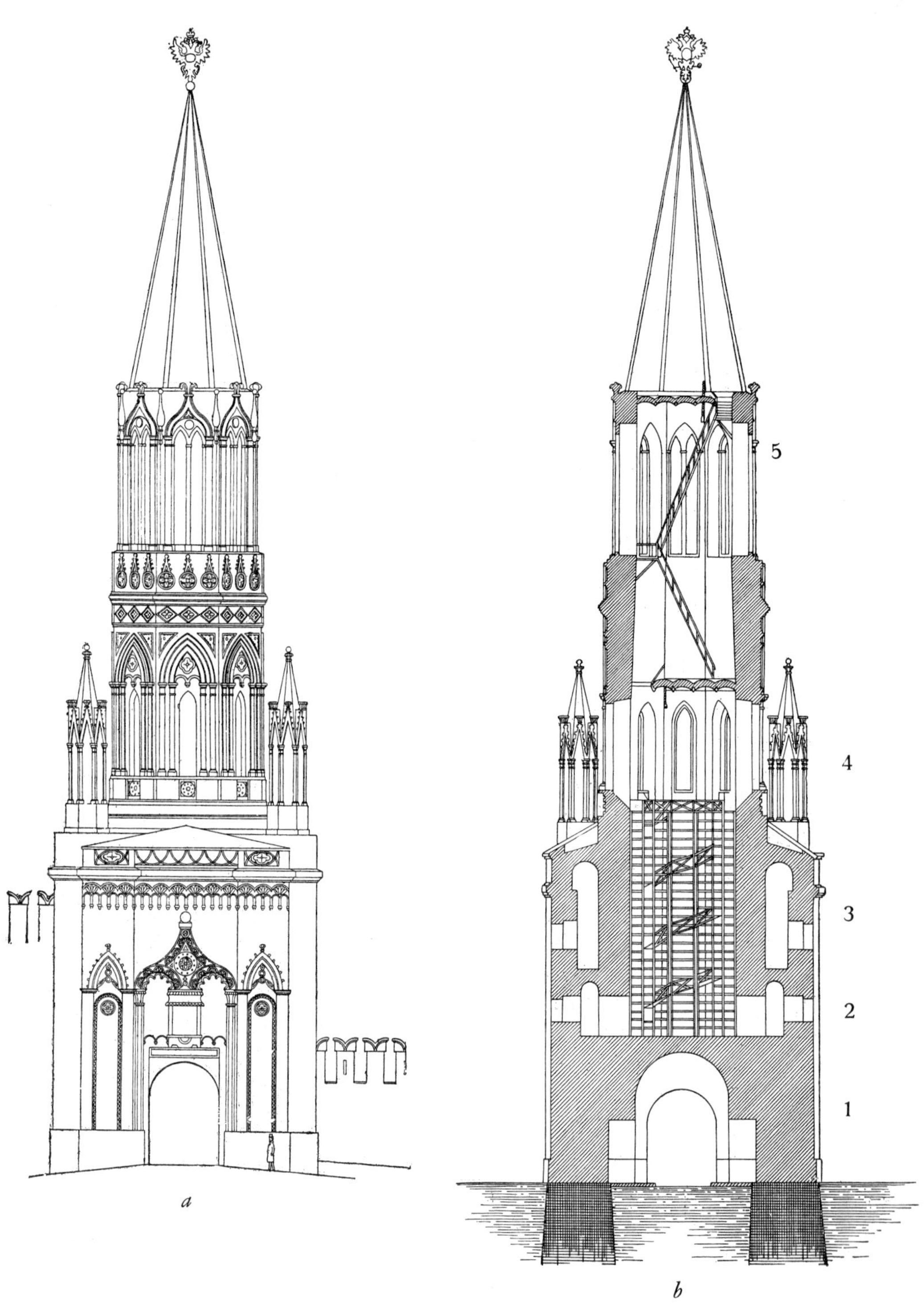

22

ELEVATION AND SECTION
OF THE NICHOLAS TOWER

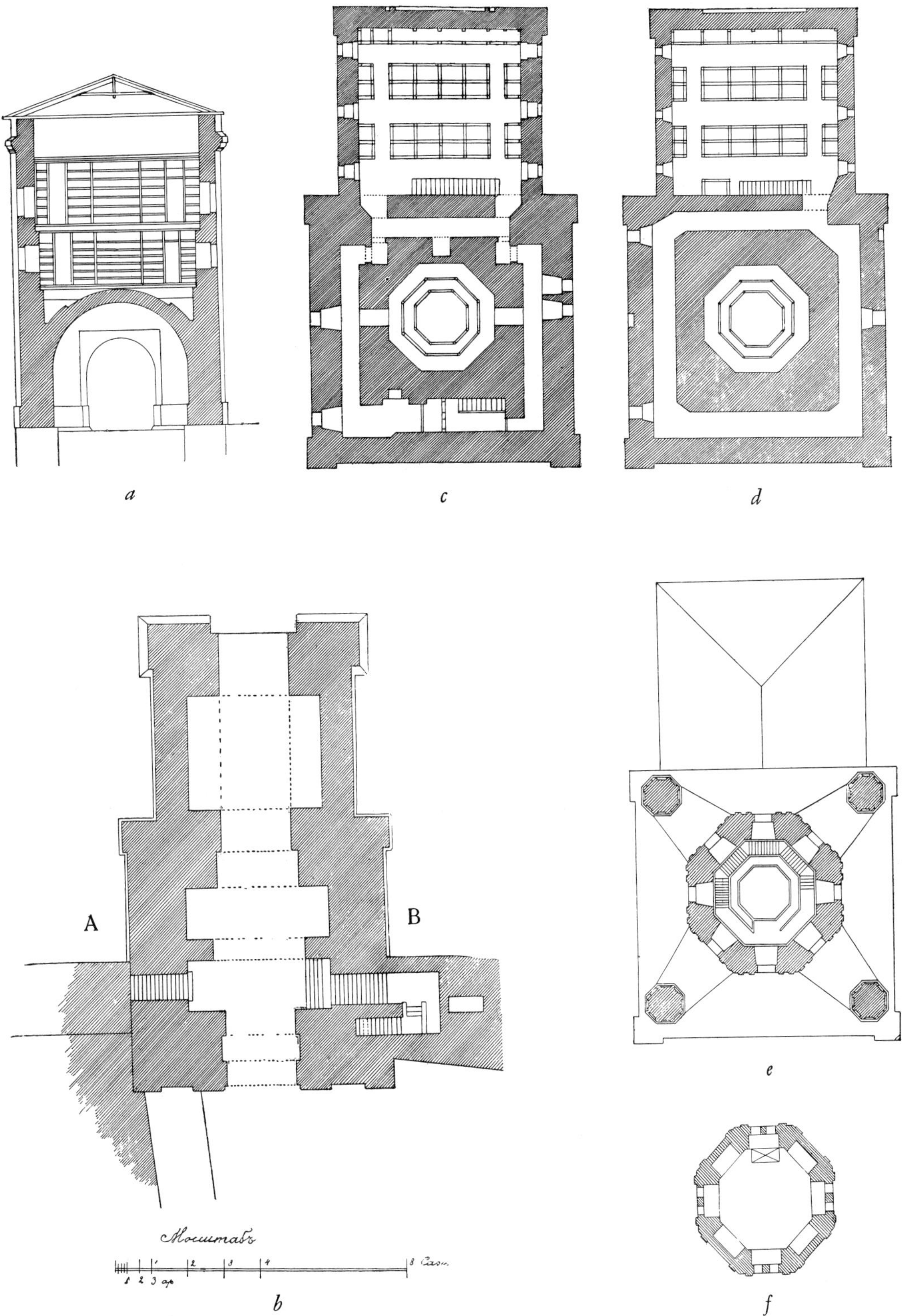

23

FLOOR PLANS OF THE NICHOLAS TOWER

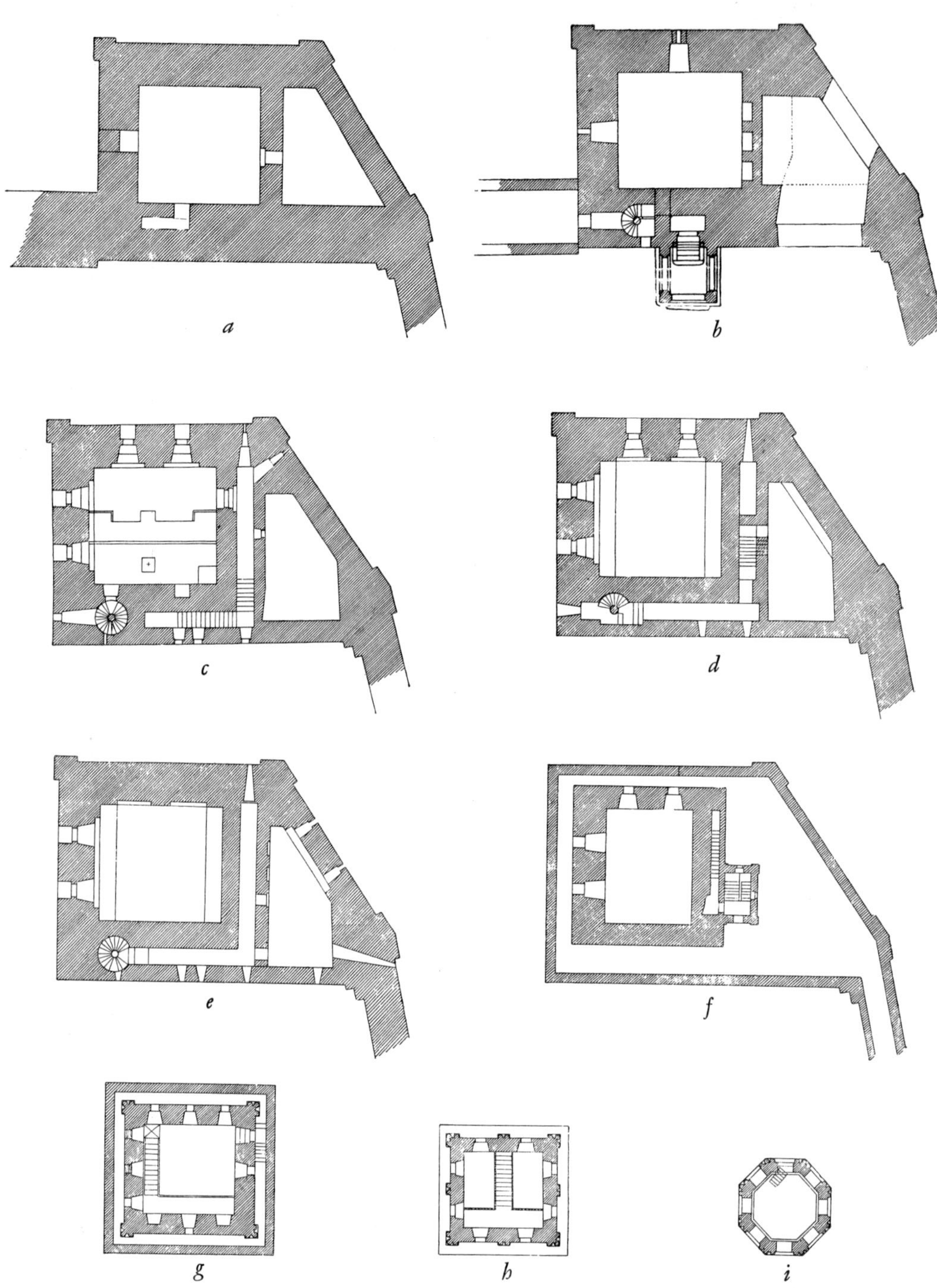

24

FLOOR PLANS OF THE FOREST TOWER

25

ELEVATION AND SECTION OF THE TRINITY TOWER

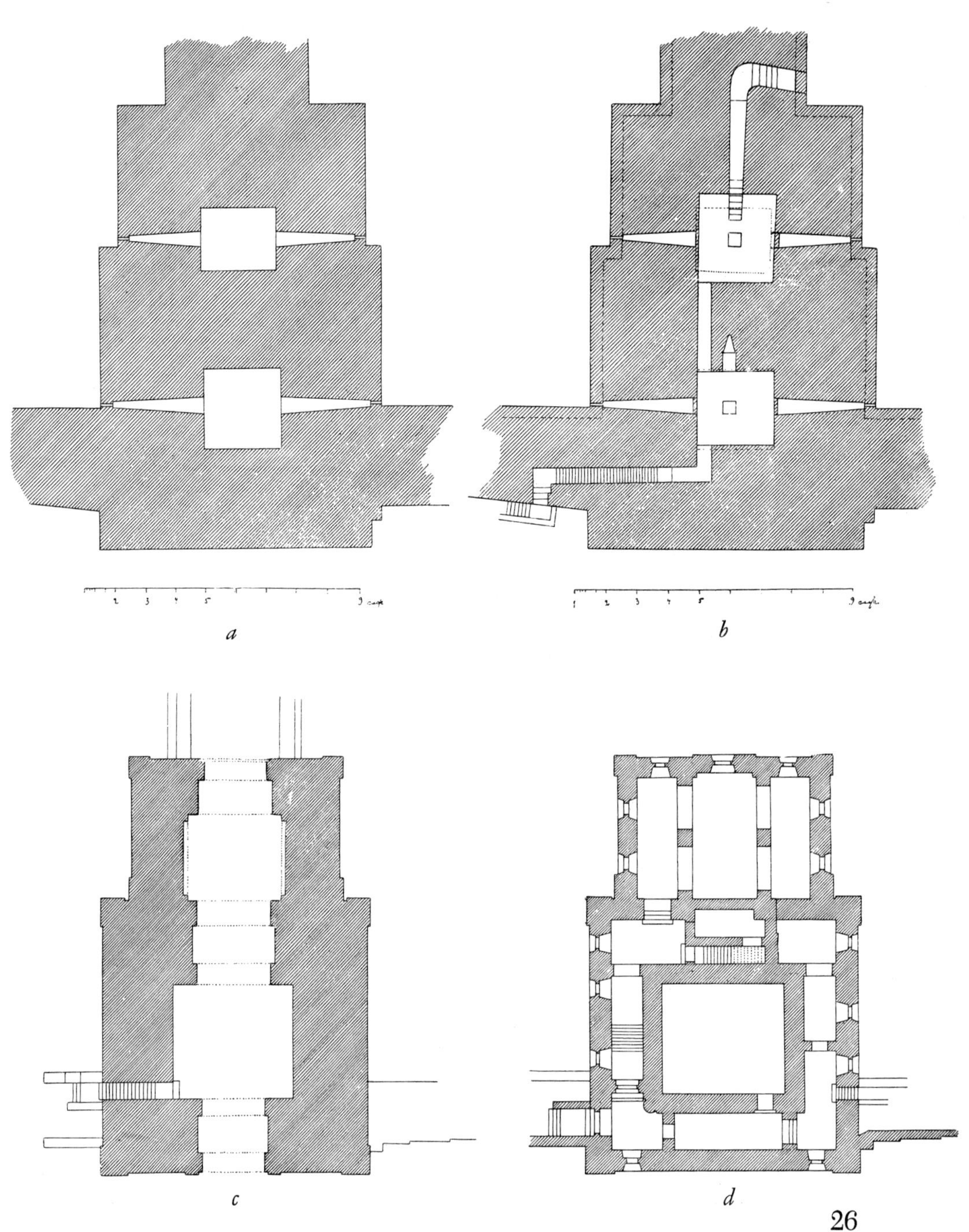

26

FLOOR PLANS OF THE TRINITY TOWER

27

ELEVATION AND SECTION
OF THE CORNER ARSENAL TOWER

a

b

28

ELEVATION AND SECTION
OF THE WATER-PUMPING TOWER

On Cathedral Square, against the background of the huge bulk of the Grand Palace, surrounded by a tall early nineteenth-century metal screen, stand the architectural monuments of medieval Moscow—edifices that have served as a starting point, a stimulus, and an inspiration for the architectural activities and for the development of the aesthetics of Moscow. These monuments were built and decorated by men of diverse backgrounds, schools, and tastes; yet, in spite of this diversity in aesthetic approach, there is a remarkable harmony in the ensemble. The beauty and charm of the scene seem not the result of a haphazard contribution of this or that architect, but an expression of medieval Russia. The forms are austere, the masses restrained and heavy; the interiors are dimly lighted, and the vaulting is almost lost in semidarkness. A faint silvery light plays on the gold frames and nimbuses of the icons[2] and on the moldings and carving of the iconostases. The stern figures of the saints and elders of the Church gaze with wide-open eyes and seem to threaten even as they bless. The effect is awesome, evocative of the unique religious feeling of the fourteenth and fifteenth centuries pervaded with meekness and the fear that hung so heavily over the heads of the Moscow populace of those days.

The most celebrated of the Kremlin churches is the Uspenskii Sobor, (Cathedral of the Assumption or Repose of the Virgin). From the fifteenth century the Russian sovereigns were always crowned in this cathedral, which is thus the Russian counterpart of the Cathedral of Reims; the Church metropolitans and the Moscow patriarchs are buried here. The dimensions of the Uspenskii Sobor are rather small—in the West it would be called a chapel rather than a cathedral—but it is so fraught with recollections, so crowded with furnishings, frescoes, and icons, from the floor to the cupola, that its smallness of space is forgotten in the fullness of its contents. The fine situation of the cathedral, its splendid domes, and internal grandeur, all excite attention. Its connection with the ecclesiastical, civil, and political history of Russia give it more than ordinary importance.

The construction of this cathedral was begun in 1326 (in the reign of the Grand Prince Ivan Danilovich Kalita) by Peter, the metropolitan of Moscow (the titular saint protector of Moscow), who may therefore be called its founder. When the Italian architect Fieravanti was summoned by Ivan III to reconstruct the old church in 1475, he was advised to go to Vladimir and study the Uspenskii Cathedral, built in 1158.

Russian historians (Solov'ev, Zabelin) point out that neither Fieravanti nor the other foreign architects had a free hand in the design of the commissioned buildings. The fact that the Uspenskii Cathedral at Vladimir was suggested to Fieravanti as a model can be explained on the ground that the design of a great cathedral, the very see of the Orthodox faith, could hardly be entrusted to a foreigner, a Roman Catholic at that. By-

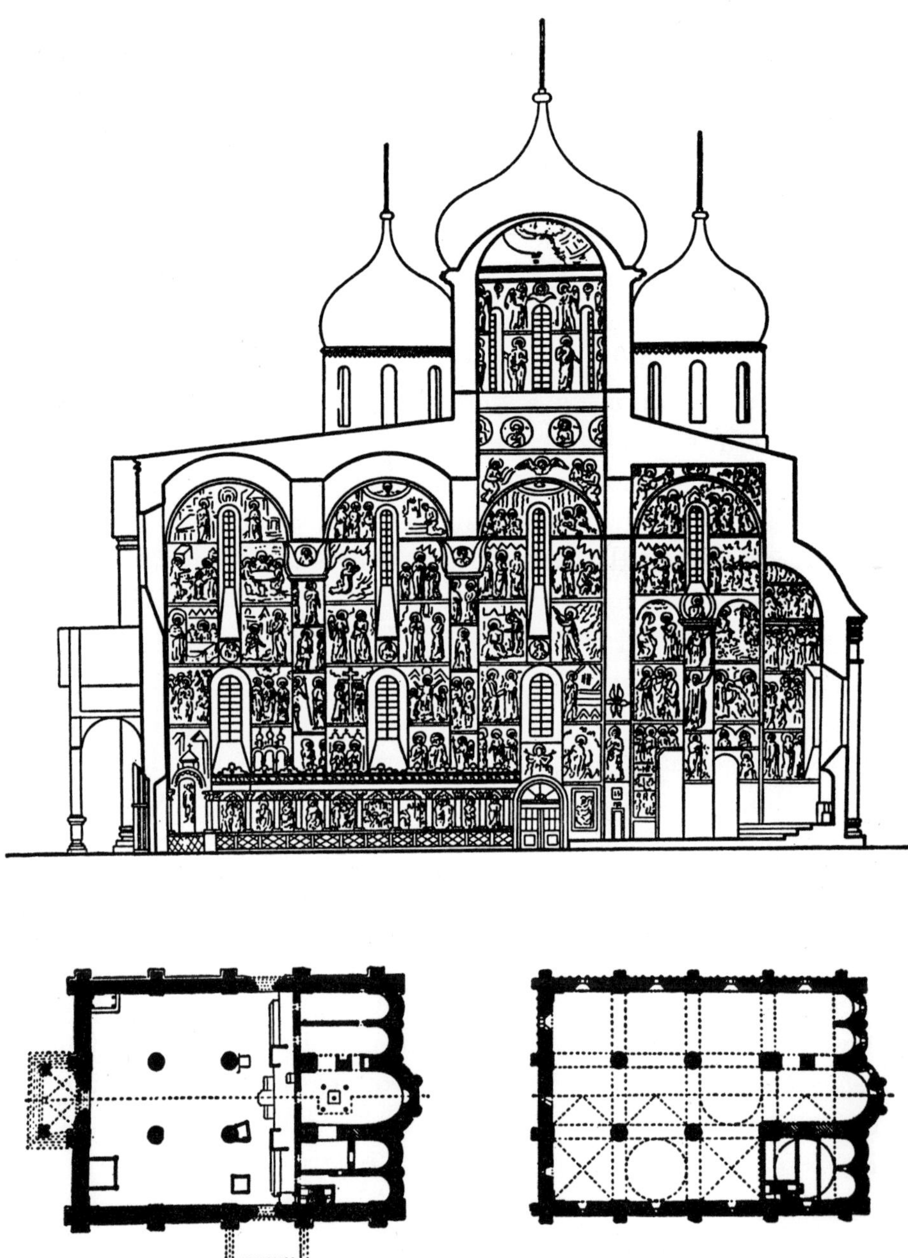

Figure 2. Plans and section of the Cathedral of the Assumption.

zantine traditions were still very strong, and the Russian clergy, ever on guard against any possible heresy or the slightest sign of "Latinity," would not tolerate revolutionary innovations in church design. On the other hand, many wooden churches in the Moscow of that period had little in common with Byzantine forms—suggesting that there were no fixed types of church architecture.

Fieravanti visited not only Vladimir, but also Rostov and Iaroslavl', where he became acquainted with the local masonry cathedrals and churches. On the shores of the White Sea he saw many of the ancient wooden churches. On his return trip he visited Old Ladoga, with its twelfth-century churches, and undoubtedly passed through Novgorod and saw St. Sophia Cathedral, built in 1045–1052. Thus the Italian architect had an opportunity to get first-hand information on Russian religious architecture and to grasp the essential features of its traditions.[3]

The Moscow Uspenskii Cathedral, completed in 1479, resembles its Vladimir namesake but is far from being a literal copy. The two cathedrals are of the same width, but the Moscow one is much longer; the Moscow cathedral has five apses, the Vladimir three; furthermore, the latter's choir galleries are suppressed. The vaulting of the Moscow Uspenskii rests on six pillars, four of which—huge circular columns—support the central cupola, which rests on a flat roof and is surrounded with four smaller cupolas. This very simple disposition produces a grandiose effect, and the massive pillars give an extraordinary stability without heaviness to the body of the cathedral. The influence of the Vladimir architecture is noticeable mainly in the façade, decorated at mid-height with a band of arcatures forming small niches *(kiotsy)*[4] that the architect used very successfully as window embrasures.

The interior of the cathedral is approximately similar to that of St. Mark's in Venice, but the body of the Kremlin church rises in a single reach toward the sky whereas the lower arches of St. Mark's create a cryptlike impression. The Uspenskii Cathedral has close-barred apertures in the walls, admitting only a faint light. This pale glow suffuses the massive columns covered with burnished gold and frescoes; it shimmers upon the magnificent iconostasis;[5] it barely lights the Last Judgment and the End of the World painted on the walls.

According to the "Sophia Annalist," the frescoes were so wonderfully executed that when the grand prince, the bishops, and the boyars entered the temple they exclaimed, "We see heaven!" We must remember that the rapturous remarks of the annalist pertain to the years 1514–1515, when the cathedral was for the first time embellished with wall paintings. A few of these can still be seen on the masonry partition separating the sanctuary from the nave. They are hidden by the high iconostasis, first built in 1482, rebuilt in 1690, and renovated in 1813 and again in 1881–1883, when it was covered with *repoussé* silver ornament. In 1642 and 1643 the cathedral was "done over with a new set of wall paintings on the gold background,"[6] some of the finest Russian painters of the period participating in the work. The paintings have been frequently restored, but not always in the strict spirit of the original. In the 1920's a number of important experiments were conducted in cleaning and restoring certain eighteenth-century paintings in the cathedral. During these experiments an excellent seventeenth-century fresco in fine condition was uncovered. In spite of the many renovations and restorations, the Uspenskii Cathedral interior is still the closest in expression to the aesthetics of the fifteenth and sixteenth centuries; it is the most rewarding and inspiring of Moscow churches.

The present smoke-gray wall coating probably did not exist in the sixteenth century. The interior of the cathedral was undoubtedly aglow with warm, bright colors and clear-cut, sharp outlines, recalling the churches of Iaroslavl'. The faces of the images must have been less stern, less grim than they appear now. The main efforts of the ancient Russian prince-builders and artists-decorators were concentrated on imparting to the church a sense of opulence and magnificence, an equivalent to an imagined "dwelling in paradise," the "Lord's Temple."

The wall paintings of the Uspenskii Cathedral served as a prototype for the works of many Russian painters of later generations. In wall painting as well as in architecture the Uspenskii Cathedral was regarded as a model as late as the reign of Empress Elizabeth (1741–1761). The St. Petersburg architects of the early eighteenth century perfected their own type of a single-cupola church, but during Elizabeth's reign an order was issued making the Uspenskii Cathedral a prototype for future churches. Even the great Rastrelli, the favorite architect of the empress, had to incorporate the basic forms of the Uspenskii Cathedral in the design of his most elegant baroque churches. All the interior surfaces of the Uspenskii Cathedral—the masonry partition (which at one time served as an iconostasis), the columns, vaults, cupolas, and window embrasures—are covered with paintings. On the columns are gigantic figures of the martyrs and figures from the New Testament; on the walls are scenes from the Gospels and the *acathyst*[7] to the Virgin; and in the window embrasures of the north wall are portraits of Saints Vladimir and Ol'ga, the first Christian prince and princess of Russia. The entire west wall is occupied by a painting of the Last Judgment, an incredibly complicated composition containing hundreds of figures.

The iconostasis, a high, gilded partition with five rows of figures, dazzles the eye with its glowing splendor. The iconographic material illustrates two themes: Church and State. The religious theme stresses the idea of the universal Church—the union of the Old Testament with the New. The State theme dwells on the importance of the unification of all the Russian states by Moscow. Through apertures in the gold and silver encasements appear the heads and hands of the saints. Their aureoles, incrusted with precious stones, stand out in relief. The images have breastplates of gold and silver and collars and pendants of diamonds, sapphires, rubies, emeralds, and pearls. From the center of the ceiling hangs a massive, silver, circular chandelier, which was installed after the original had been carried off during Napoleon's invasion.[8]

Several religious furnishings of the Uspenskii Cathedral and its sacristy are of great artistic value. Many of the ancient icons were painted by some of the great Russian masters, but they are so nearly covered by gold sheathings incrusted with precious stones that only the faces and hands of the saints are visible. Several of these icons were painted by the seventeenth-century artist F. N. Roshnov, who also did the altar paintings of the Crucifixion and each of the Twelve Apostles. The present iconostasis was erected at the end of the seventeenth century; curiously, it contains none of the wood carving that was popular at the time and that was widely used in other contemporary churches.

Near the south portal of the Uspenskii Cathedral stands the canopied tsar's stall or throne of Vladimir Monomakh.[9] This throne, a curious monument of the epoch that ushered in the change from the period of the appanage to that of the grand prince, was traditionally used as a coronation chair for the Russian rulers. Legend claims that it was originally built for Vladimir Monomakh, grand prince of Kiev, and that it was transferred from Kiev to Vladimir and from there, during the reign of Grand Duke Ivan Danilovich, to Moscow. According to most Russian historians, however, the original throne was built in 1551 for Ivan the Terrible and, because of the damage it suffered during the Time of Troubles[10] and the Polish occupation, was rebuilt for Tsar Mikhail Feodorovich.

The throne is justly considered one of the finest examples of Russian medieval wood carving. It is made of walnut and lime and is decorated with relief and pierced carving painted dark brown, although traces of gold visible here and there indicate that it was once gilded. On the cornice frieze, just below the base of the canopy and on the door leaves, a series of inscriptions in interlaced and cursive Slavonic characters add a decorative touch.

Four sculptured mythical beasts serve as supports for the throne. The contemporary chronicler speaks of them as awe-inspiring savage beasts rendered so realistically as to give the impression of being alive.

The twelve carved bas-reliefs on the side panels and door leaves are masterpieces of decorative art depicting scenes from the campaigns, battles, and other activities of an unidentified ancient Russian prince. The composition, with a keen sense of rhythm and mass organization, is reminiscent of ancient icon painting, except for a marked quality of dynamic realism lacking in the icons. The sense of movement is especially strong in the battle scenes, where the attacking knights are depicted in full war panoply, including sabers and lances, on their galloping chargers.

The octagonal, tent-shaped canopy, its form somewhat reminiscent of the crown of Monomakh (Plate 79), rises above the square stage of the throne in a series of receding tiers of *kokoshniki*[11] and steep gables. Derived from the forms of the wood architecture of northern Russia, this canopy *(shatior)* served as a prototype for later ones.

The Cathedral of the Archangel Michael (Arkhangel'skii Sobor), originally built of wood in the middle of the thirteenth century, was rebuilt of stone in 1333 as a final resting place for the Moscow princes. (Plate 37).

In 1505 Ivan III decided to build a new and larger cathedral worthy to stand beside the newly erected Uspenskii and Blagoveshchenskii, entrusting the design and construction to the Milanese architect Alevisio Novyi. Like Fieravanti before him, Novyi was compelled to incorporate the basic features of Orthodox church planning and design into the new cathedral, but in the exterior decoration he succeeded in introducing Italian architectural forms of the fifteenth century, which were adapted and reworked by Russian artists of later generations. The Arkhangel'skii Sobor rests on a stone base; its walls are of red brick, but the decorative elements are of white stone. The lower story is embellished with pilasters and arcatures containing small windows; the upper is divided into rectangles crowned with elaborate cornices. Novyi treated the *zakomary*[12] as purely decorative features by converting them into scallop-shell niches. The result was a structure endowed with a beauty radically different from that of the preceding Moscow churches. If the Uspenskii Cathedral can be considered as the epitome of the past and the embodiment of the traditional Moscow and Vladimir forms, the Arkhangel'skii was the first step toward a new art—the incarnation of the contribution that Italian art made to Moscow architecture.

Ivan III removed to this cathedral the remains of the earlier princes who had been buried in a more ancient church built by Ivan Kalita. Russian sovereigns were interred here until the time of Peter the Great. Along the wall the tombs of princes and tsars, from the founder of Moscow to the predecessor of the founder of Petersburg, are arranged in genealogical order, and form "a sepulchral chronicle of the Russian monarchy." (Only Boris Godunov is absent—his tomb is in the Troitsko-Sergievskaia Lavra.) Ivan the Terrible and his two sons occupy the most sacred spot—the narrow, fresco-covered Diaconicon next to the altar. Above each brass-covered coffin is a figure painted in a long white robe with a halo round his head—not the halo of saintly canonization, but of imperial investiture. These figures have been repainted and renovated many times and in the process have lost much of the quality of the original.

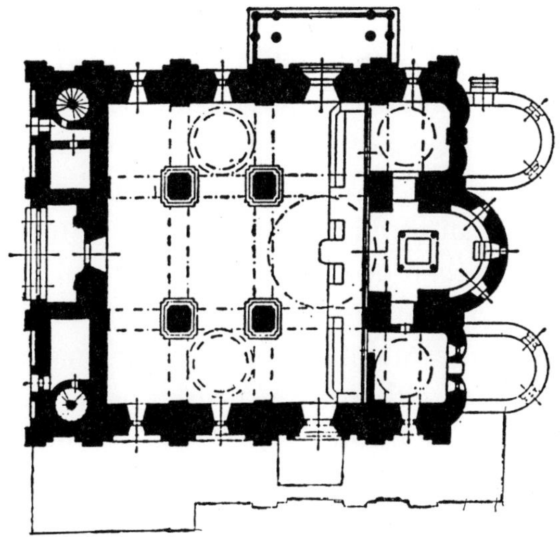

Figure 3. Plan of the Cathedral of the Archangel Michael.

The sacristy and library of the cathedral contain some of the great treasures of Russian ecclesiastical art, including the famous twelfth-century Mstislav Book of the Gospels that belonged to the Novgorodian Prince Mstislav Vladimirovich (Plate 67).

The Cathedral of the Annunciation, built by Pskov architects in 1482-1490 on the site of the original founded by Grand Prince Vasilii Dmitrievich (1389-1425), differs in certain details from the other two cathedrals of the Kremlin. The central cubical element, surmounted by five cupolas, closely resembles the forms of the Vladimir Uspenskii Cathedral. In the Cathedral of the Annunciation, however, the Pskov architects introduced an architectural motif destined to play an important role in the development of Moscow architecture of the sixteenth century and to become a theme for endless variations in the field of the decorative arts—the *kokoshnik*. The form, borrowed from the ogee-shaped roof, indicated a tendency to replace the forms of the Byzantine arch by more elongated silhouettes. The Pskov architects supported the elements of the superstructure with corbeled arches arranged in tiers and receding in steps. The cupola drums consequently seem to grow out of these elements, and the semicircular *zakomary* of the Vladimir and Moscow Uspenskii cathedrals acquire the characteristic shape of the ogee arch.

In 1547 the Cathedral of the Annunciation was damaged by a fire. While it was being repaired, open porches were added to three of its sides. This was the first such use of porches in a Russian church, a feature that became popular in the Moscow and Iaroslavl' churches of the second half of the seventeenth century (Plate 36).

At the time of the construction of the porches an anonymous Italian built the deep-shadowed portals with their engaged columns, pilasters, and archivolts, and decorated them with the richly carved, dark blue and gold ornament that winds and twists around the arches, columns, and door architraves. The Russians restudied and reworked this ornamental vocabulary, transforming it into something more suited to their taste and introducing their own ornamental elements—the *busy* (a type of beading) and the *perekhvaty* (a type of belt or band ornament).

The Cathedral of the Annunciation is much smaller and of a more intimate character than either the Uspenskii or the Arkhangel'skii; its proportions and decorations are in better taste. The internal arrangement is similar to that of the other Kremlin cathedrals. The floor is paved with mosaics of jasper and agate, and the walls are covered with frescoes by Feodosii (1518), Ivan Filatov (1648), and others. The altar is elegant and richly adorned; the iconostasis is decorated with the works of Theophanos the Greek, Andrei Rublev, Prokhor, and Daniil Chernyi. Among the images encased in gold and silver and adorned with precious stones and pearls, those of the Saviour and of the Virgin Mary are the most ornate; the case of the image of the Annunciation is said to contain eighteen pounds of pure gold besides pearls and precious stones.

The Tower of Ivan Velikii (Ivan the Great) stands on the brow of the hill to the east of and nearly equidistant from the Cathedrals of the Assumption and of the Archangel Michael. Situated almost exactly in the center of the Kremlin and rising above the gleaming cupolas, multicolored spires, and shining crosses of the surrounding cathedrals and palaces, this tower commands the entire scene and consolidates the various groups into one architectural composition (Plate 40).

The Tower of Ivan Velikii, including the cross, is 270 feet high; it rests on a stone foundation the bottom of which is said to extend down to the level of the Moskva River. The base is of white stone, and the walls are of brick reinforced with iron bars. The lower stories are octag-

29

THE CATHEDRAL OF THE ASSUMPTION

30

INTERIOR OF THE CATHEDRAL OF THE ASSUMPTION

31

THE SEAT OF THE PATRIARCH IN THE CATHEDRAL OF THE ASSUMPTION

32

THE REPOSITORY OF THE
ROBE OF OUR LORD
IN THE CATHEDRAL OF THE ASSUMPTION

33

THE THRONE OF IVAN THE TERRIBLE
IN THE CATHEDRAL OF THE ASSUMPTION

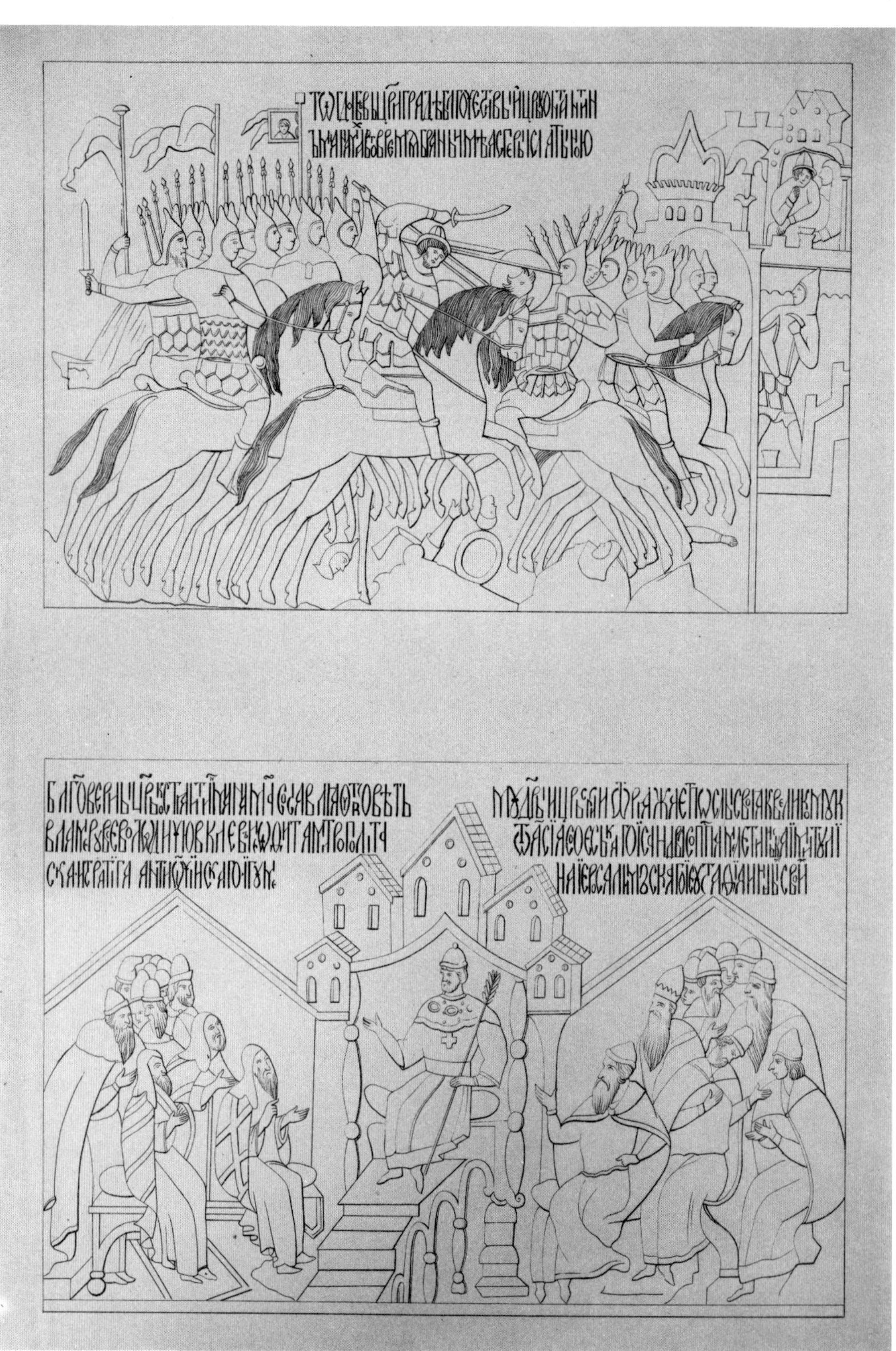

34

DETAILS OF THE THRONE OF IVAN THE TERRIBLE

35

THE CHURCH OF THE SAVIOUR IN THE FOREST

36

THE CATHEDRAL OF THE ANNUNCIATION

37

THE CATHEDRAL OF ARCHANGEL MICHAEL

38

THE CATHEDRAL OF OUR SAVIOUR
BEHIND THE GOLDEN GRILLE

39

THE CHURCH OF THE TWELVE APOSTLES

40

THE BELFRY OF IVAN THE GREAT

onal in plan, receding progressively in size and height and leading up to a cylindrical drum crowned by a cupola and terminated by a large cross.

The entire composition of the tower is based on the principle of lightening the successive architectural masses as they rise, progressing from

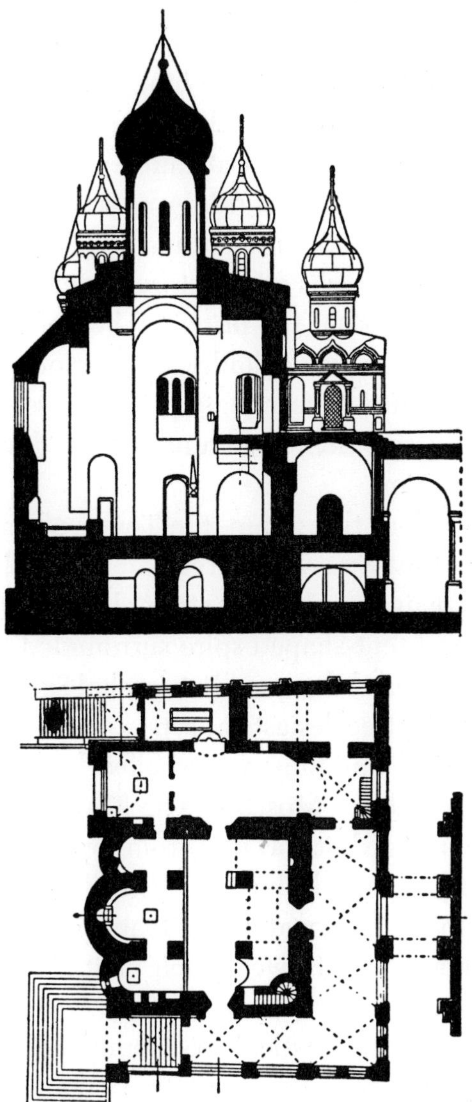

Figure 4. Plan and section of the Cathedral of the Annunciation.

the large, heavy, simple elements at the bottom to the smaller, lighter, more complicated at the top—carrying them, as it were, through the cross into space. The effectiveness of this design is largely the result of the subtle transition from the dominant horizontality below to the verticality and broken lines of the architectural elements above.

This tower was built during the reign of Tsar Boris Godunov[13] in 1600, as indicated by an inscription in three rows of huge, gilded, interlaced, cursive Slavonic characters, forming a highly decorative frieze just below the gilded cupola.[14] The imposing structure is a definite expression of an age, of a political and social era, reflecting the tastes, material aspirations, and political ambitions of Tsar Boris Godunov, who dreamt of perpetuating his dynasty. It is as though Godunov felt that by erecting it he had created a symbol of grandeur, a monument dominating everything created before him by the House of Rurik.

The Tower of Ivan Velikii is the dominating element in a group of three contiguous buildings erected at different dates but forming one unit. The central and oldest part of this group is the Bono Tower, begun in 1532 and finished in 1543, antedating the Tower of Ivan by some sixty years. The Bono Tower is a four-story structure, from which rises a two-story belfry that houses the principal bell of Moscow. This two-story belfry is surmounted by a cylindrical tower of considerable height crowned by a golden cupola terminating in a cross. The architect followed the ancient Russian belfries as a model but developed a complex architectural composition.

The second building of this group, the Tower of Patriarch Philaret,[15] was built in 1624, in the reign of Philaret's son Mikhail Feodorovich, the first Romanov. The main tower is four stories high; a fifth story of arches is topped by a central tent-shaped spire surrounded by Gothic turrets. This tower formerly housed the great Patriarchal Sacristy, with its priceless collection of ancient ecclesiastical art.

This entire group of buildings was shelled by the French in 1812 before their departure from Moscow. The Tower of Ivan Velikii was the most severely damaged; it was rent from top to bottom, but did not fall. Now completely repaired, the tower is still somewhat out of line—the Russians refer to it affectionately as "Ivan slightly tipsy."

The Tower of Ivan Velikii owes much of its imposing effect to its elevation and singularly conspicuous site. The placing of the huge tower in this spot created a salient vertical axis, commanding the neighboring cathedrals and all the other towers of the Kremlin. This axis of the Kremlin became at the same time the axis of all Moscow. The Ivan Tower houses thirty-three bells, including (it is said) the famous bell of Novgorod that once summoned the people to important gatherings in the public square. These bells are in the three upper tiers, the very large ones on the first tier and the smaller ones on the second and third tiers.[16]

The Russians have always had a fondness for bells, which at the end of the sixteenth century seem to have been regarded as sacred instruments of worship. The bells were cast in copper and silver in many sizes and varieties of timbre, power, and beauty of sound. Infinite tone-color effects were created by the various choirs of bells giving utterance to religious and lay emotions—ranging from alarm, tragedy, and sorrow to joy and exaltation. On days of disaster or funerals, certain bells were tolled; on days commemorating some happy event, other bells were used; on holidays or days of celebration, all the bells went into action. The first stroke was usually sounded from the Bono Belfry (which houses the largest bell) and then taken up by the bells of the Tower of Ivan Velikii, followed by all the bells of the "forty-forties" *(sorok-sorokov)* of churches in Moscow, booming and rolling in unison over the city like the waves of the sea or ringing out singly in soft resonance like a song of meditation.

Near the Tower of Ivan Velikii on a granite base is the so-called "King of Bells" (Tsar Kolokol). Boris Godunov intended that this huge bell[17] should hang in the Ivan Bell Tower, but it was found too heavy for the building to support. It was therefore hung on a platform outside the tower, but a few years later a fire in the Kremlin destroyed the platform and the bell was broken. Recast and hung in the belfry during the reign of Aleksei Mikhailovich, the bell fell, when the beam supporting it was damaged by fire, and broke into several pieces. In 1735, during the reign of Empress Anne, it was recast by the Russian master Ivan Matorin and his son, and much metal was added to it. It is said that everyone wishing to contribute to it threw gold or silver into the four casting furnaces, thus increasing its weight from the original 8,000 to 12,000 *pud* (432,000 pounds). The finished bell remained in its hole until 1737, when a fire broke out and destroyed the scaffolding and the roof over it. The bell became overheated and cracked on contact with the streams of water and a huge piece split off, leaving an aperture large enough to admit two persons abreast. It remained half buried at the foot of the tower for nearly a hundred years, until Montferrand (the architect of St. Isaac's in Leningrad) had it excavated and mounted on its present base in 1835 by order of Nicholas I.

The bell is believed to weigh about two hundred tons. The sides are decorated with effigies of Tsar Aleksei and Empress Anne and several icons; a globe and cross surmount the top.

At the corner of the barrack buildings (on the south side of Communist Street) is the "King of Cannon" (Tsar Pushka), weighing about forty tons. Designed for cannon balls one meter in diameter, this cannon is a purely decorative piece of artillery cast by Andrei Chokhov in 1586 at the command of Tsar Feodor, who was anxious to have the biggest cannon in the world. Tsar Feodor's equestrian portrait in relief appears upon it. A pile of giant cannon balls is arranged near by. Along the barrack walls and the façade of the arsenal are a number of old Russian and captured foreign cannon.

The remnants of the two Kremlin monasteries—the Ascension (Voznesenskii) and the Miracle (Chudov)—were removed after the Bolshevik revolution, and a large office building was erected on the site.

The Chudov Monastery was founded in 1365 by St. Aleksei on the grounds of the Court of the Tartar Khans, beyond the walls of the Kalita Kremlin. According to legend, the ground was given by the Tartar Khan Chenibek in gratitude for the miraculous cure of his ailing wife Taidula by St. Aleksei. In 1440 the Metropolitan Isidor, who attended the Council of Florence and horrified the Russian orthodoxy by acknowledging the supremacy of the pope, was imprisoned in this monastery. In the middle of the sixteenth century Maxim the Greek[18] worked here, and somewhat later one of its monastic cells was occupied by the notorious False Dimitrii under the name of Grigorii.[19] Pushkin's dramatic tale *Boris Godunov,* which was adapted as a libretto by Mussorgsky for his opera of the same name, opens with the scene in a cell of this monastery between the old monk Pimen and the young ambitious novice Grigorii, who soon was to become the crowned tsar. Here also the Patriarch Ignatius, who had blessed the False Dimitrii, was imprisoned in 1606; and here in 1612 the Patriarch Hermogen[20] was starved to death, the Tsar Vasilii Shuiskii having already been compelled to become a monk in the convent.

The Ascension Convent, formerly in a court near the Saviour's Gate, was founded in 1389 by Grand Princess Eudoxia (Evdokiia), wife of Dmitrii Donskoi. The monastery church, built in 1519, became the burying place of all the Moscow grand princesses and tsaritsas from Eudoxia, the wife of Dmitrii, to Natal'ia Alekseevna, sister of Peter I, who was buried there in 1728. The Tsaritsa Marpha, one of the wives of Ivan the Terrible and mother of the murdered Dmitrii, was brought here from Beloe Ozero. She was treated with feigned respect, but was forced to recognize the pretender as her son and to receive his Polish bride Marina Mniszek as her future daughter-in-law. She eventually denounced the usurper, and caused his downfall and murder.

VII

PALACES

The Kremlin Terem[1] Palace (Teremnoi Dvorets) is one of the oldest in the world. During the six centuries of its history the palace has been enlarged, demolished, burned, and rebuilt many times. From the end of the fifteenth century nearly every passing decade brought to it something new, leaving traces of the aesthetics and mode of life of the particular age.

The top of the Kremlin hill was chosen by the Russian rulers as a site for their estate and residence as early as the twelfth century. Here the wooden mansions *(khoromy)* of the vanished princes were located. In the fourteenth century this group of palatial residences was already famous for its beauty and wealth; frequent fires and other disasters failed to prevent the group's expanding and developing into a large complex of buildings dominating all Moscow.

At the end of the fifteenth century, with the arrival of the Italian architects and the erection of the masonry cathedrals, there was a general movement among the wealthy patricians of the day to build new palaces and mansions in masonry—the princes of the Church and of the reigning house in the lead. The Kremlin soon began to lose the primitive character of an ancient Russian wooden city and to take on the appearance of a European citadel.

The first masonry structures—somewhat out of key with the prevailing wooden architecture of the day—were erected by Ivan III, not for residential purposes, but for formal, official needs. The masonry cathedrals, churches, and palaces were to demonstrate to his rivals—the native and foreign princes—his power, his wealth, and the importance of Moscow as the dominant principality in Russia.

In 1487 Ivan III commissioned the Italian architect Marco Ruffo to build the Palace of the Facets (Granovitaia Palata),[2] which was to serve him and many of his successors as a formal location for throne and audience chamber. This gray stone building, the oldest civil structure in Moscow, stands on the west side of Cathedral Square, adjoining the huge cream-colored mass of the nineteenth-century Grand Palace. Its construction was begun by Marco Ruffo but was finished by his compatriot Pietro Solario. The diamond rustications of the original façade recall the wall treatment of the Castello in Ferrara and the Pitti Palace in Florence. The Granovitaia, together with the Holy Vestibule to the west of it, is all that remains of the old palace of Ivan III. The Holy Vestibule (Sviatyia Seni) was renovated during the construction of the Grand Kremlin Palace in 1848.

The palace contains a large, square, vaulted chamber, about seventy-seven by seventy feet, whose size and effect of spaciousness are greatly accentuated by the single central massive pier, which made possible the use of four cross vaults to span the entire room. The chamber was admirably adapted for the great formal receptions of foreign ambassadors, the installations of the metropolitans and patriarchs, and the openings of the national assemblies. In 1552 Ivan IV celebrated the conquest of Kazan' in this room; in 1709 Peter I gave a banquet here to celebrate his victory over the Swedish at Poltava; here in 1761 Catherine II opened the first conference of the commission to draft the new law code *(ulozhenie)*.

The throne formerly stood on the south side of the chamber. In the west wall of the chamber, close to the ceiling, is a curtained opening through which the distaff members of the royal family who were not present in the hall itself could observe the ceremonies from an upper-level secret chamber without being seen.

The base of the central pier is surrounded by shelves forming a buffet; on great occasions the magnificent treasures of ancient gold and silver plate and vessels from the royal household were displayed here.

At the end of the fifteenth century Tsar Ivan III began to plan new living quarters for himself. The foundation for this palace was laid in 1499; the work was supervised by the architect Alevisio Novyi, who had previously demonstrated his abilities in the construction of religious edifices. These living quarters, constituting the lower floors of the still existing Teremnoi Dvorets, were finished in 1508 after the death of Ivan. During the construction of the palace, work also proceeded on the erection of a masonry wall to protect the palace from the constantly menacing Tartars.

In the sixteenth and seventeenth centuries each member of the royal family had his own court and quarters, each of which had a large substructure for retainers and servants, baths, kitchens, and storage area. All these structures were interconnected with corridors and covered passageways; dominating them all was the Terem Palace of the tsar.

The Terem Palace is a brick structure; the window architraves, portals, entablatures, and parapets are of white stone covered with carved strapwork, foliage, and figures of beasts and birds painted in bright colors. This ornamentation dates from the sixteenth and seventeenth centuries; it was renovated in the early nineteenth century. The apartments, contained within a five-story structure (now forming the north side of the Grand Kremlin Palace), are a series of small, low, generally vaulted rooms decorated with polychrome ornaments and images painted on gold or other backgrounds.

The sixteenth century—called by some authorities the golden age of Russian national art—was particularly notable for its experimentation, daring, and novelty. The architecture, the iconography, and the decorative arts were distinctive and highly imaginative. The period was marked by profound historic events and social upheavals that seriously affected the contemporary artist, who in turn produced the works of art that became the nucleus of Russian aesthetics.

The first decades of the sixteenth century brought to completion Moscow's absorption of the separate patrimonial appanages into a single state under the central authority of an autocratic grand prince. During that time Chernigov (1500), Pskov (1511), and Smolensk (1514)—the gateways to the West—were annexed. Moscow became a great metropolis, the largest city in Russia and the center of society, religion, learning, and art.

The growth and aggrandizement of the Moscow Principality, in the process of becoming a centralized state, is strikingly reflected in the iconography and the architecture of that age. The desire for national independence and unity brought new life and force into Russian art, and manifested itself in a wave of construction of masonry churches, palaces, and private residences.

In the second half of the sixteenth century, during the reign of Ivan IV (the Terrible), many new territories and peoples were annexed to Russia, which gradually acquired the characteristics of a multinational empire. The period 1533-1584 saw also further centralization of the state, establishment of absolute monarchy, and the introduction of reforms into all phases of economic, cultural, and social life.

At this time there was an enormous amount of artistic activity in Moscow— the capital was being flooded with new art forms and techniques. As a result, there emerged a clearer creative consciousness and a sense of liberation from the stifling Byzantine traditions.

Ivan the Terrible, grandson of Ivan the Great, was born in 1530, became grand prince of Moscow at the age of three, and in 1547 was crowned tsar—the first Russian ruler formally to use this title. His character has been interpreted in many different ways by historians, most of whom paint him in the blackest of colors. On the other hand, some modern historians (Zabelin, Kliuchevskii, Pokrovskii, and Wipper) have entirely reappraised the character of Ivan and his stormy career. Even the translation of his very appellation *Grozny*[3] has been criticized.

Ivan believed himself the descendant of Augustus Caesar and, according to Josephite doctrine,[4] God's vicar upon earth. He assumed the dazzling title of "tsar" (from the Roman "Caesar") and bitterly fought anything that challenged his one obsessing idea—the divine character of the power entrusted to him.

Widely read and a great bibliophile,[5] Ivan was one of the first Moscow rulers to appreciate the value of foreign cultures and to discover that the East as well as the West had something valuable to contribute. The conquest of the khanate of Kazan'[6] in 1552 brought into the Moscow state a territory with a relatively dense population of Moslem and pagan non-Russians. By this conquest Russia had annexed a segment of the Orient and, with the annexation of Astrakhan' in 1556, became an Oriental state itself. Muscovy now extended not only to the Urals but to the Caspian. The barrier to the Far East was lifted. The great trade routes that Kazan' controlled—the Volga highway to the Caspian and Caucasian markets, the Kama road to the Ural Mountains and the lands beyond—were at last opened.

Shortly after the fall of Kazan', Moscow received an unexpected visitor from across the seas—the Englishman Richard Chancellor.[7] The northern route that was opened as a direct result of this first visit by Chancellor provided an opportunity for greater understanding and cultural exchange between England and Russia. Ivan became a strong Anglophile, and even considered the possibility of marrying Queen Elizabeth to provide for himself an asylum in England if his dynasty fell. It is not surprising that he was called the English tsar by his intimates.

The eventful and turbulent epoch of Ivan the Terrible witnessed not only the great political and commercial expansion of the Russian state, but also the growth of cultural consciousness and the burgeoning of national culture and art. At this time the printing press was introduced[8] (1563), literature and the decorative arts were flourishing, and wood carving and metal working reached a high degree of craftsmanship.

During this period the development of Russian national culture and art was continuous; at the same time an effort was made to evolve a consistent art policy and ideology, especially in iconography. The violent controversy that flared up in Church and State clearly reflected the richness of intellectual life and the abundance of talent among the laymen and clerics who surrounded Ivan IV in the early years of his reign. Among the outstanding figures of Russian culture of the period were: the first printer and publisher Ivan Fedorov; the writers Peresvetov, Iermolai-Erasmus, the Metropolitan Makarii (compiler of the *Grand Cheti Minyei*),[9] Archpriest Silvester[10] (author of the *Domostroi*),[11] the tsar himself (who had considerable literary talent); the statesman, soldier, and author Prince Andrei Kurbskii;[12] the metal-casting specialist Andrei Chokhov; and the architects Barma and Posnik Iakovlev, builders of St. Basil's Cathedral.

Ivan IV, one of the first monarchs to make systematic attempts at exploiting art for state propaganda, gave a great impulse not only to architecture but to the development of icon painting and the applied arts and crafts. Ivan was endowed with a keen appreciation of the arts of the jeweler, the goldsmith, and the enameler, and was fully conscious of their value in enhancing the prestige of his regime. A conscientious dilettante and collector, he had the gift of discovering talented Russian artists and craftsmen, putting them to work, and getting the best from them. Ivan himself closely participated in the activity of his workshops. A number of works of art were begun at his order; when they were completed, he would accept or reject them according to his personal likes and dislikes. During his outbursts of piety and repentance, many churches and monasteries were the recipients of his gifts of icons, iconostases, vestments, and church vessels. The icon encasements, relic containers, ciboria, chalices, and censers made during his reign are among the finest examples of the art of embossing, chiseling, engraving, filigree, enameling, and niello work. Until the closing years of the sixteenth century, when the Stroganovs came to the fore as patrons of the arts, the tsar, with his immediate advisers among the clergy, remained the chief arbiter and customer of art.

The wealth of Moscow and the furnishings of the Kremlin court dazzled visiting foreigners. English travelers of that period, especially those who had an eye for precious metals and gems, described Moscow as another Peru.

Richard Chancellor described a royal banquet given by Ivan the Terrible in 1553:

> The Emperor sitting upon a high and stately seat, apparelled with a robe of silver, and with another diadem on his head; our men, being placed over against him, sit down. In the midst of the room stood a mighty cupboard upon a square foot, whereupon stood also a round board, in manner of a diamond, broad beneath, and towards the top narrow, and every step rose up more narrow than the other. Upon this cupboard was placed the Emperor's plate, which was so much that the very cupboard itself was scant able to sustain the weight of it. The better part of all the vessels and goblets was made of very fine gold; and amongst the rest, there were four pots of very large bigness, which did adorn the rest of the plate in great measure, for they were so high, that they thought them at the least five feet long. There also upon this cupboard certain silver casks, not much differing from the quantity of our firkins, wherein was reserved the Emperors' drink. . . .
>
> On Christmas day we were all willed to dine with the Emperor's Majesty, where for bread, meat, and drink we were served as at other times before. But for goodly and rich plate we never saw the like or so much before. There dined that day in the Emperor's presence above 500 strangers and 200 Russians, and all they were served in vessels of gold, and that as much as could stand one by another upon the tables. Besides this there were four cupboards garnished with goodly plate, both of gold and silver. Among the which there were twelve barrels of silver containing about twelve gallons apiece, and at each end of every barrel were six hoops of fine gold. This dinner continued about six hours.[13]

On June 21, 1547, shortly after the wedding of Ivan IV to Anastasia Zakharin Romanov, a great fire broke out in Moscow. The first thing to burn was one of the innumerable wooden churches of the Arbat quarter. The fire spread to the Kremlin, exploding the powder magazines, which were built into its walls and towers. The flames enveloped the monasteries, the treasury, the armory, and the palace containing Ivan's apartments. The roof of the palace burned, and the royal chambers were gutted.

By order of the tsar the palace was rebuilt and its exterior was decorated with carvings and statuary. Barberini, who visited Moscow in

1565, states that the roof of Ivan's palace was golden. Another traveler, Mikhalon Litvin, writes that the palace was adorned with Greek statues in the manner of Phidias. The walls and vaulting of this palace, known as the Middle Golden (Sredniaia Zolotaia Palata), were frescoed in 1553 under the direction of the priest Silvester, who had been largely responsible for the religious and moral training of the boy Ivan.

Miliukov[14] says that at this time the state, to its own glorification, was collecting Russian Orthodox relics from every part of the country. The Metropolitan Makarii ordered all icon painters to be brought from Novgorod and Pskov to Moscow. These painters, working in the shops of the Oruzheinaia Palata under the general supervision of the tsar and his close advisers, developed their own school of painting, which gradually took the place of the Novgorod School. They introduced a series of allegorical and historical themes, glorifying the power and wisdom of the tsar, teaching obedience and humility, and bringing into Russian art an element of worldliness that clashed with the sacred quality of the art of icon painting but significantly widened the circle of artistic possibilities. This school opened new horizons for individual creation, freed art from the chains of ecclesiastical tradition, and made it more national and essentially much more Russian in feeling than the painting of the Novgorod school, which had followed the Byzantine tradition.

The frescoes and ornamentation of the Zolotaia Palata are of special interest, because the thematic material and manner of its presentation illustrate the new phase in the development of Russian aesthetics that took place during the reign of Ivan the Terrible. These decorations show a change not only in direction, turning the Byzantine iconographic tradition toward feeling and expression, but in the very types—from Greek to Russian; most strikingly, these decorations exemplify the characteristic trait of the epoch—the subservience of painting to the general directives of the central government. Here for the first time secular subjects appear in paintings having a definite program character and literary content.

The celebrated icon painter Simon Ushakov[15] and another court official left a detailed description of the frescoes as they existed at the end of the seventeenth century. According to this description, sacred and profane subjects were intermingled in the wall paintings of the palace chamber. These paintings depicted scenes drawn from the Bible as well as: the earth with its waters and winds; the fiery circle of the sun and the circle of the moon; the air in the shape of a maiden; time winged with the four seasons; the circle of the creation; the sainted Russian princes; the story of the baptism of St. Vladimir and Russia; scenes from the life of Vladimir Monomakh; the story of Princes Boris and Gleb; the symbolic figures of Chastity, Reason, Purity, and Righteouusness.

The corridor frescoes[16] contain an entire theory of government. The tsar, youthful in appearance, is extolled as a righteous judge and fearless warrior; he distributes alms to the poor; from his hands flows water that sanctifies the people; he vanquishes impious foes. The inspirer of this series of pictures for molding the mind and heart of the tsar (thought to be the priest Silvester) is depicted in the guise of a wise hermit who acts as the young ruler's mentor.

These allegorical frescoes were quite a distinct innovation and many were offended, particularly by the nude and seminude figures. One "wench with naked arms, dancing with abandon," intended to represent "Lust," caused a storm. Viskovaty[17] indignantly expressed to the tsar his doubts as to the merits of the new trend in icon painting in general and of the frescoes in particular. He resented the artists' painting "according to their own understanding and not according to sacred writings." However, Viskovaty dwelt only on minor details, his criticism evidently being aimed at annoying his rival Silvester, the tsar's favorite at the moment. In 1554 an ecclesiastical council was convened to settle this matter, and the Metropolitan Makarii succeeded in proving Viskovaty's misgivings groundless and caused him to withdraw his accusations.

The frescoes of Ivan's Golden Chamber reveal the influence of German and Italian-Flemish engravings. This influence of Western engraving on Russian painting grew steadily and perceptibly. These early frescoes were in effect the precursors of those that appeared a century later on the walls of the Iaroslavl' churches.

Ivan's successor, his son Feodor (1584–1598), showed great interest in the arts and contributed to their further development. The number of painters, workers in mosaics and gold, embroiderers, lapidaries, and enamelers increased rapidly. The historian Karamzin writes that the Greek Archbishop Arsenius, who accompanied the Constantinople Patriarch Jeremiah on his visit to the court of the tsar in 1588, was amazed to see the exquisite mosaics on the walls of the Irene Palace (also known as the Small Golden Tsaritsa Palace) and the many enormous gold and silver vases in the shapes of unicorn, lion, bear, stag, pelicans, swans, pheasants, peacocks. These vases, so heavy that twelve men could carry them only with difficulty, were manufactured in Moscow.

The Golden Tsaritsa Palace (Zolotaia Tsaritsyna Palata) was described by Archbishop Arsenius, who visited Ivan's daughter-in-law the Tsaritsa Irina, sister of Boris Godunov.

> The apartment of the Tsaritsa, which was spherical in shape, shone with the purest gold; and by the ingenious design of the master builder, even words spoken in a whisper were distinctly audible. The vault was covered with gold and decorated with wonderful paintings. The walls were adorned with the costliest mosaics, which portrayed the acts of the saints, hosts of angels, martyrs and elders of the church; while above the magnificent throne, adorned with a blaze of jewels, a large icon of the Most Holy Immaculate Virgin, with the Eternal Child in her arms, surrounded by saints in golden crowns adorned with pearls, rubies and sapphires. The floor was covered with cunningly wrought carpets, on which the sports of hunting and hawking were represented lifelike; other figures of birds and beasts, carved in precious metals, glittered on all sides of the apartment. In the center of the vaulted ceiling, an exquisitely sculptured lion held in his mouth a serpent twisted into a ring, from which a golden chandelier was suspended.[18]

The Golden Chamber is about thirty-two feet square. The two intersecting arches that support the vaulting were reinforced in 1683 by gilded iron cross bars. The room has seven arched, deeply splayed windows with built-in seats, and on the walls and vaults are a series of frescoes, on legendary ecclesiastical and historical themes, painted on a gold background (hence the name "Golden Chamber"). As a reception salon for the tsaritsas (hence the name "Tsaritsyna Palata") the room was used for family activities—such as celebration of birthdays and christenings—as well as for a formal audience chamber for receiving patriarchs, high-ranking boyars, and the princes of vassal states.

The Golden Chamber was decorated with frescoes at the order of Tsar Aleksei Mikhailovich; it was renovated on the occasion of the coronation of Paul I, and again during the reign of Nicholas I. At present it is part of the ancient wing in the Grand Kremlin Palace.

During the reign of Feodor Ivanovich and the regency of Boris Godunov, the chamber of the Granovitaia Palata was decorated with frescoes similar to those in the Golden Palace. According to Ushakov, who restored the paintings in 1663, these frescoes also contain a mélange of Biblical and quasi-historical subjects, edifying parables, and allegorical figures. The thematic material was drawn from history, nature, and moral and philosophical subjects. Legendary scenes linking the Russian rulers with a representative of the world's oldest monarchy—Augustus Caesar—were allotted even more space, and political significance was highly stressed. One scene shows the aging Augustus Caesar "organizing the world" and sending his own brother Prus to the banks of the Vistula—the country that was thereafter called "Prus." Rurik, supposedly a fourteenth-generation descendant of the Roman Prus—and consequently of Augustus Caesar—was invited to be prince of Rus. Hence Ivan the

Terrible's claim that his family traced its descent to Augustus Caesar. Another scene depicts the Byzantine Emperor Constantine Monomakh sending the imperial regalia—the crown and mantlets *(barmy)*—to the Kievan Prince Vladimir. Tsar Feodor Ivanovich, wearing his crown and dressed in imperial robes, is seated on his throne; at the right stands Boris Godunov magnificently attired. They are flanked by many boyars in their colorful caftans and caps. The innovation is characteristic of the Moscow school, which from that time became more and more independent of the Novgorod school, setting itself to the study of nature and the human form. While Novgorod, imbued with the old traditions, was adhering to dark flesh tints, idealization of expression, simplicity of composition, and close harmony between its figures and background, Moscow strove for picturesqueness, used warmer colors, more accurately portrayed the human forms, and endowed human features with a certain grace and worldly expression.

The Ushakov frescoes remained on the walls of the Granovitaia Palata for more than two centuries. The years and the elements had taken their toll, and in 1881 the faded and damaged frescoes were repainted by the brothers V. and I. Belousov of the Palekh Sofonov Studio.

In the reign of Tsar Aleksei Mikhailovich the Gentlest (1645–1676) the old palace attained its most beautiful and luxurious aspect. The five apartments of the fourth story were renovated and refurnished as his private quarters. The first room (Peredniaia), its walls frescoed with images of the saints (originals by Ushakov, restored by Solntsev in 1837), functioned as a waiting room for the boyars seeking audience with the tsar. The second room, the Room of the Cross (Krestovaia Palata), served as a reception room for the tsar and occasionally for boyar councils. Near the window stood a silver casket containing the original document of the Act of Election of Mikhail Feodorovich (the first tsar of the House of Romanov). At the back of the room was a casket containing the charter of the Patriarchate. The third room, sometimes called the Golden (Zolotaia), was the tsar's study where the high officials of state were received. This room contained a dais for the throne and some benches along the walls, where the boyars were seated according to seniority. An embossed casket contained the original manuscript of the book that gives an account of the election *(izbranie)* of Mikhail Feodorovich as tsar of Russia. This volume, with its colored illuminations and miniatures, is one of the most valuable monuments of the history of Russian civilization and seventeenth-century art. The center window of the Golden Room, known as the Petitioners' Window (Chelobitnoe Okno), had a device for raising and lowering a small box between the room and the ground. Into this box the poor and the wronged could place their petitions and complaints addressed directly to the tsar. The next room, the tsar's bedroom, has a carved four-poster with curtains of brocade and silk. Along its walls are benches upholstered in Venetian velvet. The fifth room was the tsar's private chapel or oratory (Plate 47), which has a pulpit and a fourteenth-century illuminated manuscript of the Book of the Gospels.

Outstanding as decorative features in all these rooms are the great faïence tile stoves. The stoves in the tsar's study and in the chapel are especially noteworthy as monuments to the great skill and artistry of the seventeenth-century Russian craftsmen in producing colored and glazed tiles and pottery *(tsenina)*.

Back of these rooms is a long narrow corridor with a carved stone floor. According to tradition, this corridor served as the inspection place for girls eligible to become the tsar's bride. On appointed days the most beautiful daughters of the best families of the land would be lined up in this corridor; the tsar, walking slowly up and down, would look them over three times, and when his "luminous" eyes fell upon the most desirable he would present her with a specially embroidered towel as a token of his favor.

The fifth floor or penthouse apartment *(palata na cherdake)* has heavily ornamented vault webbing, pendant keys, door entablatures, window frames, and colored tile stoves.

This remnant of the past is a labyrinth of low corridors and vaulted chambers adorned with barbaric magnificence. The few extant architectural and decorative elements are truly authentic remains of ancient Russian art. Except for a few modern details and perhaps well-meant but unfortunate restorations, these chambers—with their massive gilt girders, narrow, deeply splayed mica windows, ceilings of polychrome arabesques on gold ground, and fresco-covered walls—offer a complete picture of the art and environmental culture of the royal court of the late seventeenth century.

The furniture and accessories remained practically unchanged from the death of Tsar Feodor in 1682 until the restoration in 1830. Then much of the feeling of antiquity was destroyed, giving these chambers a somewhat artificial toylike appearance, but there is still a strong seventeenth-century aura about them, especially in the interiors.

The decoration of the exterior of the Teremnoi Dvorets is in some ways even more striking than the interior. Alongside the Western classical decorative elements are ornamental motifs of a decidedly Russian folk character, especially in the windows and the entrance portals, that are the most interesting decorative details of the Terem façades. The builders of the palace, using the foreign architectural novelties as basic themes, embellished them with luxurious carving—the motifs borrowed from the wooden *khoromy* of the tsar—and thus transformed them into highly individual creations.

Alongside the Granovitaia Palata is the so-called Krasnoe Kryl'tso, the former grand or main entrance to the palace.

The Russian word "*krasnoe*" ("red") formerly had a wide meaning and was most often used as a synonym for "beautiful" or "goodly." Thus the name "Krasnoe Kryl'tso" admits of a double interpretation: first, it may signify "beautiful entrance or beautiful stairway"; or, literally, it may mean "red stairway or entrance" (on festivals and great state occasions, when the emperor used to visit Moscow, the whole staircase, and even part of the street, used to be covered with scarlet carpets). The stair is about sixteen feet wide; at its base are two fine arcades, one fronting the east, the other the south, and the parapet is adorned with reclining and upright painted and gilded lions.

The Red Stairway witnessed many scenes of violence and bloodshed during the disturbances that followed the death of Feodor Alekseevich in 1682. Power had been disputed by the court parties who represented the two wives of Tsar Aleksei—Maria Miloslavskii, mother of the sickly Feodor and Ivan, and Natal'ia Naryshkin, mother of Peter (the Great). The intriguing Tsarevna Sophia, eldest daughter of Tsar Aleksei and a woman of great intellect and energy, gave her important support to the Miloslavskiis. By circulating a rumor that her young brother Ivan had been strangled by the Naryshkins, she roused the people and the garrison of Moscow—the *strel'tsy,* who had grievances of their own against the Naryshkins—to mutiny. The *strel'tsy,* followed by crowds of the citizenry, marched upon the Kremlin. Under the eyes of the Tsaritsa Natal'ia, who appeared with young Peter on the Red Stairway, the crowd murdered her uncle Artamon Matveev[19] and then rushed through the palace exterminating all the members of the Naryshkin clan who fell into their hands. A brother of the tsaritsa, Afanasii Naryshkin, was thrown from the window upon the pikes of the *strel'tsy.* On the following day the tsaritsa's father Kirill and her brother Ivan were surrendered; Ivan was tortured and cut to pieces, and Kirill was maltreated and confined to a monastery. Seven years later, after having put down another uprising of the *strel'tsy* by mass executions and having confined the Tsarevna Sophia to a convent, Peter, clad in his robes of state, stood again at the top of the Red Stairway, this time showing himself to the people as their undisputed ruler.

The Red Stairway has been rebuilt several times—especially during the reign of Nicholas I, when it was radically altered. However, the architecture of the Granovitaia as a whole remains as it was in the fifteenth century, the only changes having been made in the formerly steep roof and in the richly carved seventeenth-century windows. The double windows on the south side, the door architraves off the Red Stairway, and the Holy Vestibule are suggestive of the original decoration.

Among the seventeenth-century palaces in the Kremlin is the one that belonged to the boyar Ilia Miloslavskii, who first occupied it in 1651. When Miloslavskii died, Tsar Aleksei Mikhailovich remodeled it into a theater and a place for the entertainment and diversion of his family and court. Known as Poteshnyi Dvorets (Amusement Palace), it still exists, though it has been considerably changed. Its projecting cantilevered balcony, especially constructed to support a house chapel,[20] is particularly interesting.

Between 1680 and 1690 many gardens, balconies, and stairways were added to the Kremlin. Near the Church of the Saviour behind the Golden Grille stone passageways, covered and open arcades, hanging gardens, and cupolas crowning the roofs of various chapels were built—the passages and galleries permitting the tsar to communicate with the patriarch without having to leave cover.

At the end of the seventeenth century the short but important reign of Feodor Alekseevich (1676–1682) was marked by the greatest achievements in architecture and decoration. Between 1670 and 1700 the Kremlin reached its mature beauty when the ancient and traditional forms merged harmoniously with the elements of the Moscow baroque.

After the transfer of the capital to St. Petersburg in 1713 all the Kremlin palaces were abandoned; they were unoccupied until 1753, when the Empress Elizabeth (daughter of Peter I) decided to return to Moscow. Elizabeth commissioned Rastrelli[21] to build her a new palace facing the Moskva River. (Napoleon lived there before the fire of 1812.) Appearances were more or less kept up during her lifetime, but the buildings were poorly maintained and were gradually crumbling away.

The eighteenth century, notably its first half, was a period of decline in the architectural activities of Moscow and of advancing decay of the Kremlin. Peter the Great, who detested Moscow and all it represented, was busy building a new capital. All his energies and resources that could be spared from waging war were concentrated on the establishment of a new center of Russian civilization. Moscow and the Kremlin, associated in his mind with the bitter memories and frightful events of his childhood, were purposely neglected. His immediate successors followed his example. Not until after 1750 did the government do anything concrete about replanning the old capital, widening its streets,[22] and reviving the dying Kremlin. Commissions were created to take charge of cleaning up the accumulated debris and restoring the old structures, but little was accomplished. Here and there among its more imaginative caretakers were a few who dreamed of bringing back to the Kremlin its former glory and of investing it with a new beauty.

Such a visionary was the young Russian architect Vasilii Ivanovich Bazhenov, who was attached to an artillery engineering unit in the Kremlin Arsenal, serving as chief architect for the artillery services.

Bazhenov (1737–1799), the son of a poor church deacon, studied for the priesthood at the Slavonic-Greek-Latin Academy in Moscow, but it was soon discovered that his talents lay elsewhere. The boy was forever drawing, sketching, and carving. He was transferred first to the gymnasium attached to the Moscow University and then to the newly opened school of architecture at the Academy of Fine Arts in St. Petersburg. On graduation in 1760 he served for a while on the staff of Rastrelli "the Magnificent," and then was chosen to be one of the first pensioners to be sent by the academy to Paris for further study and additional polish. There he studied under de Wailly, and was greatly influenced by eighteenth-century French classicism. He was particularly fascinated by the works of Gabriel, Soufflot, and Peyre, who were the great architectural leaders of the epoch and who directly or indirectly helped to form his architectural tastes.

He traveled extensively in France, and in 1762 he was encouraged by the Russian authorities to go to Italy, where he studied at the academies of fine arts in Rome, Florence, and Bologna. Rome offered him a professorship, and Florence and Bologna conferred upon him the title of academician—honors that had never before been granted to Russian artists. On his return to Russia in 1765 he was lionized, presented to the Empress Catherine II, and given several commissions which he carried out successfully. The Petersburg Academy gave him the title of academician, but offered no professorship. He gained favor with some of the great nobles of the day, and became architect to the powerful and immensely wealthy Prince Grigorii Orlov.[23]

Soon, however, his star began to decline. The Frenchman Vallin de La Mothe and the Italian architects Rinaldi, Camporessi, and later Quarenghi were the reigning architectural figures in the capital. The French and Italians were entrusted with the most important commissions, the native Russians being relegated to unimportant tasks. Young Bazhenov was commandeered to the forgotten old capital of Russia, Moscow, to work for the artillery services. Not much is known about his professional activities at this time, but it can be surmised that as public-works officer he took part in some of the Kremlin maintenance work and carried out odd jobs under the general supervision of his commanding officer and patron Grigorii Orlov, the chief of supply services and the great favorite of Catherine II.

While serving as government architect in the Kremlin and brooding over his misfortune of being stuck in the province, burdened with dull routine and much red tape, he was inspired with the idea of redesigning the entire Kremlin. He conceived the new Kremlin as one vast structure, or rather a large complex of structures conforming in its general plan outline to the triangular site of the Kremlin—its enormous façade screening the existing cathedrals and monasteries. The principal element of this vast complex was to be the huge building of the palace itself, with a large oval court of honor fronting its main entrance (on the east side). The four-story palace was to contain a series of sumptuous formal salons, living quarters for the empress and her suite, a church, a theater, picture galleries, a library, service quarters, and all the necessary appurtenances for royal pomp, security, and luxury.

The arrangement of the main and secondary buildings of the Bazhenov Palace complex together with the old structure was intended to reorganize the entire general plan of the Kremlin, creating a series of new formal squares and arterial avenues. The main colonnaded oval court, with an obelisk in its center, was to become the nodal point of the plan. Several minor courts, all interconnected with thoroughfares lined with huge colonnades, were also projected. The principal radial avenues, which were planned as a continuation of the arterial highways of Moscow, were to converge toward the main court.

The palace was planned to occupy the entire area extending from the Saviour's Gates on the east to the Trinity Gates on the west, with the principal façade more than 2,100 feet long facing the river and with a series of terraces and stairways leading down to the water's edge. The structure was projected as a closed triangle, enclosing all the Kremlin cathedrals and monasteries, its left side abutting the arsenal, its right terminating at a point near the Saviour's Gate. Each of the three façades was designed in a different style: the principal was to have a Corinthian order; the two other, Ionic and Doric respectively.

The extant plans and elevations, and especially the model carefully prepared by Bazhenov for this gigantic project, convey a clear idea of what this third Kremlin—planned to replace the primitive wooden Kremlin of Kalita and the masonry Kremlin of Ivan III and the first

Romanovs—would have looked like. The principal façade, with its tall, double-story rusticated substructure and the colossal orders extending through the two upper stories, gives the exterior a certain grandeur of scale and imposing effect.

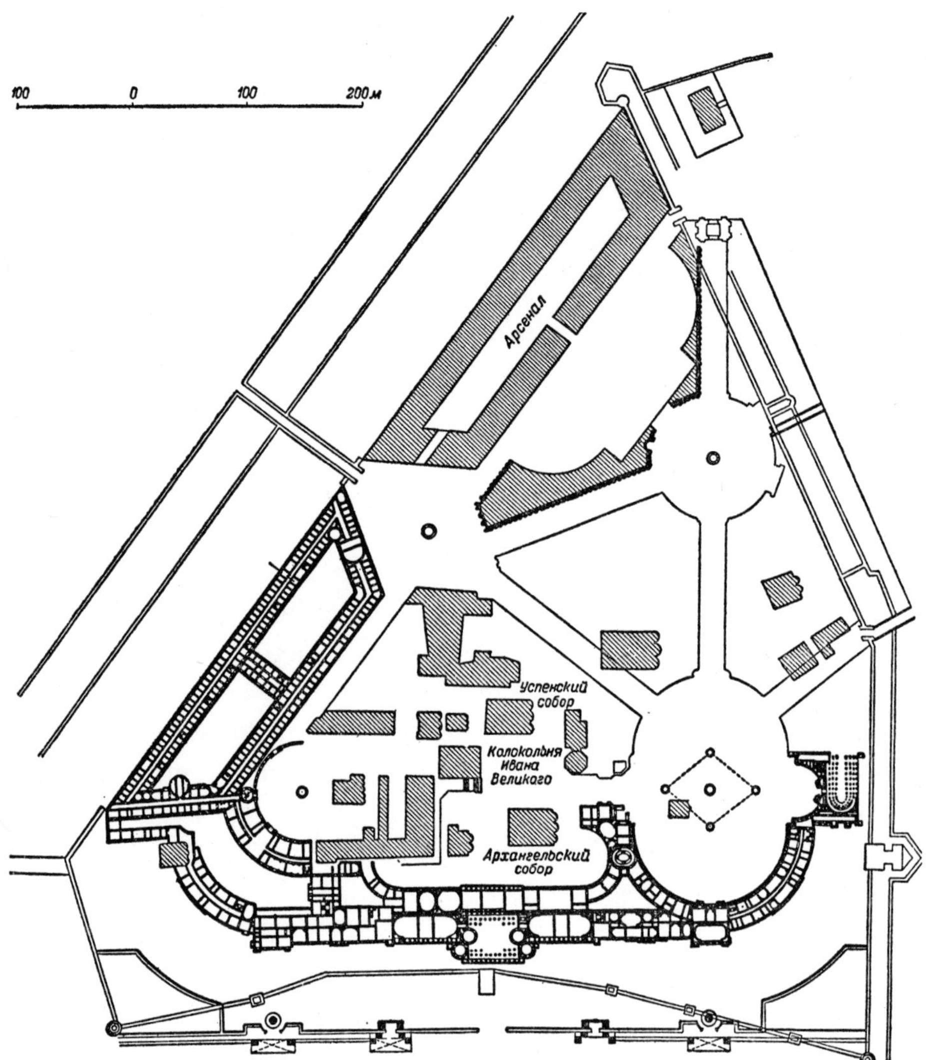

Figure 5. Bazhenov's proposed plan for the Grand Kremlin Palace.

The center of the main façade of the palace is marked by a strong projecting element with rounded corners. North of the central element is a large semienclosed court intended to contain the cathedrals and the Belfry of Ivan Velikii. South of the structure are outlined three terraces leading to the river. Opposite is an imposing semicircular peristyle.

Columns and colonnades, so much in fashion at that age, are everywhere. Entire forests of them decorate the principal façades as well as the inner courts and esplanades. Bazhenov said that his design was to be a "hymn to the column." The young architect dreamed of the vast French royal chateaus, of the old Roman Forum and the Bernini colonnades, of the Renaissance palaces with their massive substructures, archways, porticoes, and pediments; yet he never lost sight of the historical, sentimental, and artistic values of the ancient Kremlin monuments, the best of which he was determined to restore and preserve within the new structure.

Although Orlov—with whom Bazhenov discussed his plans—knew little about art, he was sufficiently impressed to bring the project to the attention of the empress. The empress—a prodigious builder, forever associating with artists and architects, and ready for anything new in artistic expression—was overwhelmed by the boldness, scale, and imaginative quality of the project. The time was ripe for doing something of this kind. This was the age of worship of the antique by architects and painters as well as by such philosophers and aesthetes as Voltaire, Diderot, and Grimm, who were Catherine's personal friends and artistic mentors. There were other, even more important reasons. There were no suitable quarters in the Kremlin, or in all Moscow, to accommodate the empress and her court on her visits to the old capital. Then too, this "Russian Minerva," highly skilled in setting the diplomatic stage and manipulating public opinion abroad, felt that some such stupendous and costly bit of construction was the proper antidote for the rumors circulating in the capitals of Western Europe that Russia, as a result of her current war with Turkey, was financially bankrupt. So huge and so magnificent a project would draw the attention of all the European chancellories and prove that Russia had enough power and resources not only to wage war, but to build on a grand scale. What is more, it would carry down Catherine's name in history and make her forever famous as one of the greatest builders of all times and all nations.

The cost of construction was estimated by the architect to be between twenty and thirty million rubles (at present equal to about 210,000,000 gold rubles). Camporessi, a contemporary architect, thought that the cost would be at least fifty million rubles (now, 350,000,000 gold rubles).

The empress approved the project, assigned 120,000 rubles for preparing working drawings and a model, and gave orders that the preliminary work of clearing the ground was to be started at once. The architect and his assistants spent nearly four years in preparing the model, which was built to a scale of 1 : 48 by the German woodcarver Witman at the enormous cost (for those days) of 50,000 rubles.[24]

Edward Clarke, who inspected the model, describes it in his book *Travels in Europe:*

The plan was to unite the whole Kremlin, having a circumference of two miles, into one magnificent palace. Its triangular form, and the number of churches it contains, offered some difficulties; but the model was rendered complete. Its fronts are ornamented with ranges of beautiful pillars, according to different orders of architecture. Every part of it was finished in the most beautiful manner, even to the fresco painting on the ceilings of the rooms, and the colouring of the various marble columns intended to decorate the interior. It encloses a theatre, and magnificent apartments. Had the work been completed, no edifice could ever have been compared with it. It would have surpassed the Temple of Solomon, the Propylaeum of Amasis, the Villa of Adrian, or the Forum of Trajan. Camporesi spoke of it in terms of equal praise, but at the same time he confessed to me, that Quarenghi, his countryman, at Petersburg, an architect well known for his works in that city, entertained different sentiments. Quarenghi allowed it to be grand, as it must necessarily be, from its stupendous nature; but thought it too much ornamented, and too heavy in many of its parts.[25]

In 1769 work was begun on the preparation and clearing of the site. Many ancient structures—including the seventeenth-century office buildings *(prikazy)*, the Treasury Building (Kazennyi Dvor) erected in 1483 by the Italian architect Marco Ruffo, and a few churches—were razed. Somewhat later the Tainitskaia Tower, the two neighboring Nameless (Bezymiannyia) Towers, and the entire wall between the Petrovskaia and Annunciation (Blagoveshchenskaia) towers were removed.

When the old underground passages, cellars, dungeons, and some forgotten graves were uncovered, the stench of putrefied matter (the "balsam odor" as one of the writers of the day described it) was so overpowering and sickening that the empress thought it advisable to postpone the excavations until winter.

The formal excavation ceremony was held with great pomp in August, 1772, but the cornerstone was not laid until almost a year later. Work was progressing rather slowly. The empress made constant changes in the plans she had previously approved, and Bazhenov himself had to report to her frequently and personally to explain every detail. Even the model was transported to Petersburg for her inspection.

Finally, when everything was approved and confirmed by Catherine, the ceremony of laying the cornerstone was held on June 1, 1773. There was a colorful procession by the large brilliantly uniformed architectural and engineering staff; the architect and other dignitaries made speeches; and a flowery ode to the "Semiramis of the North," especially composed for the occasion, was rendered by a choir; a casket, containing the enabling act and the data about the project's author and his principal assistants, was lowered into place—the crowd roared, the cannons boomed.

This was probably the most memorable day in the life of the thirty-six-year-old Bazhenov—it seemed as though his dream was about to become a reality, his name destined to be placed alongside the greatest world architects, but the empress had other plans.

The war with Turkey was going favorably for Russia. There was no further need for impressing the outside world with the inexhaustible resources of the empire. The previous highly publicized descriptions of the project and reports of its progress had served their purpose. Peace with Turkey was signed in 1774, and Catherine was already thinking of other projects—and other architects. Money for the continuation of the Kremlin reconstruction was withheld, and in 1775 Catherine issued an order to stop the work altogether.

The official excuse was that the structure was too massive, that the soil of the Kremlin hill could not support such a heavy load—a flimsy excuse, because Bazhenov and his very able and practical assistant Kazakov, of whom more later, thoroughly investigated and tested the soil and provided for every contingency.

Thus ended this greatest of all eighteenth-century architectural dream projects. There are some who think that its sad ending was a blessing in disguise; they argue that it would have dwarfed all the ancient monuments, and that the Kremlin would have become an odd conglomeration of Italian, Muscovite, late baroque, and resurgent classic architectural influences. On the other hand, there are those who feel that Bazhenov was extremely conscious of the possible clash between the existing old and the proposed new; that in developing his design he was aiming to create an architectural complex that would harmonize with the best of the old remnants; and that, by replanning the Kremlin and by laying out his new great plazas, arterial thoroughfares, and imposing approaches, he was providing a magnificent setting for the ancient monuments and reëmphasizing the beauty of the whole.

Of the entire ambitious project, nothing remains except the large wooden model.[26] The excavations were filled; the wall and towers were rebuilt by Bazhenov on a line slightly removed from their former position. Conscious of the historical and sentimental significance of his work, the architect restored those elements to their original state.

The Kremlin, however, could not entirely escape being affected by the wave of classicism that was then sweeping all over Russia. Shortly after the Bazhenov fiasco Matvei Kazakov, formerly second in command on the reconstruction project, was commissioned to design a number of buildings in the Kremlin. He was more fortunate than his predecessor. Of the several projects that he submitted, two were accepted and actually built: the Archbishop's House (1775) and the Senate Building (1776–1787), housing at present the offices of the USSR Supreme Soviet.

The simple and compact plan of the Senate Building is in the form of a triangle, its inner court broken up by connecting wings into three segments: two small triangles and one large pentagon. The triangular

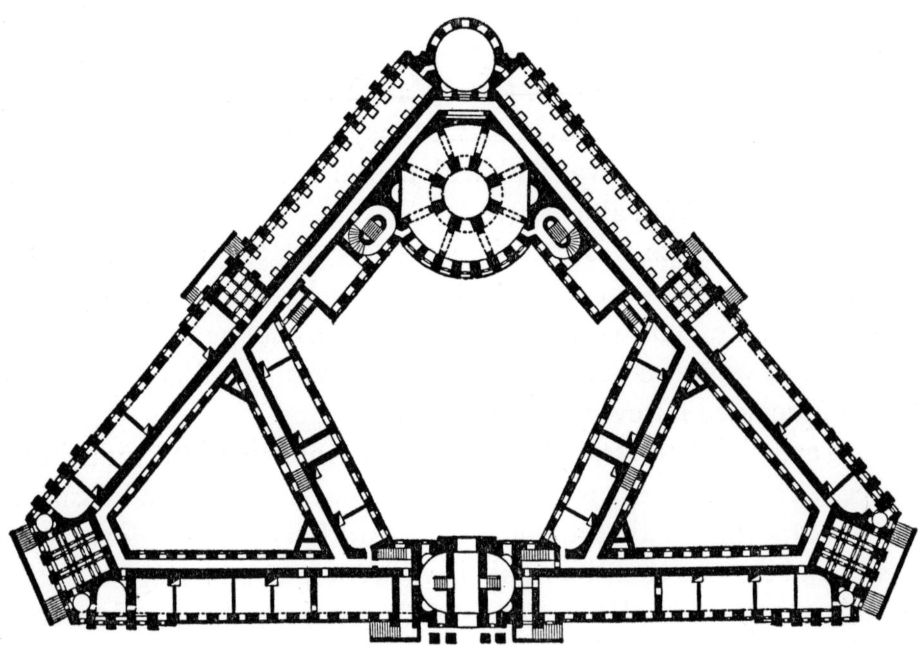

Figure 6. Plan of the Senate Building.

plan was dicated by the fact that the site was hemmed in between the Kremlin wall, the former Chudov Monastery, and the Arsenal Building. The dominant feature of the composition is the large circular domed senate chamber, (eighty-three feet in diameter and ninety feet high) at the apex of the triangle. The interior of this Russian Pantheon is decorated by a magnificent Corinthian colonnade supporting a cupola with a coffered ceiling. Especially notable are the allegorical bas-reliefs depicting the history of the reign of Catherine II.

In contrast to the sumptuous interior, the exterior is distinguished by the simple and severe treatment of its long façades. Kazakov achieved an effect of classic dignity by placing the two upper stories on a rusticated substructure, including them in one order of flat pilasters, and crowning them with a handsome cornice. The main façade is fronted by a four-columned Ionic portico that frames the arched carriage entrance. The building is a remarkable example of early Russian classicism, displaying a great fertility of invention and profound familiarity with the

41

THE TEREM PALACE

42

THE RED STAIRWAY AND PALACE OF FACETS

43

INTERIOR OF THE PALACE OF FACETS

44

CHAMBER IN THE TEREM PALACE

45

THE GOLDEN TSARITSA CHAMBER IN THE TEREM PALACE

46

BEDROOM IN THE TEREM PALACE

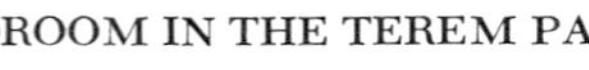

47

THE TSAR'S PRIVATE CHAPEL
IN THE TEREM PALACE

48

STAIRWAY IN THE TEREM PALACE

49

WINDOW IN THE TEREM PALACE

50

WINDOW IN THE TEREM PALACE

51

WINDOW IN THE TEREM PALACE

52

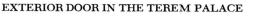

EXTERIOR DOOR IN THE TEREM PALACE

53

WINDOW IN THE PALACE OF FACETS

54

DOOR ARCHITRAVE IN THE TEREM PALACE

55

THE GRAND KREMLIN PALACE

56

THE HALL OF ST. VLADIMIR
IN THE GRAND KREMLIN PALACE

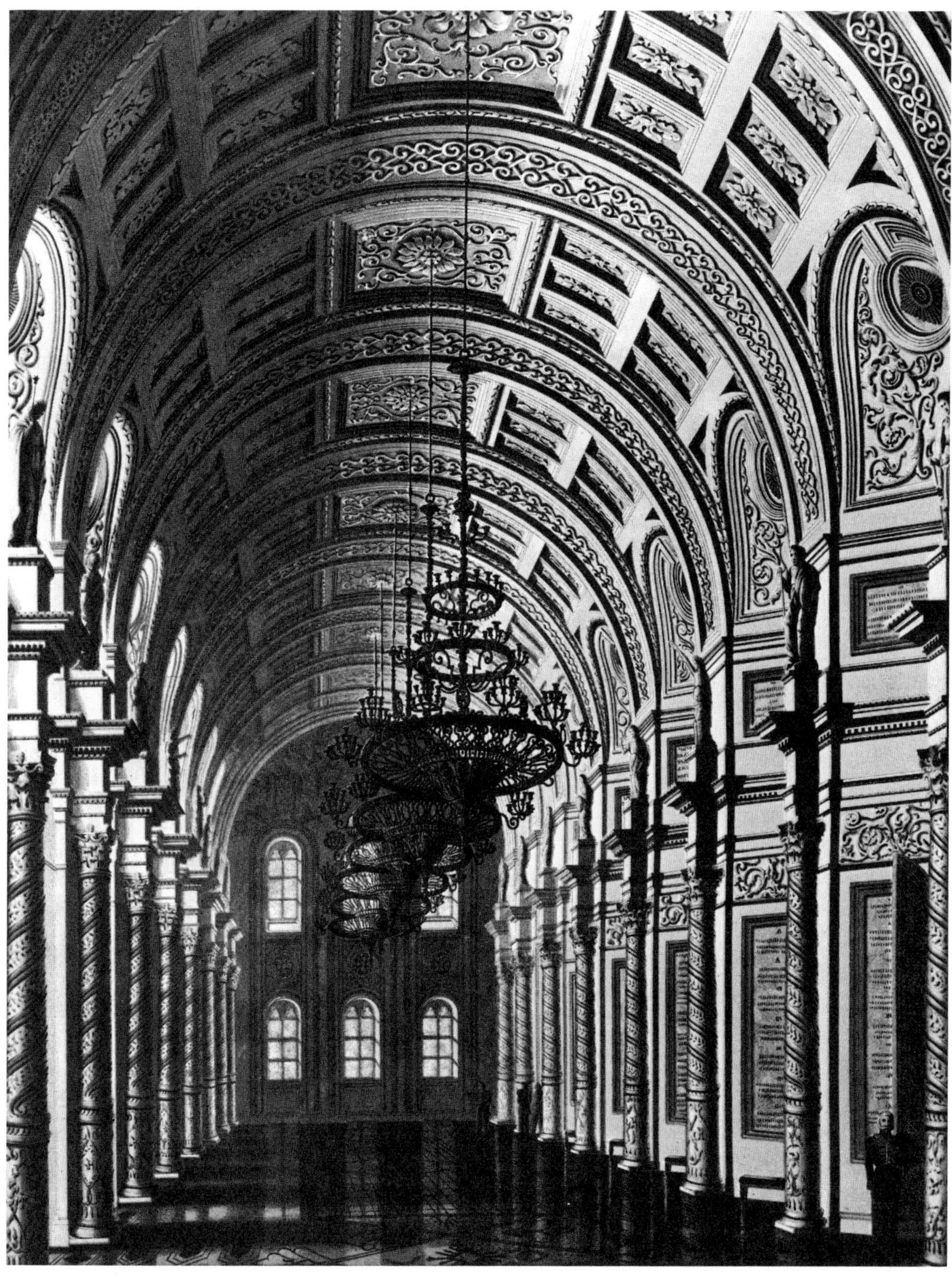

57

THE HALL OF ST. GEORGE
IN THE GRAND KREMLIN PALACE

58

THE HALL OF ST. ANDREW
IN THE GRAND KREMLIN PALACE

classic orders, but it gives the impression of being out of key with the surrounding golden-domed cathedrals and tent-covered towers.

For more than half a century after the completion of the Senate Building, hardly anything of importance was added to the Kremlin. Construction in St. Petersburg and vicinity was still absorbing most of the nation's energies and resources. There was also considerable building activity in Moscow and its suburbs and in some of the provincial cities, but the Kremlin was neglected.

The suite of apartments in the old Terem Palace and the small baroque palace built for Elizabeth by Rastrelli were entirely too small, uncomfortable, and inadequate for official functions. Then too, the hodgepodge of the surrounding dingy structures was forever staring in the face of visiting royalty. Finally, about 1830, Nicholas I decided to remove a number of the old structures and build a new palace to serve as his Moscow residence.

The aesthetics of the age of Nicholas I—the age of "official nationalism" based on the Uvarov[27] formula "Orthodoxy, Autocracy, and Nationalism"—are clearly revealed in the building of the new palace; its architecture reflects the unique characteristics of the great construction wave that swept Russia during the early decades of the nineteenth century—the postwar (1812) period of awakened national pride and enthusiasm, initiating large projects in architecture, painting, and sculpture.

Classicism, which nurtured Russian creative thought for more than a century, began to seem foreign, imported. Instead the Russian architects began to look to the national forms of architecture and decorative art. Official nationalism and the growing tide of Slavophilism—two currents running parallel but issuing from different political and social sources—were instrumental in arresting the tide of Western classicism and turning the aspirations of the Russian intelligentsia toward the interrupted development of national art.

Nationalism was stimulated and guided by the reactionary regime of Nicholas I, who wanted to crush the slightest manifestation of progressive thought, and who saw in his particular brand of nationalism a means of combatting the ferment of the dreaded liberalism of the Decembrists.[28] Official nationalism in architecture was largely formulated by the Academician Konstantin Thon,[29] who sought to create a "genuine" Russian style based on old motifs derived from "Russian-Byzantine," "Russian-Gothic" and even "Russian-Hindu-Gothic" architecture.

The Slavophils—especially the more enlightened—also advocated nationalism in art, but their nationalism was based on the artistic activities of sixteenth- and seventeenth-century Russia, on the originality of the construction methods peculiar to that period, on the taste and skill of the Moscow artisans, on the churches of Novgorod and Iaroslavl', and on the peasant "izbas" of the Dvina and Volga regions. Western civilization and art, transplanted by Peter the Great and his successors, were looked upon by the Slavophils as a sickly growth in a soil that was never meant to receive it, causing an interruption in the development of national life and art and stifling the native genius and the instinctive aspirations of the nation. It was necessary to repair and restore the links of the broken chain and to imbue architecture and the other arts with the national spirit.

Unfortunately the early phase of this movement coincided with the rampant chauvinism of Nicholas I; good taste was at a low ebb, and style was almost nonexistent. Consequently little was accomplished.

Official nationalism found its clearest expression in the architectural projects of Thon. Ostensibly the idea underlying the design of his two principal works—the Grand Kremlin Palace and the Church of Christ the Saviour[30]—was the creation of monuments embodying the forms and expressing the spirit of national architecture. Actually these buildings fall far short of their purported aim. Only details here and there have superficial national characteristics—such as the decoration of the window architraves, the "tent" over the roof of the Grand Palace; essentially they are only a lifeless imitation of ancient Russian forms.

The huge Grand Kremlin Palace (Bol'shoi Kremlevskii Dvorets), occupying an area of nearly half a million square feet, was erected between 1839 and 1849 on the site of the old estate of the medieval Russian princes and tsars (Plate 55). In clearing the site for this palace many old structures were demolished. Fortunately the Golden Tsaritsa Chamber, the apartment of Tsar Aleksei, the Granovitaia Palata, and a few old churches were spared; all were incorporated in the new palace, which was built in the form of a quadrangle.

The Grand Palace covers a large part of the Kremlin hill, and its dome-shaped, gilt belvedere is visible for miles. The architecture is an incongruous mixture of various periods and forms of Italian Renaissance and pseudo Russian. The most noteworthy features of the Grand Palace are immensity and the sumptuousness of its materials. The principal wing (four hundred feet long and ninety-two feet high) faces south, and contains some of the great state salons. The north wing contains the old apartments of the Terem Palace. On the east are the Cathedral of Annunciation and the Granovitaia Palata with its Red Stairway; on its west side are the Oruzheinaia Palata (the old armory) and the Poteshnyi

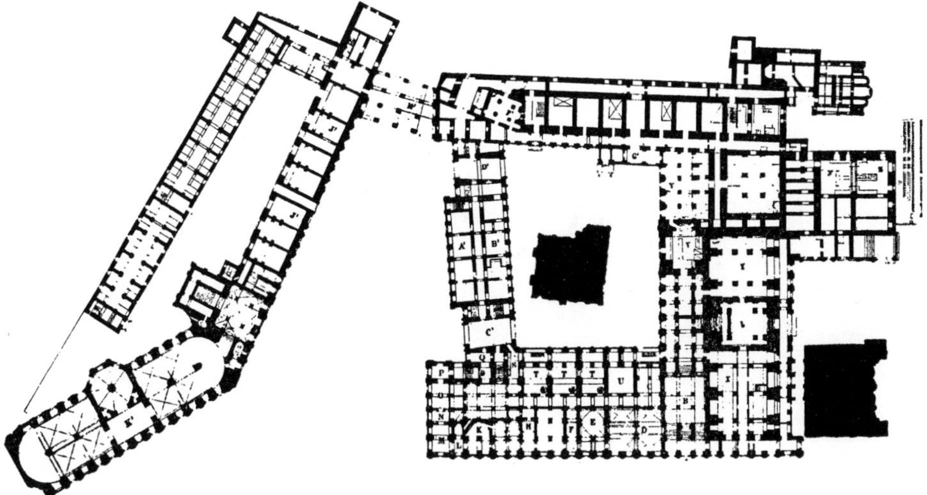

Figure 7. Plan of the lower floor of the Grand Kremlin Palace, with the Oruzheinaia Palata at the left.

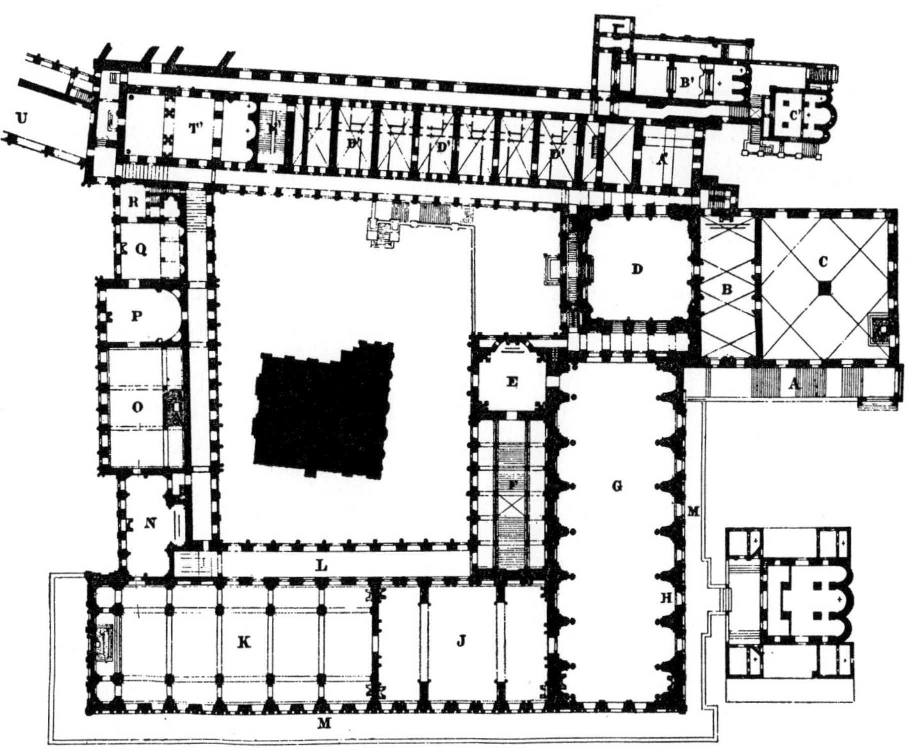

Figure 8. Plan of the upper floor of the Grand Kremlin Palace.

Dvorets (Amusement Palace). North of the Terem Palace wing are the former barracks of the Chevaliers Guards.

In the center of the quadrangle is the fourteenth-century Church of the Saviour in the Forest (Spas na Boru), the oldest building in the Kremlin. Of its ancient mural decorations, there remains only the picture of the Transfiguration, which is ascribed to the Moscow school of the fifteenth century. The rest date from the nineteenth century.

The magnificent granite staircase of the main wing of the Grand Palace, consisting of fifty-eight steps in five flights, leads to the State Parade Antechamber, the vault of which is supported by four monoliths of gray marble. On the first floor, to the left of the vestibule, is the so-called *sobstvennaia polovina* (own half), formerly the private apartments of the tsars, richly furnished in the style of the mid-nineteenth century.

The antechamber, at the head of the main stairway, contains a large canvas by the great Russian painter Repin, representing a group of peasants doing homage to Alexander III. A door to the right leads into the great festal halls.

The interiors are decorated with rare woods, malachite pilasters, marble and alabaster columns, crystal chandeliers, and much gold. The general impression is of great luxury and opulence, of great decorative architectural ambitions. The halls or salons, dedicated to different orders of chivalry, are ornamented with appropriate glittering heraldic motifs. The furniture and walls of each hall are draped with silk in the colors of the particular order.

The Hall of St. George (Georgievskaia Zala) is located on the site of the "Middle Golden Palace" of Ivan IV. This gigantic hall (Plate 57), the largest in the Kremlin (200 feet long, 68 feet wide, and 58 feet high), receives its name from the Order of St. George the Victorious, the highest imperial military order. Inscribed in gold upon the marble slabs in niches along the wall are the names and dates of the Russian regiments that distinguish themselves in battle as well as the names of individual knights of the Order of St. George the Victorious. Alexander Hall (dedicated to the Order of Alexander Nevskii) has pink walls of imitation marble decorated in gold. The Hall of St. Andrew (Andreevskaia Zala), the former imperial throne room, has square columns and vaulted ceiling decorated with flowers of gold and heraldic devices (Plate 58); the inlaid floor is of striking design—more than twenty kinds of wood were used to produce intricate and elaborate patterns of scrolls and flowers. The Halls of St. Andrew and of Alexander have been combined into one large chamber to accommodate the yearly meetings of the Supreme Soviet.

Most of these halls are arranged along the principal south façade of the Grand Palace. In the west wing are the Guard Room, the Hall of St. Catherine, the State Drawing Room, the State Bedroom, and the Winter Garden.

The Hall of St. Vladimir (Vladimirskaia Zala) serves as a connecting link between the remainder of the old Terem Palace and the new (Plate 56). To the east is the Holy Vestibule (Sviatyia Seni), which connects with the Red Staircase and the Granovitaia Palata. A stairway leads out of it into the old palace. From the first landing there opens a view of an old terrace, the Verkhospasskaia ploshchadka, which is surrounded by an ornamental gilded railing (Zolotaia reshotka). This railing was cast in 1670 from the copper coins that, because of their decrease in value, caused the bloody uprising in 1662 (the Copper Revolt),[31] and were therefore withdrawn from circulation.

To the right of the terrace is the entrance to the small Chapel of the Saviour behind the Golden Grille (Spas za Zolotoi Reshetkoi), often called the Upper Cathedral of the Saviour (Verkhospasskii Sobor). This highly decorated chapel (Plate 38) was built above the Zolotaia Tsaritsyna Palata from 1678 to 1681 by the architects Ogurtsov, Konstantinov, Sharutin, and Ilarion Ushakov, who also built the upper floors of the old palace. The builders designed the chapel as an ornamental feature of the tsar's palace, and concentrated special attention on its group of eleven cupolas. The cornice and the cupola drums are embellished with colored tiles designed by the Elder Ippolit, one of the best craftsmen of the late seventeenth century. Drastic changes were made in the interior decoration at the end of the eighteenth century.

VIII

ART TREASURES

The Kremlin is not only one of the greatest monuments of Russian medieval architecture, it is also one of Russia's richest treasure houses of decorative art. Large collections of sacred and secular art objects—church vessels and furnishings, illuminated manuscripts, carving, embroidery, jewelry, and enamels—are contained in the sanctuaries, sacristies, palaces, and, most of all, in the Oruzheinaia Palata[1] museum. The treasure of the Kremlin is in many ways a chronicle of the aesthetic development of the country. It contains a history in precious metals and jewels as well as in the stones and bricks of the walls and towers.

In the design and ornamentation of the art objects two principal styles may be distinguished: the geometric, primarily of Eastern origin; the naturalistic, of Western. From these styles Russia borrowed many elements and suggestions, reworking them, fusing and imbuing them with a spirit entirely her own, and incorporating them into the very heart of her national art.

Influenced by its geographical position and by extensive trade with the Near and Far East, Russia naturally borrowed and preserved many elements of various Eastern sources during the early period of its history. The influence of Persia, India, China, Asia Minor, Byzantium, and of the frequent invasions of the Mongols is highly evident.

The influence of Western art is, at the same time, far from negligible. Art historians disagree about the importance of this Western influence as compared with the purely Eastern elements in the arts of Russia. Viollet le Duc, in his *L'Art Russe,* analyzes the origins of Russian art in general and the elements of which it consists, and arrives at the conclusion that Russian art is composed of elements borrowed from the East to the almost complete exclusion of all others. This historian says that Russian art is the product of three basic elements: the local Scythian, the Byzantine, and the Mongol. Nine-tenths of these elements, he maintains, are Eastern.[2]

On the other hand, a number of Russian historians hold that the West and Scandinavia exercised a more marked influence on the art of Russia than is commonly supposed, especially before the sixteenth century, after which time Western influence is commonly acknowledged. These historians point out that Russia was early influenced by Roman art (at Novgorod), by the Italian Renaissance (the Moscow Kremlin), and by the Polish-Italian phases of the baroque (the churches of the so-called Naryshkin style at the end of the seventeenth century). Russian art was thus affected by all the phases of Western art, with the possible exception of the Gothic, whose birth and development practically coincide with the period of the Tartar domination over Russia.

From the middle of the seventeenth century these Western influences, which for a long time were more or less sporadic and superficial, assumed a more and more dominant role at the expense of Byzantine traditions. Icon painting gave way to the painting of portraits; the shops of the Oruzheinaia Palata became crowded with foreign artists and craftsmen. The "Friazin"—Frankish or Italian—art triumphed over the Byzantine.

Many foreign artists and craftsmen played an important role in the formation of Russian art. Byzantium, Persia, and Syria contributed large contingents; Italians, Germans, Poles, and Hungarians also entered the workshops of the tsars and the patriarchs—each brought an element of his native art and skill.

These artists, who were necessarily men of adventurous natures and often of wide education and many talents, both gave and received; they adapted themselves to their changed conditions and engrafted motifs and elements found in their new country upon their own art, with the result that their productions, though recalling the art of their original fatherlands, were imbued with the spirit of their adopted country.

Russian decoration, in all its variety of design and color, can be studied in the apartments of the old Terem Palace on every wall, every window and door architrave, as well as on the enameled tile *(tsenina)* of the stoves. This decoration is to be found also in the sanctuaries on the altars, on the baldaquins, iconostases, and royal doors of the churches; on the arms, saddles, and harness; and on the metalwork, jewelry, embroidery, and other objects exhibited in the Oruzheinaia Palata of the Kremlin. The spectator may perhaps be dismayed by the excessive barbaric magnificence, by the lavish display of jewels and precious metals; he may feel that the refinement of the Persian and Byzantine art is lacking—but he cannot escape the grandeur and marked originality of Russian art.

In the Russian concept of the silhouette and form of an object, a peculiar elegance and grace and nearly always a concern for the pictorial effect are clearly evident. Whether the object is a *bratina* (loving cup), the façade of an iconostasis, or the frame and breastplate of an icon, the Russians (like the Persians and Arabs) use ornamentation to clarify proportion and to enliven what would otherwise be a blank space. The ornament of the Russian architect, for example, is nearly always a sort of tapestry or embroidery in low relief—an interlacing of floral, animal, and geometric ornament—which entirely fills the surface to be decorated and yet does not interfere with the architectonic or structural lines of the edifice or room.

Among the Russian collections of ancient vestments, manuscripts, books, and church furnishings, the first place in importance is rightly held by the Patriarchal Vestry (Patriarshaia Riznitsa), situated in the former Palace of the Patriarchs in the Kremlin. This collection is truly outstanding, not only because of the intrinsic value of its objects in precious metals and rare gems, but also because of the significance of its treasures in the history of Orthodox iconography and early Russian applied art.

The objects in this collection came from the personal belongings of the Moscow metropolitans and patriarchs, as well as from the various vestments, crowns, croziers, and other furnishings used by them during the church services and rituals.

After the abolition of the patriarchate and the institution of the Holy Synod by Peter I in 1721, the Patriarchal Vestry became known as the Synodical Vestry (Sinodal'naia Riznitsa) and the Patriarchal Library was made into a separate establishment.

Many of the objects contained in the Synodical Vestry and in the sac-

59

THE IMAGE OF OUR LADY

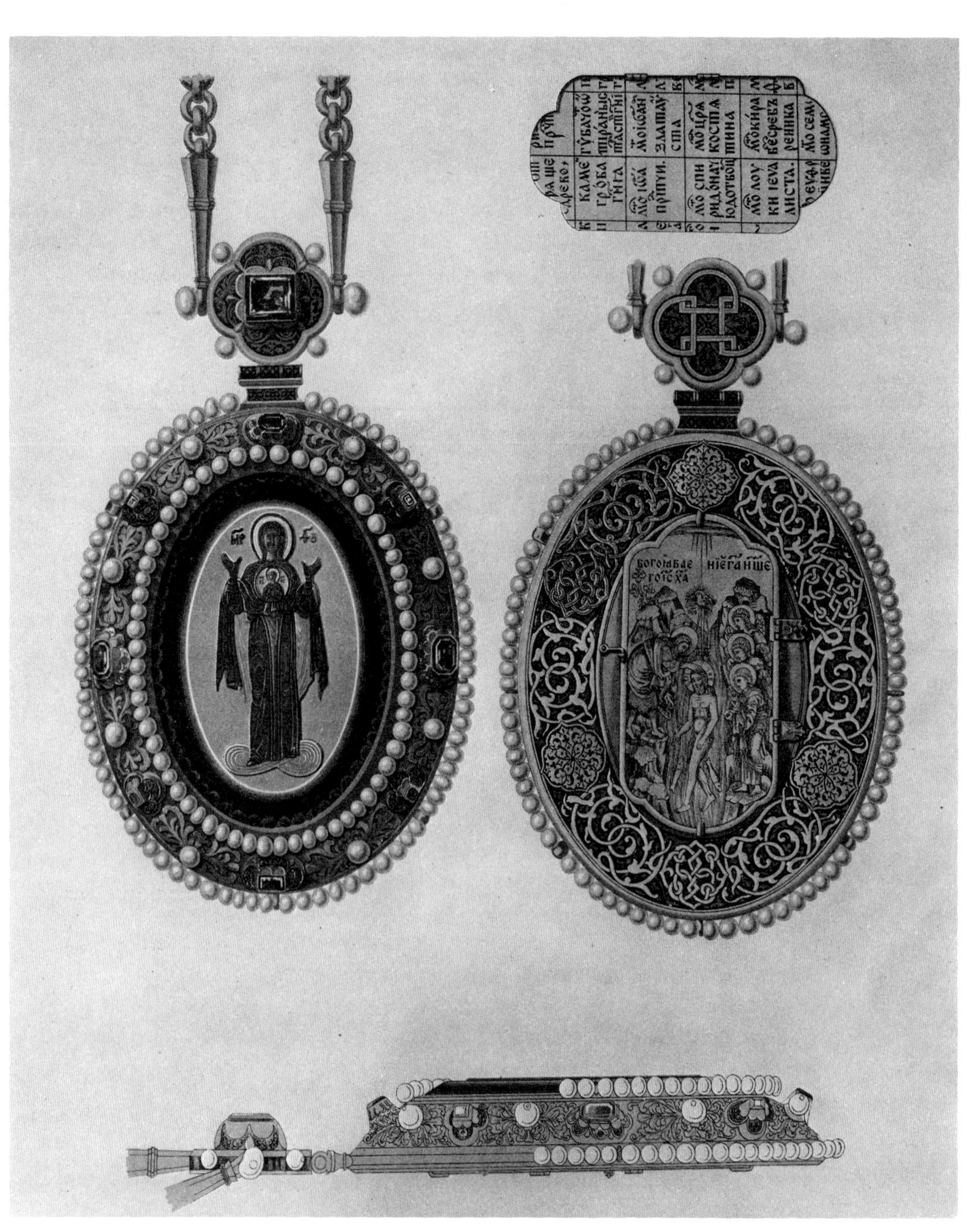

60

THE PANAGIA OF PATRIARCH PHILARET

61

THE "JERUSALEM" TABERNACLE

62

GOLD CENSER

63

THE ARMLETS OF PATRIARCH NIKON

64

THE CROWN OF PATRIARCH NIKON

65

THE PECTORAL CROSS
OF TSAR MIKHAIL FEODOROVICH

66

SILVER PANAGIA WITH GILT ORNAMENT

67

FRONT COVER OF THE MSTISLAV GOSPELS

68

FRONT COVER OF THE BOOK OF THE GOSPELS

69

FRONT COVER OF THE BOOK OF THE GOSPELS

70

THE SACCOS OF METROPOLITAN DIONISII

71

DETAIL OF THE SACCOS
OF METROPOLITAN DIONISII

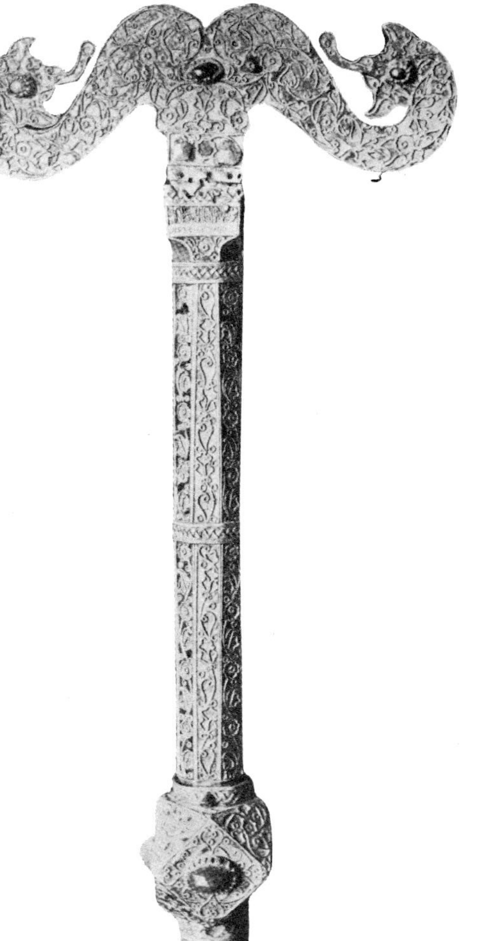

72

THE PASTORAL STAFF
OF PATRIARCH NIKON

73

THE PASTORAL STAFF
OF PATRIARCH PHILARET

74

CARVED WOOD ALTAR CROSSES

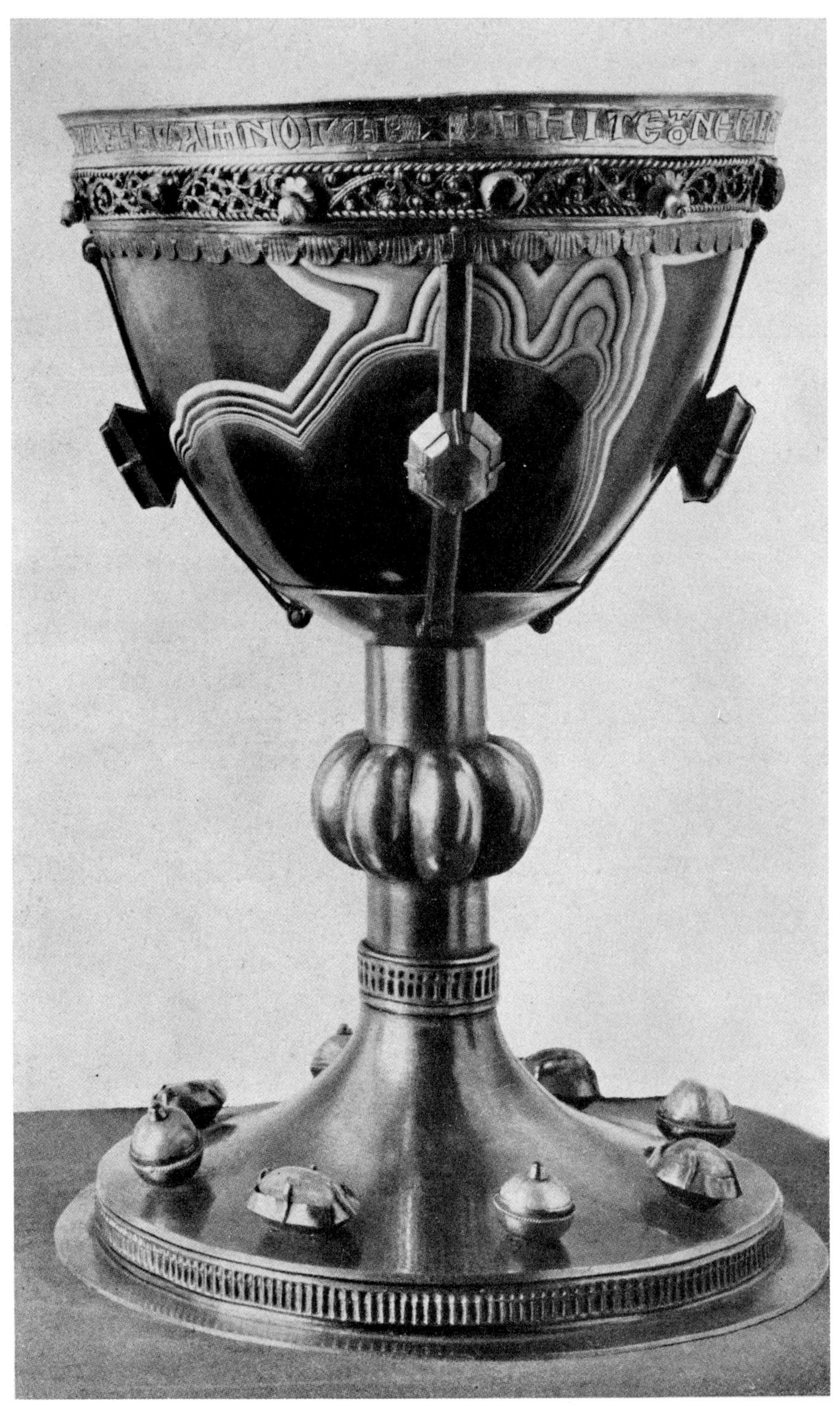

75

CHALICE

76

SEVENTEENTH-CENTURY COSTUMES
OF THE TSAR AND HIS ATTENDANTS

77

EMBROIDERED REGALIA COLLARS (BARMY)

78

THE ORB OF
GRAND PRINCE VLADIMIR MONOMAKH

79

THE CROWN OF
GRAND PRINCE VLADIMIR MONOMAKH

risties of the Kremlin churches do not exist in their original state—most of them have been altered or entirely remade. Yet these collections are still the finest and most significant depositories of ecclesiastical art in Russia, containing as they do some of the richest collections of church furnishings—sacredotal robes and vestments embroidered with pearls and precious stones, crowns, miters, panagias, pectoral crosses, pastoral staffs, censers, chalices, communion plate, and quantities of beautifully bound and illuminated service books.

Russian ecclesiastical jewelry is frankly designed for richness of effect; extensive surfaces of precious metals are displayed, and the gems are large and of dazzling color. Although flamboyant, the style is not in vulgar taste. The designs are well executed, and the color effects produced by the precious stones and enamels are harmonious. The decoration is based on the principles of flat design in sharply contrasted colors, and is infused with the spirit of the Orient.

The human figure is freely used in the representation of religious subjects. Ornament consists largely of foliate designs and scrolls or of systems of repeating scrolls; a relation with similar designs in textiles or decorative sculpture is apparent. Gems and pearls enrich the more precious objects; the gems in box settings or gold cells, the pearls threaded on gold wire to form borders around medallions or compartments or as frame edgings.

One of the unique and interesting specialties of the art of the Moscow goldsmiths—a specialty that became highly developed at the beginning of the seventeenth century—was the decorative encasement *(oklad)* of icons. This custom of enriching the painted image with gold and jewels became a thoroughly established tradition. Spurred on by the pious zeal of the donors and yielding to the general taste for opulent backgrounds, the goldsmiths began adorning the icons with precious metal plaques that were embossed, chiseled, or engraved with arabesques, or nielloed or enameled in color on a silver or gold background and studded with precious stones and pearls. The borders of the frames were covered with similar silver strips that were often set with jewels. The flat golden nimbus of early times was given relief as a halo *(venchik)* and adorned with *repoussé* or with filigree or twisted gold wire *(skan')* sometimes picked out with enamel; later the halo became an actual crown. But the zeal of the donors did not stop at these symbolic ornaments. The artists began to decorate icons with silver-gilt collars *(grivny)* in the symbolic form of crescents, and with pendants *(tsaty)* attached to them. To the haloes they began to add earrings and strings of pearls, diamonds, sapphires, rubies, and emeralds to hang along the forehead. The passion for magnificence and opulence in the design of religious objects became truly extravagant.

As early as the fourteenth century, under Greek influence, the Russians began to cover even the figures in the icons with plates of silver, showing in more or less relief the outlines and folds of the clothes and vestments. Such a plate (*riza*—properly speaking, a religious vestment, especially a chasuble or alb) was first applied to the large stationary icons and later to those that individuals received as gifts at baptism or on special occasions. Paul of Aleppo[3] described the icons in the Uspenskii Cathedral: "All around the church and about the four piers are set great icons of which you can see nothing but the hands and faces. Hardly any of the clothing can be distinguished (i.e. the painting); the rest is thick *repoussé* silver and niello. . . . " Even more opulent were the trappings of the icons in the Cathedral of the Annunciation, the favorite church of the wives and daughters of the tsars. "No goldsmith," said Paul of Aleppo, "however skilled, could evaluate the great stones, diamonds, rubies and emeralds, set upon the icons and haloes of Our Saviour and Our Lady; the jewels glow in the darkness like burning coals. The gilding of the icons with pure gold, the many-hued enamel executed with the finest art, all arouses the admiration of the keen observer. The value of the icons in this church would fill several treasuries."

The outstanding examples of ecclesiastical metal craftsmanship are the various articles and vessels used in the preparation and celebration of the Holy Eucharist, as prescribed by the Orthodox Church: the chalice, the paten, the astericos (*zvezditsa*) used to cover the paten, a star-shaped object with rays bent to form feet, and the spoon (*lzhitsa*) used with the chalice—all of chiseled or enameled gold. A host of other objects were used during the liturgical services or great ceremonial processions; censers (*kadila*), ciboria, reliquaries, crucifixes, croziers, and processional lanterns. These were all given special attention in careful workmanship and lavish decoration.

The panagia is a peculiar ornament or sacred vessel of the Russo-Greek Church. The Greek word "*panagiia*" (most holy) refers figuratively to the Holy Virgin and by extension to the triangular communion wafers and to their containers, which are of two kinds: the pectoral panagia (*naperstnaia panagiia*) is a jewel worn suspended from the neck by the high dignitaries of the Church as a symbol of office, an object on which much care and rich decoration are lavished; the portable or travel panagia (*putevaia panagiia*), usually in the form of a circular or elliptical locket, made of two hinged, concave pieces, is worn by priests in the same way, and used for carrying the communion wafers on a journey or when visiting the sick. The panagiar is a small round plate, decorated with the image of the Virgin, on which the communion bread is placed for the rite of Elevation.

Many of the panagias in the patriarchal sacristy of the Kremlin are fine specimens of craftsmanship; they are of gold or silver, enameled and set with precious stones and occasionally with remarkable cameos (Plate 66).

Several types of crosses are used on different occasions. These crosses vary in size, design, material, and richness of decoration—from the simple, rudely stamped brass crosses of the poor peasantry to the enameled and bejeweled crosses of the patriarchs, metropolitans, tsars, and wealthy nobles. Very often a plain cross is set in the center of another, more elaborate or conventional, and nearly always sacred monograms and inscriptions in Slavonic characters are engraved on the field.

The small pectoral cross *(tel'nik* from the Russian word "*telo,*" meaning "body") is the most common, and is worn directly on the body.

Crosses, somewhat larger than the pectoral, worn by the members of the clergy over their vestments usually have an image of the crucifixion on them; these are called bosom crosses *(naperstnyie kresty).*

The large wood, ivory, or metal altar crosses *(naprestol'nyie kresty)* are used by the priest for blessing the worshippers and also at various other ceremonies.

The tau-shaped crozier or pastoral staffs *(posokh)* of Russian bishops are usually made of silver-gilt, except for a few good examples of ivory. The staff of Patriarch Philaret (1619–1633), silver-gilt, hexagonal, diminishing slightly toward the foot, is embossed on its entire surface with vertical bands of floral arabesques of the kind frequently found on Russian metalwork. There are three bosses set alternately with rubies and turquoises; on the ends of the head are two large sapphires. On the top are inscriptions deeply engraved, and on the sides are representations of the Passion.

Another staff of the same patriarch has for its head a curved piece of walrus ivory set in silver-gilt, chased and nielloed at the extremities with representations of cherubim. On the top is an inscription in Slavonic: "Philaret, Patriarch of Moscow and of All-Russia"; the upper boss is decorated with green enamel (Plate 73).

The top of the pastoral staff of Patriarch Nikon (1652–1658) is more elaborate, a curved ram's horn Oriental in character, and of the Indo-Tartar type (Plate 72).

The censer (Plate 62), the use of which seems to have derived from the ancient Hebrew ceremonial, is one of the most important sacred utensils, and is in constant use in the Russo-Greek church.

As in the West, certain architectural forms occur frequently in church vessels, and it is not surprising that certain features of Russian ecclesiastical architecture and ornament are prominent, especially the bulbous cupola *(lukovitsa)*. A square or hexagon-shaped body with a cover is often used, suggesting a series of *kokoshniki* supporting one or several drums that bear cupolas, each surmounted with a cross.

Representations of the Saviour and of the saints are usually arranged on the sides of the principal element in *repoussé* and chased niches. The hieratic characteristics of Byzantine iconography have been preserved, but Russia's distinctive treatment of the figures of saints and groups is manifest. The foot is often ornamented with niello tracery and with decorative inscriptions of interlaced Slavonic letters in compartments. The chains are of simple oval links, with now and then a small cross; the thumb pieces are similar to the cover in style, and are highly decorated.

The tabernacle or ciborium, the vessel for Eucharistic wafers *(darokhranitelnitsa)*—often called "Zion" or "Jerusalem"—is usually in the form of a church or shrine with domes or cupolas surmounted by a cross. One such tabernacle made during the reign of Ivan the Terrible is in the sacristy of the Uspenskii Cathedral. It is built in the form of a cupola-church, and is a characteristic specimen of Russian art of that period (Plate 61).

Bible covers are usually of precious metals enriched with filigree or *repoussé* ornament and gems. Pearls often serve to form borders around Biblical scenes and figures of saints executed in enamels or in embossed work. Smaller scenes of figures are usually arranged along the margins and at the corners. The cover of the Mstislav Gospels, 1103–1551 (Plate 67), and that of the Gospels presented to the Uspenskii Cathedral by Tsaritsa Natal'ia Kirillovna in 1689 (Plate 68) are but two of the outstanding examples of the art of the book and its covering.

The Oruzheinaia Palata is one of the oldest, richest, and most interesting museums in the world, containing the hereditary treasures of a long line of grand princes, tsars, and emperors—one of the great decorative art collections in Europe.

The Kremlin collections came into being through no conscious planning of any single prince or tsar. No premeditated scheme shaped their formation. Rather, they represent the collective creative life of the Russian people, whose rulers—the dual representatives of Church and State—were inveterate collectors of arms and armor, gold and silver plate, precious stones, jewelry, snuffboxes, watches, and other objects of ecclesiastical and secular art, reflecting the history, the ambitions, the tastes, manners, and customs, the love of splendor of the nation—above all, its predilection for solidity and opulence and its appreciation of the colorful and picturesque. In wealth, craftsmanship, and historical interest, these treasures are rivaled only by the collections of the Louvre, the Cluny, the Tower of London, and the Kensington Museum.

The objects of art displayed in the vestibule and halls of the Oruzheinaia Palata are mostly from the seventeenth century, with a few from the twelfth, fifteenth, and sixteenth centuries. Richard Chancellor hints at the collections existing in 1555 when he mentions "goodly gownes, two of them as heavie as a man could easily carrie, all set with pearles over and over, and the borders garnished with sapphires and other good stone abundantly."

The Hall of Armor (Bronnaia Zala) houses a complete collection of Russian armor from the thirteenth to the seventeenth century, representing the accouterments and battle equipment of every branch of service and rank—from the commander in chief *(pervyi voevoda)* to the private *(prostoi ratnik)*.

The Hall of Arms (Oruzheinaia Zala) displays the firearms—military, hunting, and parade—the shields, quivers, standards, and even the medallions and portraits of the Russian sovereigns, mostly from the seventeenth and eighteenth centuries.

The Crown Hall (Koronnaia Zala) has a number of coronation robes on display, including the robe of Catherine II that was so heavy with gold and jewels that it needed twelve chamberlains to support it. Here also are the jewels and insignia of former tsars, including the crown attributed to Vladimir Monomakh (Plate 79) and the crowns of Kazan', Astrakhan', Georgia, Siberia—"crowns upon crowns, scepters upon scepters, rivers of diamonds, oceans of pearls." Here also is the famous orb, said to have been sent to Vladimir Monomakh (Plate 78) with other treasures by the Greek Emperors Basil and Constantine. The Crown Hall also houses a number of coronation chairs, including the ivory throne of Ivan III (Plate 80); a jeweled throne of Aleksei Mikhailovich brought from Persia in 1660, still sparkling with hundreds of gems (Plate 82); and, under a canopy of velvet and gold, the imperial chair upon which sat, as joint sovereigns, the two brothers of whom one was destined to rule alone under the name of Peter the Great.

The Hall of Silver (Serebrianaia Zala), on the second floor, contains one of the richest collections of ancient and modern gold and silver plate and jeweled cups from the twelfth century to the reign of Nicholas II. Some are of Russian workmanship, others of foreign manufacture—gifts to the Russian tsars from Western and Eastern royalty. A striking picture of the great collection, as it existed before the Polish occupation of 1612, is presented by the Burgundian captain Jacques Margeret, who served under Boris Godunov and Dmitrii the Pretender.

> The treasury of the tsars *(raskhodnaia kazna)* is filled with all sorts of jewels. . . . There is a large number of gold and silver vessels of various sizes. Besides this there is an infinite number of gilt and non-gilt silver plate. I've seen a half dozen huge casks made of silver and a large number of enormous and very heavy bowls with ring-shaped handles attached to each side, so that when filled with mead they could be conveniently carried. These vessels require the services of four attendants each to carry and distribute them among the guests, usually one bowl per table. With each bowl there were provided a number of large boat-shaped ladles *(kovshi)* used for dipping into the contents of the bowl. All those vessels are of Russian work. Besides those, there were a large number of silver vessels of German, English, and Polish make—either gifts of various kings and princes, sent through their ambassadors, or items acquired by the Russian tsars because of the beauty of their workmanship.[4]

The frequent fires and especially the melting down of the ancient plate, during the Time of Troubles, have greatly diminished this collection, and help to explain the scarcity of examples of gold and silver work made before the accession of the Romanov dynasty.

The Oruzheinaia Palata was created at the beginning of the sixteenth century as an arsenal. It became successively a technical, scientific, pedagogical, and art institute, and contained shops and studios of icon and portrait painting, gold and silversmith work, keeping at the same time its original purpose—the manufacture of arms. By 1628 some of its artifacts were already worthy of being museum pieces. After St. Petersburg was built, the Oruzheinaia Palata was used as a simple storehouse; from 1737, when a fire destroyed the building, to 1810 its collections were dispersed among several of the older Kremlin buildings. In 1812, during the Napoleonic invasion, the treasures were hastily dispatched to Nizhnii-Novgorod for safekeeping; many valuable art objects were lost at this time, but the remaining collections were returned after 1814. In 1851 all the collections were housed in the still existing, specially constructed building, adjoining the Grand Kremlin Palace, that until the Bolshevik revolution of 1917 served as both storehouse and museum.

The postrevolutionary museum administration removed many articles valuable and interesting historically, ethnographically, or technically and distributed them among various special museums, reserving for the Oruzheinaia Palata only objects that could be considered real art pieces.

Until its reorganization in the 1920's the oldest and most valuable section of the Oruzheinaia Palata—its very core—consisted of the remnants of the Grand Treasury (Bol'shaia Kazna), which had been the treasury of the Moscow grand princes and tsars since the fifteenth century, and contained not only the hereditary regalia but also the personal valuables of the sovereigns.

The officer in charge of the tsar's treasury *(kazennyi dvor)*,[5] organized during the reign of Ivan III and mentioned for the first time in 1494, consisted of three sections: the Grand Treasury, which contained the tsar's regalia presented to Vladimir Monomakh by the Byzantine emperor; the Armory (Oruzheinaia or Oruzhnichia Palata), which housed shops for the manufacture of the tsar's arms; and the storehouse or depot (Zapasnoi Dvor) that contained the imperial robes, dress, uniforms, arms, and armor for the tsar, his bodyguards, and his most trusted military units.

Even among the first employees of the shops there were not only craftsmen skilled in arms manufacture, but also goldsmiths, silversmiths, lapidaries, carvers of wood and bone, enamelers, niello and filigree workers—artists that specialized in the embellishment of the tsar's weapons, armor, trappings, and the imperial household vessels and plate.

In the icon-painting chamber (Ikonnaia Palata), which was somewhat like the Italian l'Opera del Duomo, were artists who designed the tsar's emblems and standards and embellished the icon frames and breastplates and the crosses, medallions, and Easter eggs for the tsar's immediate family. These artists also painted the frescoes in the tsar's apartments.

The manufacture of arms was at an especially high level during the reign of Aleksei Mikhailovich. The Russian craftsmen either followed the models of foreign masters or used the old Russian models as their inspiration, perfecting and elaborating them or inventing new models and decorating them in the "Moscow Style" in keeping with the rich national costumes of the period.

In 1806 a masonry building, designed by Egorov, was erected in the Kremlin facing the Senate Square to house all that remained of the tsar's treasures. During the reign of Nicholas I a two-story building, designed by Thon, was erected in the Kremlin near the Borovitskiia Gates. In 1851 this structure, connected with the Grand Kremlin Palace by a covered arcade, became the museum of the Oruzheinaia Palata.

The full catalog of this museum, containing more than ten thousand items, was compiled in 1835. Later a committee under the chairmanship of Count S. Stroganov[6] began work on the multivolume *Antiquities of the Russian Empire (Drevnosti Rossiiskago Gosudarstva),* in which the treasures of the Oruzheinaia Palata were given special prominence.

The Oruzheinaia Palata collections are mainly of metal objects, from simple cutlery to the most elaborate snuffboxes. Also included are arms of the great warriors and heroes of former days, gold and silver objects, jewelry, carved ivory, glass, porcelain, textiles, costumes, furniture, carriages, and harness.

Included in the arms collection are examples from the sixteenth and seventeenth centuries; of special interest are the arms that were manufactured in the Oruzheinaia Palata itself and whose original bearers can be identified.

The enamels and filigree, also from the sixteeenth and seventeenth centuries, are in cloisonné, champlevé, painted enamels, and niello conceived and manufactured by the tsar's designers *(tsarskie znamenshchiki)* and craftsmen *(tsarskie mastera).*

The Oruzheinaia Palata collections can be roughly divided into three groups. The first group includes filigreed and woven gold *(skan')* crowns and such regal insignia as scepters, diadems, orbs, staffs, and crosiers. The second group comprises gold and silver table service, goblets, tankards, *bratiny, charki, kovshi,* and crystal glasses. The third group consists of watches, snuffboxes, rings, and chains.

All kinds of Western and Eastern goldsmith work are housed here, representing the thousands of gifts made by foreign sovereigns to the Russian tsars over the centuries. The arts of London, Paris, Nürnberg, Augsburg, and Danzig are represented here in quantity and quality even finer than in the museums of those cities.

In medieval Russia the Oruzheinaia Palata, with its closely integrated gold and silver workshops and the private shops of the tsar and tsaritsa, was the very fountainhead of Russian national art. It was a kind of central station, where nearly everything pertaining to the arts and crafts originated, and from which its various products spread throughout the land. Although the Oruzheinaia Palata was not exactly a stronghold of tradition—more of the latest innovations could be found there than anywhere else—though the new vogues were sympathetically received and protected, even if they came from foreign lands and were tainted with heresy, still its products must be considered as the "work of Moscow" *(Moskovskoe delo)*—art largely influenced by the spirit of ancient Russia.

The particular style—often of monumental character and imposing magnificence—developed by the Oruzheinaia Palata was the result of

80

THE IVORY CHAIR
OF GRAND PRINCE IVAN III

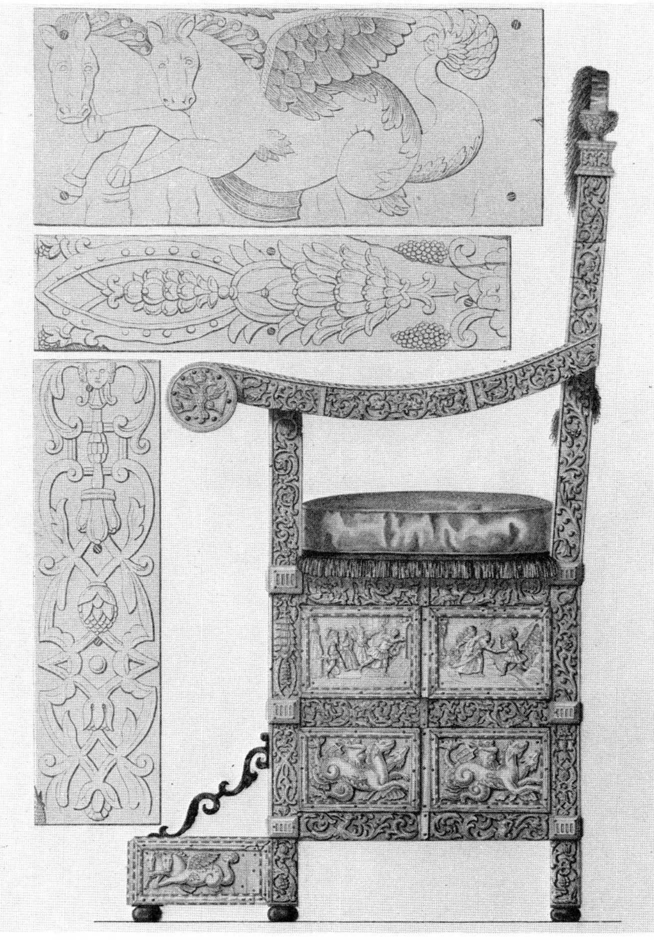

81

DETAILS OF THE IVORY CHAIR
OF GRAND PRINCE IVAN III

82

THE THRONE OF
TSAR ALEKSEI MIKHAILOVICH

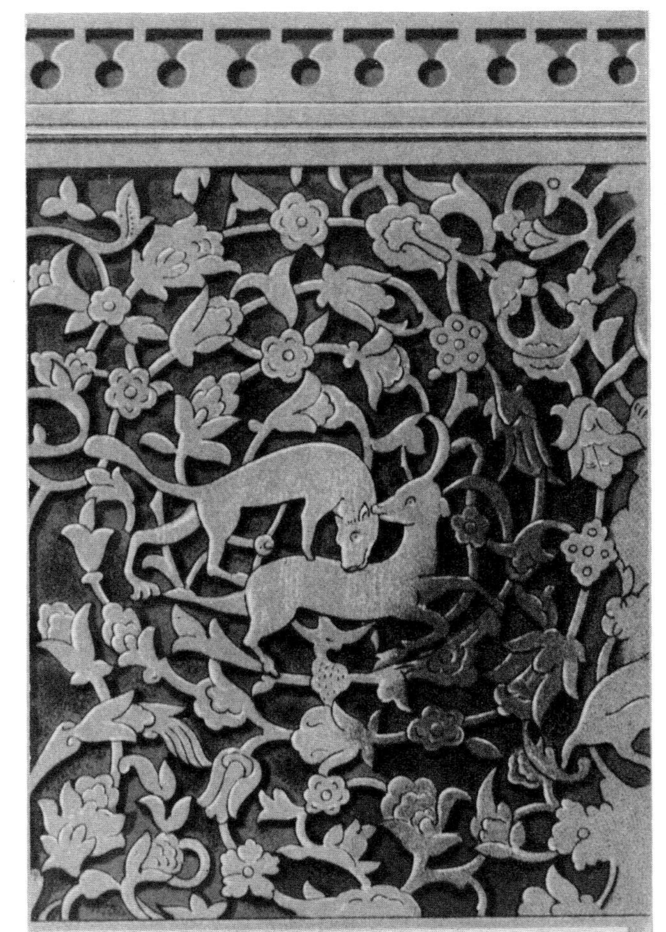

83

DETAILS OF THE THRONE
OF TSAR ALEKSEI MIKHAILOVICH

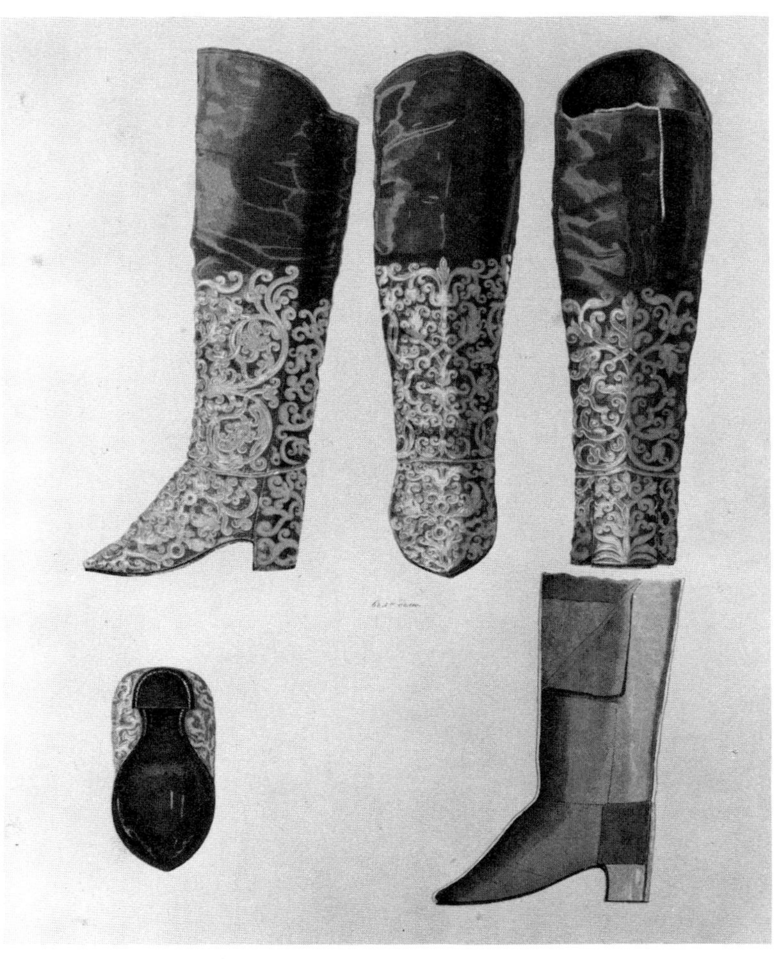

84

BOOTS

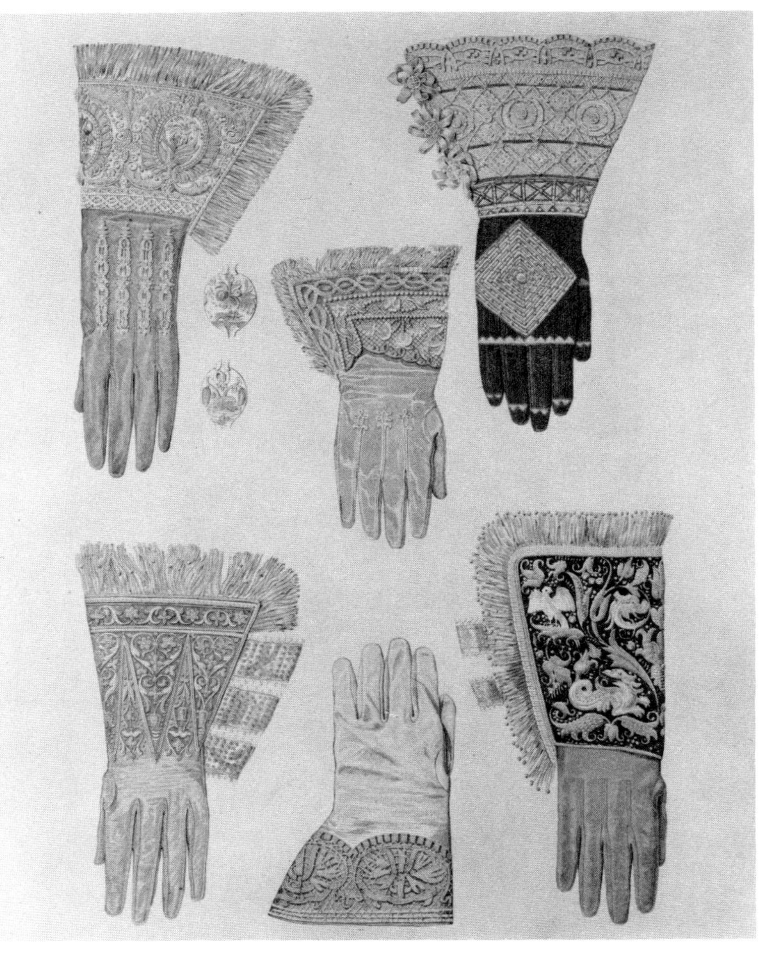

85

GLOVES

86

COSTUME ORNAMENTS

87

THE HELMET OF
GRAND PRINCE ALEXANDER NEVSKII

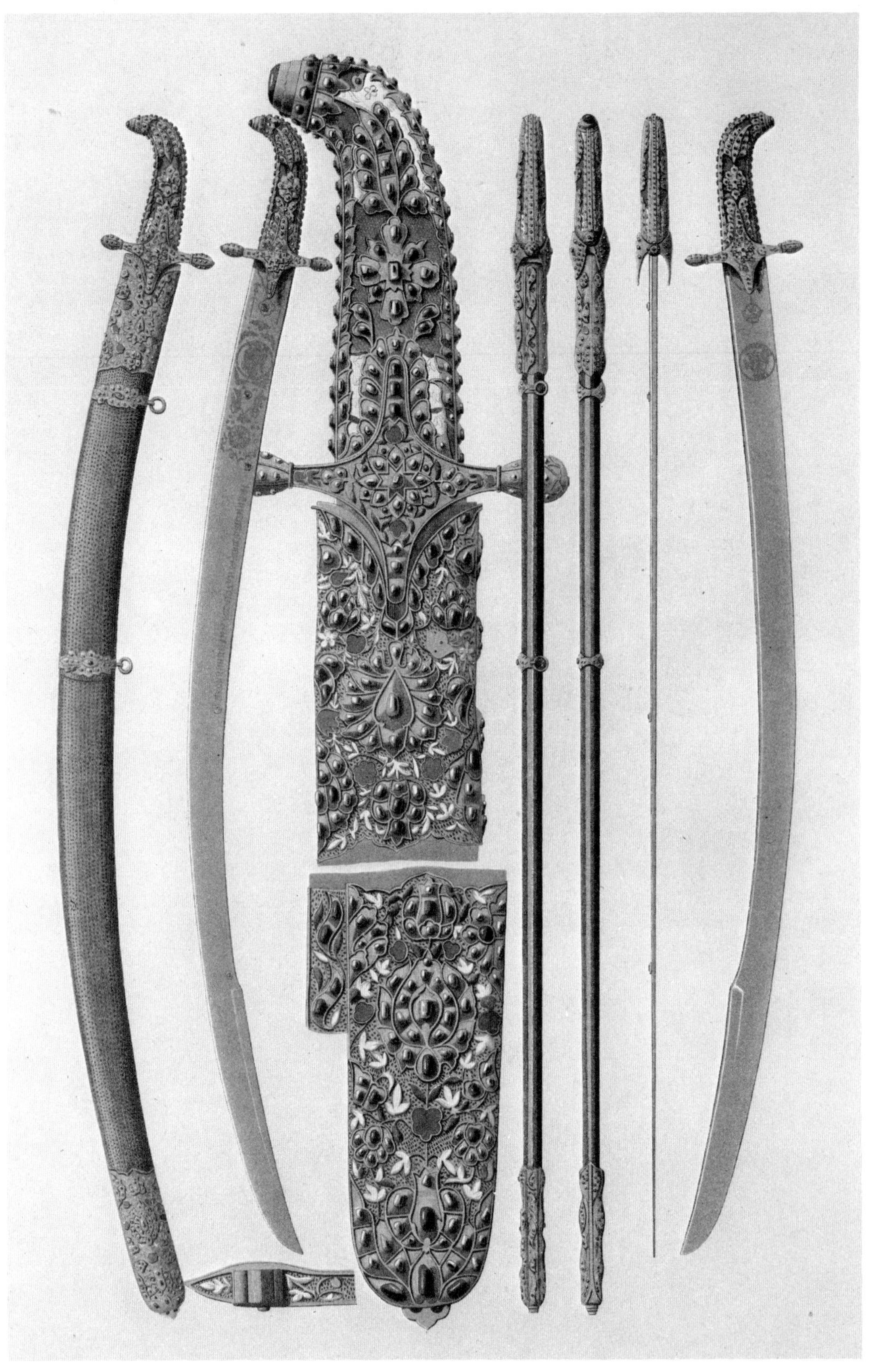

88

THE SABER OF
GRAND PRINCE VLADIMIR MONOMAKH

89

GUNPOWDER FLASK

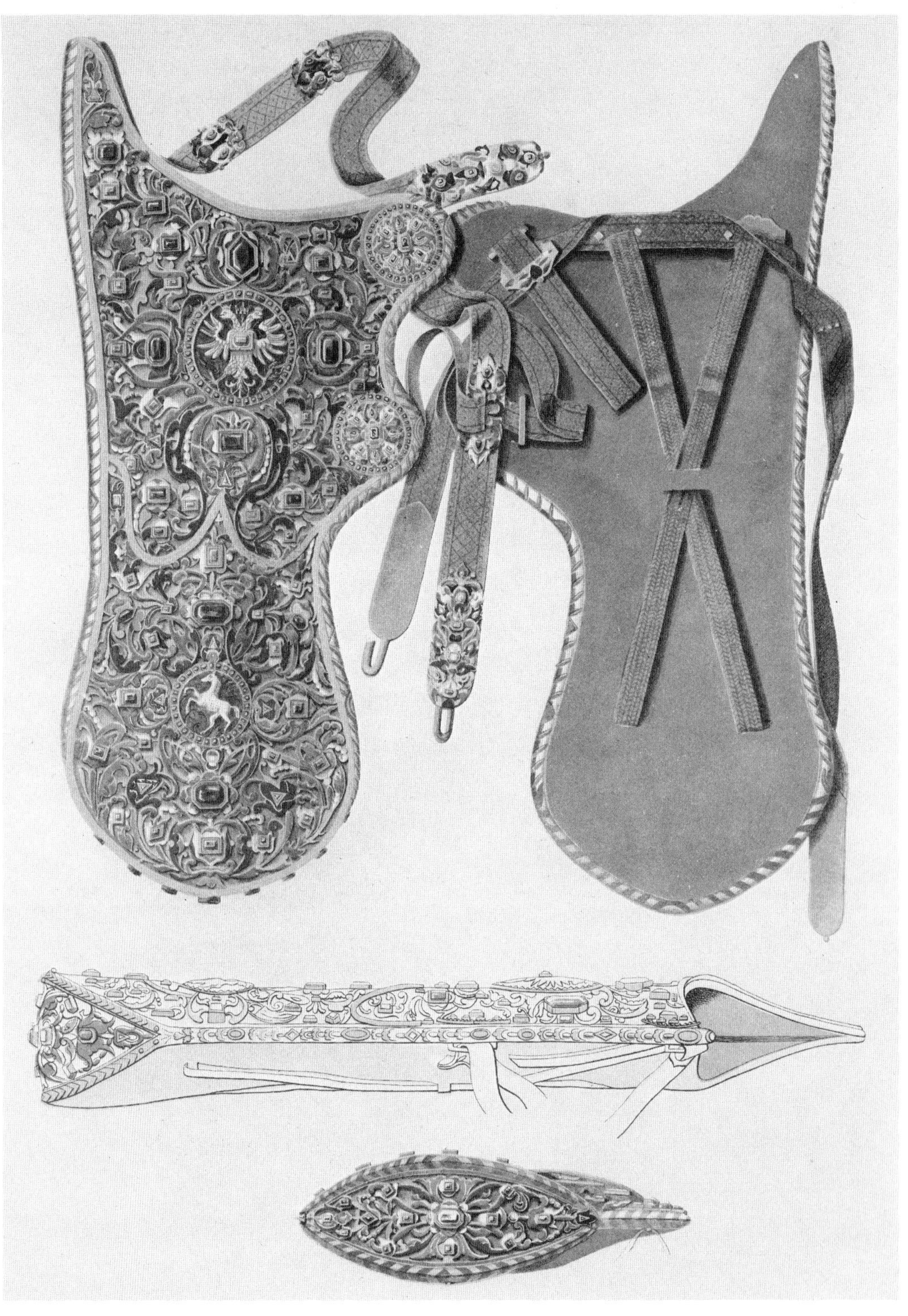

90

QUIVER

91

SERVING DISH

92

THE TEAPOT OF
TSARITSA EVDOKIA FEODOROVNA

93

THE PITCHER AND WASHBASIN
OF TSAREVICH ALEKSEI PETROVICH

94

THE GOLD PLATE OF
TSAR ALEKSEI MIKHAILOVICH

its craftsmen's study of the icons, mural decorations, manuscripts, ceramics, and gold and silver work of the times of Ivan IV and his predecessors.

We might wonder how it happened that this institution, which was originally organized as a bureau in charge of arms manufacturing and storage (Oruzheinyi Prikaz), acquired such great influence in the development of Russian art. To understand this, we must refer to the end of the fifteenth century and the beginning of the sixteenth.

At that period, which largely coincides with the reign of Ivan III, the Principality of Moscow had already reached its desired political goal when it became the strongest and most influential governing power, assuming the leadership not only in matters of state but in social and religious life, learning, and art. The essentials were accomplished and the stage framework—the walls, towers, cathedrals, and palaces of the Kremlin—was set, but additional *décor* was needed. The etiquette and ceremonial pomp of the princely court required many other things—the most important being the symbols of wealth and luxury reflecting the newly acquired power.

Weapons, armor, and other military trappings were the principal symbols of might and magnificence in those days, and the princes of ancient and medieval Russia prized them above everything else. Even the poor reigning houses lavished most of their attention and income on the collection and upkeep of arms, and every princeling had in his retinue some noble with the title of *mechenosha* (swordbearer and, by extension, armorer) who supervised the acquisition and care of weapons and armor. His was the all important office—the guardianship and glorification of the symbols of power.

Ivan's son, Grand Prince Vasilii III, contributed greatly to this practice and enhanced the importance of the armorer when in 1511 he established the vital and most responsible office, the armory, later to become known as the Oruzheinyi Prikaz. The chief armorer *(oruzhnichii* or, in its later version, *oruzheinichii),* was to be the first and most influential personage in the prince's entourage.

The armorer's duty was not only to care for and guard the prince's collection of weapons, but to superintend the manufacture of all sorts of arms, military trappings, emblematic designs, escutcheons and flags, and all other war paraphernalia. He also supervised the embellishment of the prince's arms and the pieces the prince presented to foreign potentates and their ambassadors.

Quite understandably, a people so persistently engaged in warfare and so imbued with love of colorful ornamentation attached much importance to the decoration of arms and armor. Hence in the varied forms and ornaments of helmets, shields, maces, halberds, pikes, sabers, saddlery, and harness preserved in the Oruzheinaia Palata are many splendid examples of sixteenth- and seventeenth-century pieces richly decorated with niello, enameling, damascening, and incrustation with varicolored gems.

Richard Chancellor offers us a glimpse of the military trappings of the army of Ivan the Terrible in 1553:

> All his men are horsemen. . . . The horsemen are all archers with such bows as the Turks have, and they ride short as do the Turks. Their armor is a coate of plate, with a skull on their heads. Some of their coates are covered with velvet or cloth of gold; their desire is to be sumptuous in the field, and especially the nobles and gentlemen; as I have heard their trimming is very costly, and partly I have seene it, or else I would scarcely have beleeved it; but the Duke himselfe is richly attired above all measure: his pavilion is covered either with cloth of gold or silver, and so set with stones that it is wonderful to see it. I have seene the King's Majesties of England and the French King's pavilions, which are fayre, yet not like unto his. And when they bee sent into farre or strange countreys, or that strangers come to them, they be very gorgeous. Els the Duke himselfe goeth but menaly in apparrell; and when he goeth betwix one place and another hee is but reasonably apparrelled over other times. In the while that I was in Moscow the Duke sent two ambassadours to the King of Poleland, which had at the lest five hundred horses; their sumptuousness was above measure, not onely in themselves, but also in their horses, as velvet, cloth of golds, and cloth of silver set with pearles and not scant. What shall I farther say? I never heard of nor saw men so sumptuous.[7]

The interests of the Russian medieval princes were not centered exclusively on war and the implements of war. As protectors of the faith, they devoted much attention to the encouragement of piety and morality. Before the rise of Moscow, Novgorod was the center of Russian cultural life (especially of icon painting). Moscow, as a new political power, had to assume the leadership in all things religious, cultural, and artistic.

With the passage of time and the growth of Moscow in political importance, the wealth and magnificence of its churches and princely court grew apace. Ivan IV, though better known for his cruelty than for his love of letters and art, bought stocks of precious metals and gold and silver vessels in Germany and commandeered artists, goldsmiths, enamelers, and carvers skilled in the arts of embellishment of icon encasements *(oklady)* from Novgorod. He also imported from Riga craftsmen specializing in the manufacture of religious vessels. These craftsmen became members of the staff of the Oruzheinaia Palata, contributing their knowledge and skill to the development of the arts and crafts as well as to the further growth of weapon manufacturing. The bureau grew in importance and became firmly established as an industrial, scientific, and artistic center.

During the Time of Troubles (1604–1613) the administration of the Oruzheinaia Palata ceased to function and most of its artists and craftsmen deserted to the provinces. With the accession of Tsar Mikhail Feodorovich the craftsmen and artists returned to Moscow and resumed their work. Moscow came to life again ushering in a strong revival of cultural and artistic activities.

Tsar Mikhail (1613–1645) reëstablished the Oruzheinaia Palata, but concentrated mainly on the purely technical side of arms manufacturing because the tsar felt that decoration and embellishment could wait. Mikhail imported mining engineers *(rudoznatsy)* and technicians, and built powder and firearms plants; he invited the best native and foreign specialists to his service. The bureau in charge of arms manufacturing became the most important section of the Oruzheinyi Prikaz. The goldsmithing and silversmithing sections were detached from arms manufacturing, and functioned as separate bureaus subordinated to the arms office, in which all industrial and artistic activities were centered—mining, smelting, casting; painting of icons, portraits, and miniatures; designing of emblems, blazonry, military standards, government documents, charters, and citations; manuscript illuminating and bookbinding. The administration of each of these activities, headed by a special functionary *(diak)*,[8] was housed in a separate building or buildings. The manufacture of gold articles had its own establishment and office known as the Zolotaia Palata (the Goldsmiths' Chamber); so did the manufacture of silver vessels, and its office was known as the Serebrianaia Palata (the Silversmiths' Chamber). These buildings were close to the palace, and functioned as branches of the court household—hence the name "Oruzheinaia Palata," which replaced "Oruzheinyi Prikaz."

An important period in the artistic activities of the Oruzheinaia Palata began with the appointment of Boyarin Bogdan Matveevich Khitrovo (1616–1680) to the office of *oruzheinichii.* His appointment, by Tsar Aleksei Mikhailovich in 1654, to this high post coincided with the initiation of the Nikonian reforms, which had far-reaching effects on Russian history and art.

The figure of Khitrovo, as an administrator and enlightened progressive who valued the art of medieval Russia but at the same time broke new paths for the development of the arts and crafts, is so important that it is necessary to consider both the man and the historical setting in which he moved.

About the middle of the seventeenth century, upon the initiative of Patriarch Nikon,[9] certain reforms were introduced into the religious ritual of the Russian Church. A revision of the service books was undertaken to eliminate the gross errors and even interpolations that had slipped into the Slavonic manuscripts and then into print. These reforms aimed to reconcile the Russian Church ritual, religious texts, church design, and icon painting with those of the contemporary Greek Church.

Both Nikon and the tsar who supported Nikon wanted to introduce into the art of icon painting a current of new ideas and to bring it in line with the reforms. They also decided to reintroduce the outer and inner features of the Greek Church: the basic plan, cupolas, furnishings, vessels, ambons, bishops' crosses, vestments, and cowls. For that purpose it was necessary that the head of the Ikonnaia and Zolotaia Palaty should be a man who could see eye to eye with the tsar and the patriarch and would act in agreement with them in all matters related to the Nikonian reforms.

Khitrovo happened to be the ideal man for the position. He had already distinguished himself as soldier, diplomat, judge, administrator, and builder. He was not creative, but he had a gift of sensing the problems of his artistis and craftsmen. Above all, he had a knack of combining the management and coördination of things purely technical with those that belong to the spiritual and creative world. At the same time that he had the greatest respect for the arts and crafts of the past he encouraged any new expression that fitted the temper of an age when Western art was becoming firmly established in Russia.

The thorniest problem facing Khitrovo was to determine the line of demarcation between orthodoxy and heresy in icon painting—he had to reconcile his own artistic judgment with the often divergent preferences of the tsar and the patriarch. On the one hand, he had to take into consideration many hallowed traditions in the treatment of religious subjects; on the other, he had to struggle with the technical difficulties peculiar to Russian religious painting, with the fact that the icon was not a creation of a single artist but the collective work of a number of specialists.[10] Then too, the Western influences in icon painting (especially potent in the last half of the seventeenth century) were antithetical to the very spirit of Russian icon painting—a folk creation, its content representing the confession of faith, its techniques the life of the people.

Khitrovo undertook the job with energy and boldness. In spite of the sharp protests of Nikon and the tirades of the fanatical Archpriest Avvakum,[11] he welcomed Western influences. The works of art produced during the twenty-six years of his tenure clearly indicate that he was a man of great culture, liberal, progressive, and hospitable to new ideas, and one who appreciated talent and individuality in artists, giving his greatest encouragement and support to those who could study foreign models, adapt them to the needs of Russia, and imbue the finished product with the Russian spirit.

The activities of the icon chamber were not limited to strictly sacred painting; its artists also painted portraits *(parsunnoe pis'mo)*[12] and miniatures, illuminated manuscripts, made maps and charts, designed furniture and furnishings, created frescoes and objects of gold, designed textiles for vestments—they did everything and anything that required creative power, imagination, and ability.

In 1672 and 1673 two remarkable illustrated manuscripts were produced in Moscow: the *Tituliarnik,* or *Book of Genealogy of the Tsars;* and *The Book of the Election (Izbranie) to the Throne of the Great Sovereign, Tsar and Grand Prince Mikhail Feodorovich, Autocrat of All Great Russia.* Both were compiled at the Posol'skii Prikaz (Office of Foreign Affairs), but were designed and illustrated by the artists of the Oruzheinyi Prikaz. As models of book design, illumination, water-color miniature painting, gilding, and silvering, they offer proof of the high level that the art of bookmaking had attained in those days.

The principal designer of the *Izbranie* was the icon painter Ivan Maksimov, who painted the faces *(pisal litsa).* S. D. Rozhkov painted the background and secondary figures *(dolichnoe);* A. Evdokimov and Th. Iuriev created the floral ornamentation. The director of the entire work in the design of the *Tituliarnik* was G. A. Blagushin. The blazonry and the emblematic designs were executed by the calligraphers Matvei Andreev and Feodor Lopov. The portraitists were Ivan Maksimov and D. Lvov, who worked on it five months.

In these two manuscripts it is interesting to see, Trutovskii[13] points out, the differences between the portraits of Russian dignitaries and those of foreigners. The Russian tsars, princes, and patriarchs are painted in a somewhat stilted, dry manner, with a certain sameness and lack of realism, as though the artist was afraid of his subject, fearful that he might offend and incur the disfavor of the great personage by painting him as a human being. Hence the resulting portraits often acquired the characteristics of an icon. By contrast, the portraits of foreign kings and princes are fully alive, with movement and freedom of the body, light and sparkle in the eye. These persons are presented in many kinds of costumes and uniforms, and their hair is dressed in various fashions. Convention is disregarded, and the portraits are rendered as the artist's will, talent, and imagination dictated. The approach, the brushwork, and the style seem like those of entirely different artists.

One of the most distinguished icon painters at the Oruzheinaia Palata was the celebrated Semion Ushakov (1626–1686), whose works are regarded as the best examples of the Moscow seventeenth-century school of icon painting. He was appointed court painter at the early age of twenty-one and, like Cellini in Italy, soon became the favorite of the mighty and the rich. Fascinated by Western religious art, he attempted to produce naturalistic illustrations of the Bible. He practiced etching and prepared designs for a number of successful woodcuts. His woodcut depicting the seven deadly sins is remarkable for its vigor and dignity, but his icons are somewhat flawed by excessive sentimentality and naïveté. Much of his time was spent in designing gold and enamel vessels in the ateliers of the Oruzheinaia Palata, and he is also known to have decorated arms and drawn maps. His chief work at the Palata was designing church vessels to be executed in precious metals and enamels; he is thought to have been the designer of Patriarch Nikon's miter, which has some noteworthy enameling, especially in the upper part.

During the second half of the seventeenth century the character of the large ornamental patterns of a secular nature gradually underwent a change, drifting away from the Russian and Byzantine models toward those of Western Europe. However, the floral ornamentation of manuscripts and icons was still in the ancient Russian style, featuring extensive application of gold and silver backgrounds. "Frankish" or Western ornament *(Friazheskiia travy)*—the motifs and style of the baroque—was used rarely and timidly.

The principal business of the Oruzheinaia Palata, the purely technical and industrial phase of arms manufacturing, reached a high level of competence. Along with the technical improvements in ceremonial arms—the swords, daggers, and firearms, the armor, shields, casques, and helmets, the hunting and riding equipment, blankets, saddles, and harness—their embellishment was also greatly perfected.

Khitrovo set for himself the task of producing not only an efficient and mechanically reliable gunstock, a deadly sword blade or dagger, but also something that could be richly decorated and embellished: steel to be damascened in gold; scabbards to be ornamented with precious metals and encrusted with gems; gunstocks to be carved and inlaid; helmets and nosepieces to be chased, engraved, and enameled. All such objects had to be efficient and strong, and yet light of weight, rich, and beautiful. Khitrovo's armorers became renowned for their skill in preparation of steel as well as for their artistry in damascening, nielloing, enameling, and gem-encrusting. The registers of the Oruzheinaia Palata mention blades, coats of mail, and helmets made in the Moscow, Circasian, Turkish, Persian, and German styles.

The helmets were usually hemispherical or conical, with backpieces, earpieces, and a guard for the face in the form of a movable arrow-shaped piece or nasal damascened with gold—a type common in the East.

Several varieties of maces, adapted either for use in war or as scepters, are preserved in the Oruzheinaia Palata. Some are provided at the top with six wings or projections *(shestopiery)* that served as cutting edges; others have handles that are richly damascened, neilloed, enameled, or studded with jewels, and were used only at important state affairs.

The battle axes are of various shapes; some were used by the tsar's bodyguards on ceremonial occasions. They are of silver-gilt, with crescent-shaped steel blades damascened with gold and handles decorated with arabesque designs.

Elaborate designs in *repoussé* covered the breastplates and other parts of the body armor and the large round shields or bucklers. Color was achieved by the gold inlay of damascening; niello, enamel, and jewels heightened the richness.

The Oruzheinaia Palata has some magnificent examples of arms, particularly those made during the reign of Aleksei Mikhailovich. Outstanding are a bowcase and a quiver (Plate 90), ascribed to Ivan Iuriev, used by the tsar on gala occasions *(saadaki bol'shogo nariada)*. Several other bow-and-arrow cases, recalling the ancient Scythian form, are made of various precious materials and elaborately enameled and jeweled.

A circular, silver-gilt powder flask or priming horn in the collection (Plate 89) is *repoussé* and chased in high relief on both sides. The design on one side represents the so-called Tsar's Vision *(Tsarskoe videnie)* —an eagle attacking a dragon—surrounded by a border of leaves interspersed with birds and animals, all on a matted ground. On the other side is a figure of St. George striking a dragon surrounded by a border of foliage. An inscription on the edge indicates that the flask belonged to A. I. Nesterov.[14]

Among the outstanding craftsmen of the Palata during Khitrovo's tenure was the celebrated Nikita Davydov, a gunsmith and armorer who learned his art from Eastern masters. An excellent sample of his work is the decoration of the helmet of Alexander Nevskii, which he ornamented with jewels and a medallion enameled with a figure of St. Michael the Archangel (Plate 87). Davydov was the founder of an entire school of fine armorers that included Grigorii and Afanasii Viatkin, Titov, Kobelev, and Luchanin, who were celebrated not only for their skill in producing fine gun barrels and steel blades, but for their artistry in decorating those arms.

Fine workmanship and mechanical perfection particularly distinguish the arts and crafts of that period. The tools and equipment were few and simple; but the workmen made the most of the available facilities, and displayed great skill and ingenuity in producing highly complicated and artistic objects without the aid of machines. These men were especially resourceful and dexterous in handling the embossing and chasing tools; using a simple hammer, anvil, and wooden bench, they were able to produce not only large reliefs of sharp convexity, but the most delicate designs. They embossed, chased, or engraved all sorts of patterns and ornaments; they embellished plaques in enamel, niello, or filigree; they then soldered, fastened with screws, or otherwise applied these plaques not only to the main body of the object, but to the most minute parts of the icon encasements or frames, to various vessels, scepters, crowns, diadems, buckles, buttons, or countless other items of feminine and masculine adornment.

Russian gold and silver work, like the other arts, shows considerable Oriental influence, particularly Persian and Byzantine. There are also marked traces of the influence and even imitation of the ornament and technique of Western art. This is not surprising in view of the large influx of foreign workmen from both the East and the West during the period of Russia's greatest artistic vitality in the sixteenth and seventeenth centuries.

From early times many metal objects were produced in chiseled brass and inlaid with copper, silver, and occasionally gold. The artist concentrated on beauty of form, color, and effective arrangement of ornament. He engraved scroll designs, floriated arabesques, inscriptions in cursive Slavonic, and medallions of fantastic beasts or birds. A favorite theme was the *sirin,*[15] peacock, heraldic birds, or other fantastic animals. The human figure, seldom portrayed in the nude, sometimes appeared in the shape of relief figures applied to the the sides of caskets and drinking vessels, but decoration in the round was usually restricted to solid bosses and to handles of ewers and jugs. The ewers, jugs, pitchers, and drinking vessels were skillfully designed and convey the impression of solidity. The handles, balanced by graceful spouts, are well proportioned and comfortable to use.

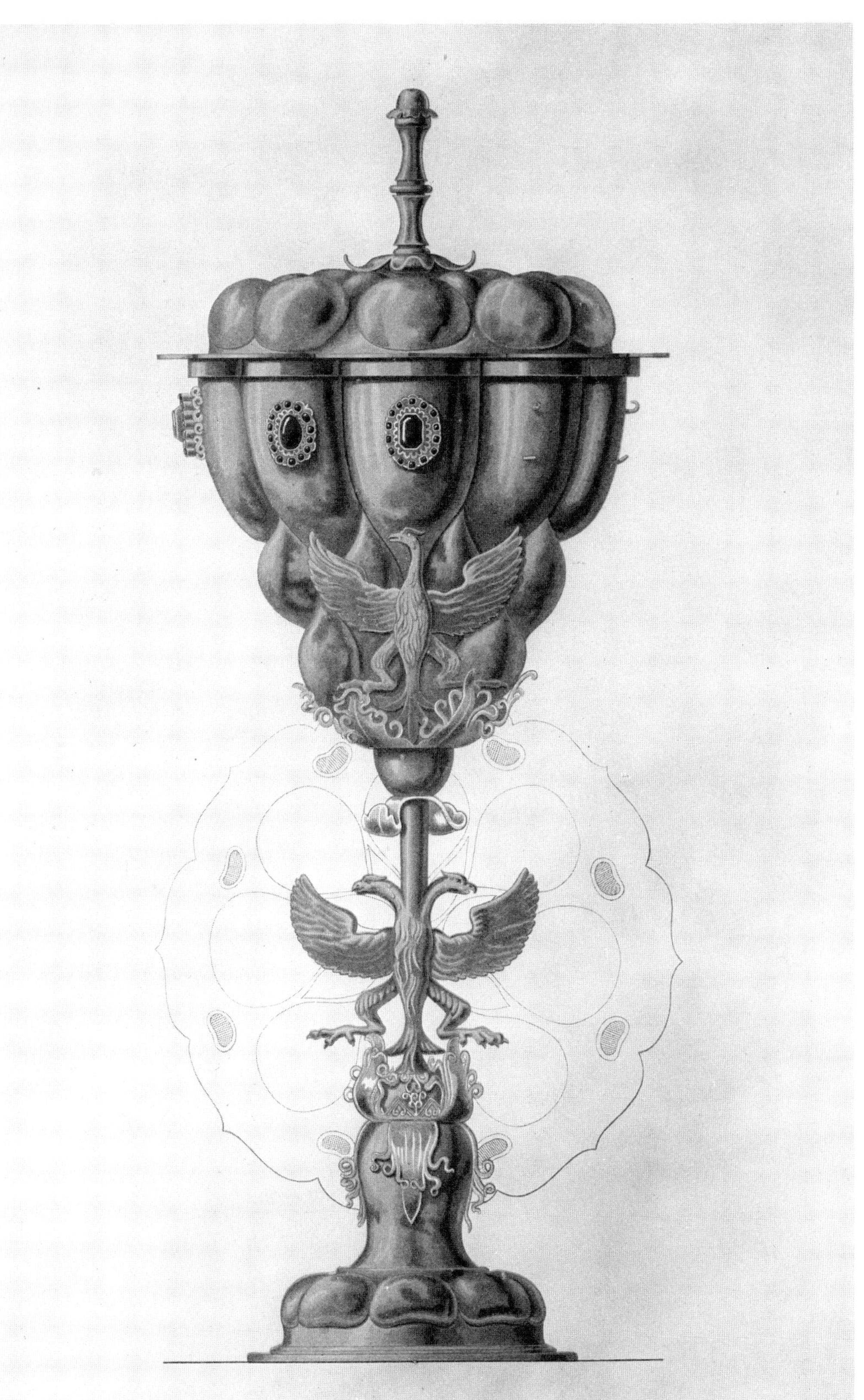

95

SILVER-GILT GOBLET

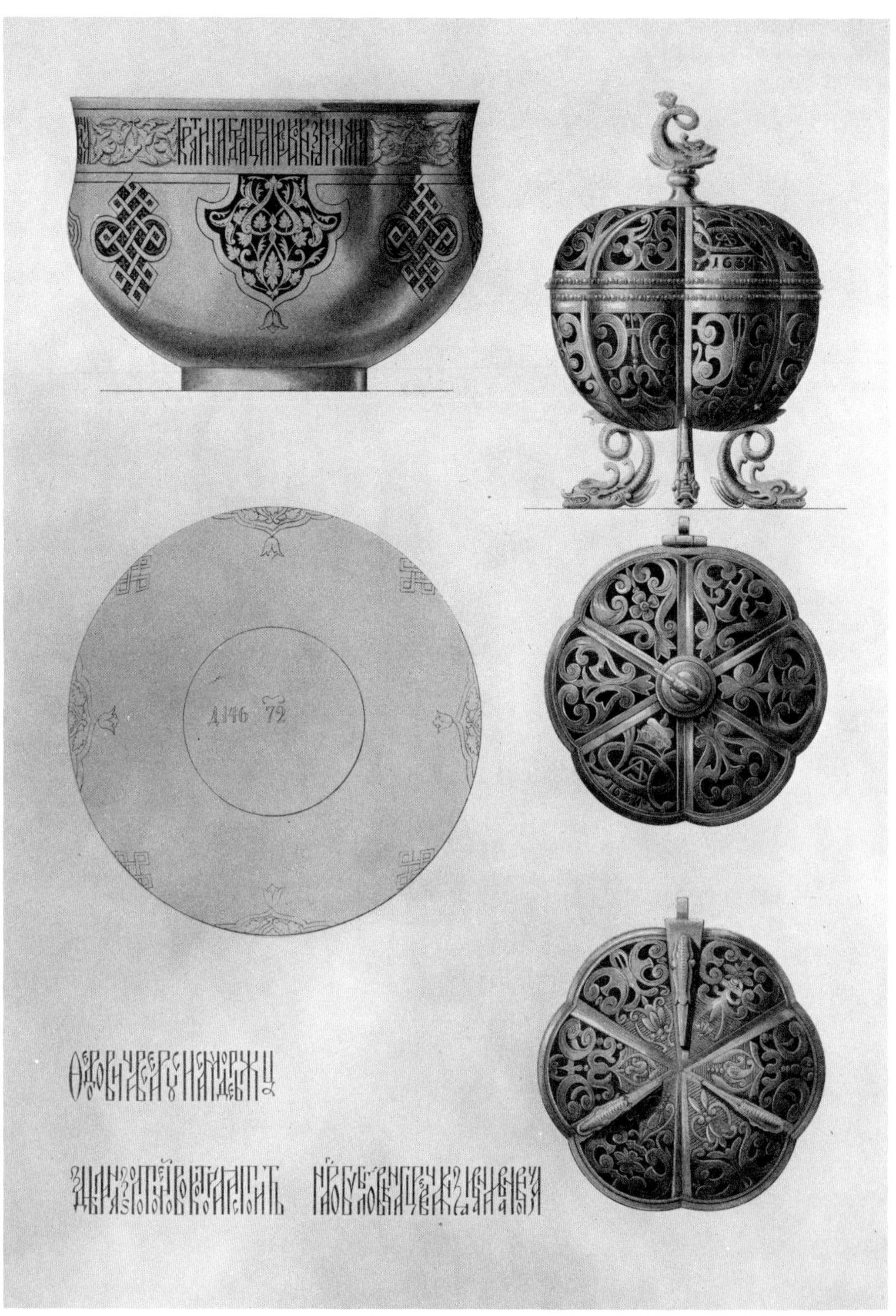

96

THE BRATINA AND INCENSE BURNER
OF TSAR MIKHAIL FEODOROVICH

97

JEWELED GOBLET

98

THE BRATINA OF PETER TRETIAKOV

99

SILVER-GILT TANKARD WITH ENAMEL

100

OXHORN AND SILVER-GILT TANKARD
WITH ENAMEL AND PRECIOUS STONES

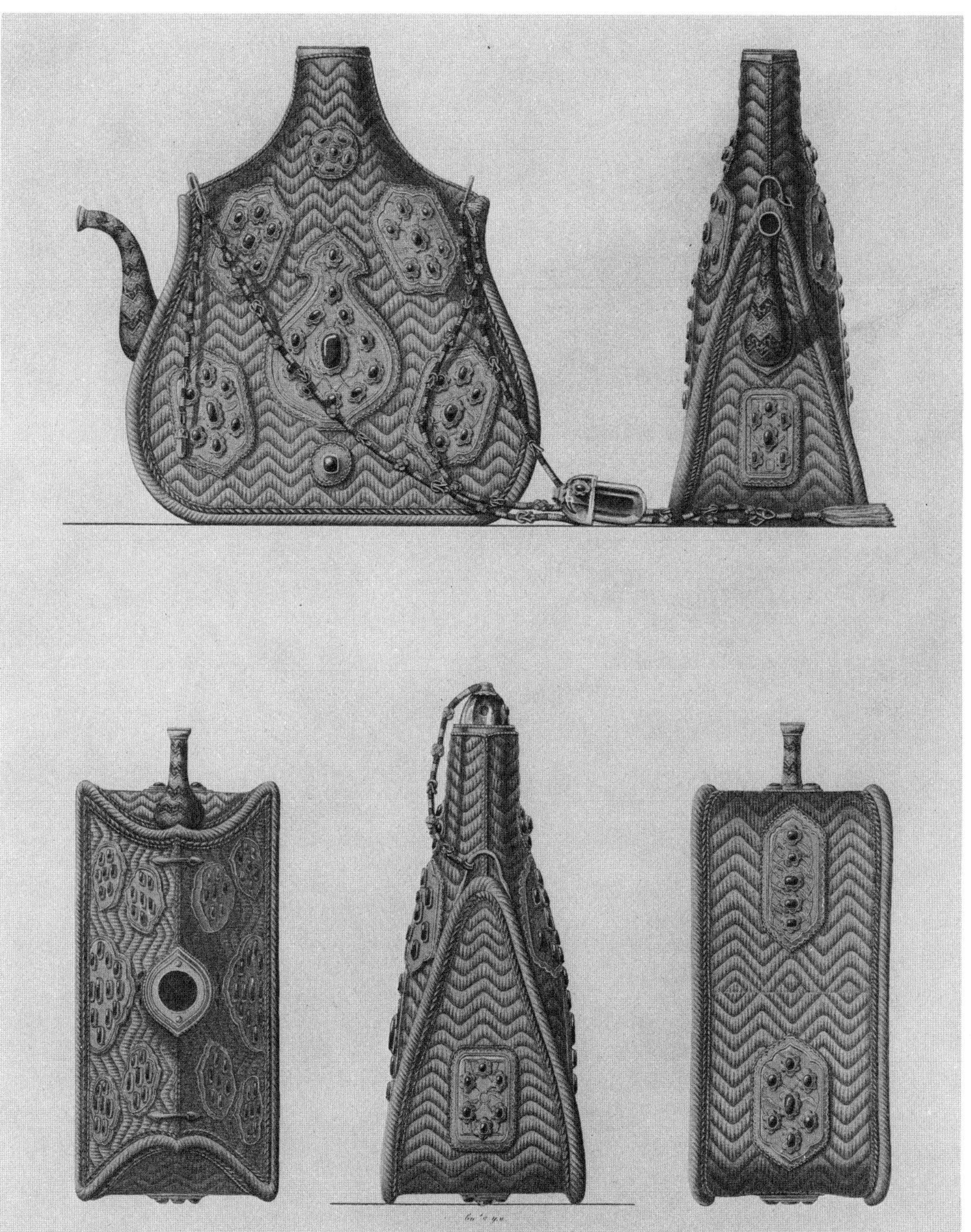

101

FLASK

102

THE PORCELAIN FLAGON
OF TSAREVICH IVAN IVANOVICH

Among the representative examples of secular gold and silver objects are the drinking vessels used at the princely courts and in the households of the great nobles on ceremonial festive occasions or at private family affairs. Some of these drinking vessels are peculiar to Russia, especially the loving cups, *bratiny;* the small cups, *charki,* used for strong liquors; and the ladles, *kovshi.*

The name "*bratina*" (from "*brat,*" "brother") was given to a peculiar sort of bowl or loving cup that was passed around the table during feasts and customarily used for drinking to the health of the guests or the hosts. Most persons of eminence and wealth had their own particular family *bratina,* which was especially valued as a gift. This fact explains why so much care was lavished upon the design, and why these cups were among the best examples of Russian craftsmanship.

The form and ornament were confined to certain traditional conventions. These cups were nearly always globular in shape, and rested on a low base or on animal feet. Some of them were provided with handles and covers.

The *bratiny* were usually of silver gilt. The body was usually decorated with *repoussé* flower ornament or foliage on a matted ground, with fruit and fretwork, or with medallions depicting hunting scenes or animals of the chase. The bottom of the bowl was often decorated with a convex and nearly hemispherical chased or engraved medallion. An almost invariable ornament was the inscription around the rim or lip, engraved or nielloed in the interlaced Slavonic lettering that so often contributed a distinctive feature to the Russian decorative arts. The inscription sometimes recorded the name of the owner, but frequently it was a toast or a sentimental motto.

Herberstein, in describing the drinking customs of the Russians and their manner of proposing toasts, was evidently referring to the *bratiny* in his travel notes of 1549:

> Silver goblets and various other vessels containing liquor are produced, and all strive to make each other drunk; and very clever they are in finding excuses for inviting men to drink, and when they are at a loss for a toast to propose, they begin at last to drink to the health of the emperor and the prince, his brother, and after that to the welfare of any others whom they believe to hold any position of dignity and honor. They think that no one ought or can refuse the cup when these names are proposed. The drinking is done in this fashion. He who proposes the toast takes his cup and goes into the middle of the room, and standing with his head uncovered, pronounces in a festive speech the name of him whose health he wishes to drink, and what he has to say in his behalf. Then after emptying the cup, he turns it upside

down over his head, so that all may see that he has emptied it, and that he sincerely gave the health of the person in honor of whom the toast was drunk. He then goes to the top of the table and orders many cups to be filled, and then hands each man his cup, pronouncing the name of the party whose health is to be drunk, on which each is obliged to go into the middle of the room, and, after emptying his cup, to return to his place. He who wishes to escape too long a drinking-bout must pretend that he is drunk or sleepy, or at least declare that, having already emptied many cups, he cannot drink any more; for they do not think that their guests are well received, or hospitably treated, unless they are sent home drunk.[16]

An interesting example is the *bratina* of Peter Alekseevich Tretiakov who was a secretary of the State Council under Mikhail Feodorovich about 1618. It is of silver and gilt, weighs about three pounds, and stands eleven and four-tenths inches high. The bowl is of the conventional form, but around the base are several figures of men supporting the bowl in their upstretched arms. The cover is coved, and from it rises a silver flower on a long stem. Most of the surface of the bowl and cover is embossed with foliage and flowers. Four attached gilt plaques are decorated with similar *repoussé* ornament and with shields flanked respectively by a heraldic lion and unicorn, two fishes, two pages, and two eagles. Beneath each plaque the same design is engraved on the plain surface. The form and floral decoration of these plaques recall the jeweled pendants *(tsaty)* hanging from the necks of icons. At the bottom of the bowl is the usual convex medallion, engraved with the question: "Man, who art thou who looketh at me, dost thou perchance desire to swallow me?" The inscription on the rim, freely translated, reads: "Know thou man, as arms are necessary to a warrior on the day of battle, so is rain in time of drought; even as the comfort of consolation from a true friend in time of misfortune and sorrow, so is the need for moderation, understanding, and companionship for all those who would partake of the sweetness. The *bratina* of Peter Alekseevich Tretiakov."[17]

The *kovsh* is a kind of boat-shaped bowl with a long handle, used for ladling out such common beverages as *kvas* (a sour-sweet drink made of water and black bread) or beer. These bowls are of different sizes, some quite large; most of them are elongated, with the front turned up to a point. They were used in the homes of the peasantry, in monastery refectories, in the mess halls of the army, and in many other places. The Russian museums contain examples dating from the fourteenth and fifteenth centuries which have been studiously imitated until comparatively recent times.

The *stopa* is a large mug-shaped covered vessel, recalling the sixteenth-century German and Italian tankards, used for serving mead, beer, and *kvas*. The *charka*, a kind of small cup used for serving strong liquors, are usually hemispherical, sometimes on small animal feet, and nearly always with one flat open-worked handle. The lip is generally engraved with Slavonic inscriptions or mottoes similar to those on the *bratiny*. The *charka* was often made of two shells decorated with lobsters, sea horses, fish-swallowing men, mermaids, or other fantastic sea creatures; some were made of semiprecious stones mounted with bands of gold.

The craft of embossing and chasing reached a high level of excellence in the second half of the seventeenth century. The objects from the tsars' and patriarchs' treasures, both religious and secular, are all outstanding examples of Russian decorative art.

The arts of enameling, niello, and filigree were even more cultivated than those of gold and silver *repoussé*. They achieved a style all their own and acquired unique distinguishing characteristics of refinement and elegance—novelties in design and technique, new fashions in the application of gold and silver, unique and entirely different color schemes—all of which was reflected in the other arts and crafts of that period.

The activities and innovations in this field were largely due to Tsar Aleksei Mikhailovich, and reflect the personal tastes of the tsar. His influence is especially revealed in two fields: gold sheet stamping *(basmenoe delo)* and enameling *(finiftianoe delo)*. Aleksei Mikhailovich was favorably disposed toward the Orthodox East and its representative arts. As a result, at the very beginning of his reign, a number of jeweled articles appeared in the Tsargrad (Constantinople) style—a combination of the art of the Turkish Musulman East with that of the Greeks and Mount Athos. The works in the style of the Western jewelers, so much in vogue during the reign of his father, receded into the background.

The Tsargrad style in jewelry was distinctive in its extensive use of thin gold plaques and sheathing *(basma)* decorated with stamped Greek-Byzantine designs and enriched with emeralds, rubies, and diamonds combined with enamels of the same shades as the gems. This style was in great favor throughout Aleksei's reign and was extensively applied to vestments, clothes, arms, thrones, vessels, and icon encasements. It seems to have been peculiar to his epoch, because it almost disappeared with the accession to the throne of his son Feodor Alekseevich.

In the art of enameling, the influence of Aleksei Mikhailovich's tastes reveals itself in his partiality toward the colors green, blue, and white, with the frequent addition of yellow and sometimes of red shades. During his reign pink Turkish foliage designs and flowers also appeared in the enamel ornamentation. These same pink flowers can be seen in the illuminations and page borders of manuscripts and in the design of chapter heads, citations, charters, and patents of nobility. Aleksei's preference for green tints was so strong as to influence even the architectural decoration of his day—for example, the exterior wall murals of the Poteshnyi Palace. His love for green is further revealed in the foliage, ornaments, and background decoration of many enamel objects. A good example is his personal plate (Plate 94), the background of which, with an eagle in niello, and all the foliage around the rim and the festoons at the bottom are green. The rosettes are brown; the festoon background at the bottom and some tendrils here and there are white; around the edge is a narrow band of blue enamel. From a distance the plate gives the impression of being green.

Partly under the influence of Mount Athos—as a representative of the Orthodox East—and with the help of Greek craftsmen, niello work *(chern')* reached a high level of development. This art was long known in Russia, but it was rarely used except for very fine lines in ornament and inscriptions. During the reign of Tsar Aleksei it was more frequently and widely applied in gold and silver work. Niello is used not only for ornament and inscriptions, but very often covers the entire background and thus becomes the forerunner of the niello ground that was so popular during the Moscow period of Peter the Great's reign.

The Oruzheinaia Palata with its many shops continued to develop and prosper until 1707. The last Oruzheinichei was Prince Peter Ivanovich Prozorovski, whose death in 1718 marked the end of a significant period in Russian art. In 1711 Peter I ordered the personnel of the Oruzheinaia Palata transferred from Moscow to the newly established armory in St. Petersburg. All the designers and craftsmen in any way connected with the arts went along. The year 1711 is considered by many historians as the darkest year in the history of Russian national art. According to Trutovskii,

> The most remarkable artistic institution, the only one of its kind, in the truest sense of the word, an institution, the like of which never existed anywhere or at any time, was destroyed with a single stroke of the pen, with the scribble of five letters [Peter]. With it died the very heart of national Russian art. It never beat again and there was never a true renaissance. It carried with it to its grave the old traditions, originality and uniqueness which so powerfully and brilliantly informed all its creations, subjugating everything foreign and external: the art of the Franks *(friazheskoe)*, of Byzantium (Tsargrad) [or Constantinople], Persia and Venice. It carried with it to the grave the very spirit and sensitivity of the Russian artistic soul.[18]

IX

THE RED SQUARE

The Red (or Beautiful) Square (Krasnaia Ploshchad') is a large oblong rectangle bounded on the west by the battlemented wall of the Kremlin, in front of which stands the Lenin Mausoleum; on the east by the grand façade of the commercial arcades; on the north by the Historical Museum and the Gates of the Resurrection (Voskresenskiia Vorota); and on the south by the Church of St. Basil.

The Red Square was the center of political and social life of medieval Moscow, in much the same way as the Roman Forum served ancient Rome. Here is the Lobnoe Mesto (Place of the Skull or Brow)—a tribune somewhat like the Roman Rostrum or the Novgorod Veche stepen' (Assembly Platform)—called by some of the medieval Russian chroniclers the "umbilicus of the world." From this low, flat-topped structure the medieval tsars delivered their speeches, and the patriarchs of the church blessed the people. Tradition has it that in 1547, on this very platform, Ivan the Terrible bewailed his misrule, confessed the sins of his youth, and promised amendment.

Crowds gathered in the Red Square for either pleasure or business.

All Moscow came here to learn the latest news, to hear the town criers and the tsar's heralds announce the new *ukazy* (edicts), and here corporal punishment was administered by order of the tsar. Centuries ago this was the place of public execution, complete with scaffolds, hanging poles, and instruments of torture, which were not removed until 1727.[1] Victims were hanged, broken on the wheel, impaled, beaten to death, buried alive, or burned in iron cages. Faithless wives were put into specially prepared holes in the ground, earth was tightly packed up to their necks, and they were left to die. Counterfeiters were stretched on the ground, and molten lead was poured down their throats. Those who had been guilty of sacrilege were torn to pieces by iron hooks.[2]

With the Red Square are associated many events in Russian history. In the Middle Ages it was often the scene of bloody battles with the Tartars. In the seventeenth century it was the scene of uprisings, and it witnessed the series of wholesale executions in the early days of Peter the Great after the rebellion of the *strel'tsy*. At the same time this square was the central market place not only of Moscow but of the whole country. The principal trade routes converged here: the Nikitskaia from Novgorod, the Tver'skaia (Gorkii Street at present) from Tver', the Nikol'skaia from the east, and the Ordynka from the south and the Golden Horde.

Here, near the Spas Gates, was the Krestets, where unemployed priests offered their services to merchants and boyars who had their private chapels, ready to say mass and to perform whatever rites were demanded of them for a small monetary consideration.

Near by, on both sides of the former Spas Bridge, which crossed the Alevisian Moat, were the many stores and booths that sold mainly educational merchandise—manuscripts (later, printed books), penny prints *(lubki)*, and pictures of local and foreign art.

In the Red Square scribes peddled their wares—pious religious texts, historical compilations, lives of the saints, tales of miracle workers, and—stealthily—also stories and verses of a secular nature.

Extensive trading was carried on in the corn chandlers' shops arranged in rows near the Moskva River. Here every row handled its own specialized merchandise: for example, Kharchevoi Riad dealt in foods, Shaposhny Riad, hats; Medovyi Riad, meads and wines; Ptichei, poultry; Ikonnyi, icons; Triapichnyi, rags, with special rows for Armenian, Persian, and Bokhara merchants of Oriental rugs, silks, spices, and jewels. Certain arcades traded in fine textiles, embossed firearms, damascened blades, silver, pewter, and other valuable articles.

The police department had its offices behind a high fence on the site of the present Historical Museum. Musketeers on duty would bring here all thieves and violators of public order.

An open, noisy brawling market spread out in front of St. Basil's Church. Merchants crying aloud urged prospective customers to inspect their wares. Vendors circulating among the motley crowd offered *pirogi* (meat pies), *sbeeten'* (hot mead), and *kvas*. Blind beggars sang at crossings, and many comedians and acrobats performed tricks and put trained bears through their paces to the great delight of the gaping throngs.

The beggars, the rouged wenches offering their charms, the peddlers, the public executions, the religious services and processions—all greatly contributed to the local color. Added to the above were the numerous pubs and taverns *(kabaki)*, the most famous of which was known as "Beneath the Cannon" (Pod Pushkoi). Foreign visitors were always amazed at the sight of stark naked people who had left their last stitch of clothing at the tavern.

The Church of St. Basil (Khram Vasiliia Blazhennago), at the top of the rather steep incline of Vasilievskaia Street, which leads from the bank of the river up to the Kremlin hillock, stands at the southeast end of Red Square. Down one long side of the square runs the battlemented brick wall of the Kremlin, with the severely simple mausoleum of Lenin against it, flanked by towers of varied design (the Nikol'skaia and Spaskaia).

The north end of the Red Square is blocked by a nineteenth-century building—the Historical Museum—on either side of which are entries to the square. The fourth side of the square is the massive gray row of arcaded commercial buildings that were once a series of shops and are now occupied by government stores and offices.

St. Basil's occupies an exceptional place in Russian architecture, and deserves to be considered at length. This boldest departure from classic or Byzantine architecture violates the academic laws of symmetry and proportions as understood by the Western world, and the structure is uniquely medieval Russian in content, form, technique, decoration, and feeling.

Long the subject of heated discussions, the architecture of St. Basil's has been either greatly ridiculed and termed as "the dream of a diseased imagination" or highly praised as an unique expression of the medieval Russian genius. Théophile Gautier compared the agglomeration of its many elements to the crystals of a giant madrepore. Other Western observers, notably such nineteenth-century travelers as the French de Gustine and the German Blazius, described its ensemble of towers and cupolas as "a bush, a plant or a bouquet of vari-colored flowers." On the other hand, many Russian art historians have said that, in spite of its seemingly incongruous jumble of architectural elements and decorative details, the church is uniquely original in conception, design, and execution—a brilliant solution of the difficult problems presented the architects by the Metropolitan Makarii and Tsar Ivan IV. Furthermore, some observers are of the opinion that the architecture of the church, in its departure from the traditional plan and distribution of masses of the Kremlin cathedrals, reflected the beginning of the new, national epoch in Russian art—an expression of the aesthetics of the rising middle classes, the traders and shopkeepers of Kitai-Gorod, and no longer that of the dwellers inside the Kremlin, the formerly powerful boyars. Its very location on the Red Square—at the people's forum and market place—points to the steadily growing importance of the districts beyond the Kremlin walls populated by the merchant, trading, and artisan classes.

These varying views and the paradoxical strangeness of this structure can perhaps be better understood in the light of the historical circumstances surrounding its construction.

As previously indicated, the epoch of Ivan the Terrible, during which St. Basil's was built, was marked by diligent searchings and novel experimentations in many phases of art which were begun several decades earlier. The native architects, in their attempt to break with the "alien" forms of Byzantine traditions, turned for inspiration to the indigenous forms of wooden churches, examples of which were common in and near Moscow. The graceful, slender "tent" roofs *(shatry)*: the chapels, galleries, and porches with their picturesque stairways, the *kokoshniki, bochki,* and cupolas—all these distinctive features of the wooden churches must have captivated the imagination of the local contemporary builders.

The Church of St. John the Precursor (Ioann Predtecha), built in 1529 at the village of Diakovo near Moscow, was one of the first significant attempts to break away from the traditional cupola-type church and to translate the forms of wooden architecture into masonry. St. John's is of special interest because St. Basil's, built some twenty-five years later, was greatly influenced by the forms of the earlier church.

St. John's (Plate 105) marked a most decisive step in the history of Russian architecture, pointing the way to bolder innovations. Ingenious, richly decorated, altogether unusual among the older Moscow masonry churches, this church remains pentacupolar as tradition demanded. However, by clever manipulation of the height of the corner chapels in relation to the central element, the architect succeeded in giving the structure the general silhouette of a pyramidal tower. The transition from the base to the tower is accomplished by two recessive rows of decorative *kokoshniki*—the upper pointed and the lower semicircular—that greatly add to the beauty of the upper elements. The wall surfaces are embellished with rectangular frescoed panels and colored tiles.

Figure 9. Plan and section of the Church of St. John the Precursor.

Above the west wall the architect placed a sharply profiled belfry similar to those developed by the Pskovian builders but with the typical Moscow decorative treatment. The general architectural masses of the church retained the austerity and somewhat heavy characteristics of early Moscow, but the decorative elements provided a new variety of richness in texture and color.

The Church of St. Basil the Blessed (or Beatified), originally known as the Cathedral of the Intercession of the Virgin (Pokrovskii Sobor), is, like St. John's at Diakovo, a votive church built by Ivan IV in commemoration of the conquest of Kazan' and Astrakhan'. At that time Russia was passing through a particularly intense phase of religious fervor. The Stoglav Council[3] had recently met; the young tsar, flushed with victory, wanted to signalize his military success as a triumph of the Cross over Islam.

At the suggestion of the Metropolitan Makarii, Ivan decided to erect a masonry church dedicated to the Intercession *(Pokrov)* of the Virgin. Because this was to be a memorial church, easy of access to all the people of Moscow, Ivan decided on a site on the Red Square at the edge of the ditch *(na rvu)* along the Kremlin. With the church as the central, dominant element, he planned eight smaller but separate churches (not chapels) of wood, each with its own altar and iconostasis, dedicated to a saint whose feast day coincided with one of the days of the eight decisive victories over the Tartars. These temporary wooden churches were later replaced by masonry. In 1588 another church was added on the northeast side of the cathedral to house the crypt of Basil the Blessed (Vasilii Blazhennyi).

St. Basil, for whom this extraordinary church was named, was a popular mendicant prophet and miracle worker of the sixteenth century who claimed as his distinctive glory that he was "idiotic for Christ's sake." This church contains relics of another saint—John the Idiot—as well as the chain and cross worn in penance by St. Basil. Idiocy was a common form of religious fervor in Russia, and these dedicated idiots *(urodivyie)* were treated with reverence.

One of the most venerated altars in the church—the third in importance—was dedicated to the entry of Jesus into Jerusalem. Foreign visitors to Moscow during the seventeenth century were impressed with the colorful Palm Sunday (Verbnoe Voskresenie) processions,[4] and referred to St. Basil's as the Church of Jerusalem.

Begun in 1553, St. Basil's was finished and consecrated in 1560. It was designed by the Russian architects Barma and Posnik Iakovlev,[5] who, in the words of the chronicler, were "very wise and eminently fit for this marvelous work." According to a persistent legend, the Church of St. Basil was designed by an Italian architect, who was then blinded by order of the tsar so that the Italian would not be able to produce a more beautiful church anywhere. Another version of the same legend says that the tsar asked the architect if he could build an even finer, more magnificent church. When the architect replied that he could, the tsar ordered him beheaded so that St. Basil's would remain an unrivaled monument.

The St. Basil group of churches is basically cross-shaped, the arms of the cross extending from a square center—the main church—over which rises the central tower covered with a tent-shaped roof and crowned with a gilt cupola. At each arm of the cross, along the principal axes, are four octagonal churches. Four other secondary churches (two square and two of irregular outline) are along the diagonal axes. All these elements are placed over a tall, vaulted substructure—the typical *podklet* of the Russian wooden churches. The pyramidal belfry at the southeast corner is separated from the church. The plan and the general massing of the elements are unusual not only in the accepted concept of church design, but in the distribution of the main masses. Rather than being merely the result of some fanciful caprice, the arrangement of the several churches and the grouping of the principal units were probably planned by Metropolitan Makarii.

The main church is of stone and brick and covered with stucco. In the seventeenth century the entire structure, originally white, was painted in variegated colors, the stairways were roofed over, the sheet-iron covering of the cupolas was replaced by tile, and the old belfry was replaced by the present tent-roofed bell tower.

Like the churches at Diakovo and Kolomenskoe, St. Basil's embodies the characteristic architectural features of the wooden churches of north Russia translated into masonry. Here too the transition from the square substructure to the main octagonal tower is accomplished by recessive, interspaced *(v perebezhku)* tiers of ornate *kokoshniki.* The same method is used to form the transition from the massive base to a smaller octagon supporting the tent-shaped spire surmounted by a small bulbous cupola. The eleven steeples are banded together like an immense bundle of fantastically shaped plants. The eight cupolas, dominated by the central pyramid, are all of the same general silhouette but are different in design—as if to single out each of the component churches in the complex. Some, with their twisted, variegated shapes, are reminiscent of Oriental turbans; some are decorated with ribbed or interlacing designs; others are faceted, giving them the appearance of pineapples; still another has

Figure 10. Plan and section of the Church of St. Basil the Blessed.

imbrications reminiscent of the aspen shingles of the wooden churches. All the cupolas are bulbous, projecting considerably beyond the diameter of the drum. This diversity of forms and decorative features is further heightened by the lavish use of colored tile. Although these heterogeneous elements are highly individual in character, they combine into a harmonious ensemble.

A striking feature of St. Basil's is its coloring: red, orange, yellow, green, blue, violet, gold, and silver mingle successfully and produce a stunning effect.

The interior is by contrast somber and cavernous. Each of the nine church chambers is prolonged upward in a kind of drum surmounted by a dome. The chambers are connected by low, vaulted passages within the thick walls, with a narrow, vaulted corridor around them. The low, arched doorways and windows are of various forms, all deeply recessed and flanked with engaged columns. The interior of the central church was frescoed in 1784 during the reign of Catherine II; the other surrounding churches were frescoed between 1839 and 1845.

St. Basil's is understandably strange, puzzling to Western eyes; yet it was well suited to the age and its former surroundings. It still exercises a singular attraction at all times of the year, but is especially fascinating in the winter. Seen in the pale sunshine, with its clump of pinnacles and cupolas illuminated against the sky, the building is most impressive. Nikol'skii, in his book, *Staraia Moskva,* had the following to say of St. Basil's:

> In the last hour of twilight, in the last moments of the dying day, when all outlines become simplified, it is not difficult to perceive the origin of the building, and what gave birth to the idea of such a building. Basil the Blessed stands out as a gigantic cluster of trees. Round a tall, old fir are grouped a number of smaller trees, forming a natural pyramid-like copse. The German traveler Blazius (in the forties of the nineteenth century) astonished by the appearance of the Church, compared it to a "colossal plant." And this similarity is not something haphazard. In all ancient-Russian buildings of the complex type, where the structure represents a group made up of several separate units joined together, there is a certain feeling of the scheme of the Russian forest landscape, organically relating the architectural monuments to their natural surroundings.[6]

At the end of the eighteenth century the Red Square, surrounded by almost unbroken rows of buildings, was a broad-walled market place resembling a closed interior court rather than an open square.

During the reconstruction of Moscow, after the fires of 1812, the first of its public plazas to receive attention was the Red Square. In 1814

Alexander I appointed Osip Ivanovich Beauvais (1784–1834), an architect educated in the traditions of Kazakov, chairman of a special commission for replanning and general design supervision.

Beauvais conceived the square ensemble not only as a civic center, but as an open parade ground, an element in the chain of planned wide boulevards and avenues of the city. He opened the square by removing the long row of old masonry buildings along the Kremlin wall, and changed the central unit of the old Commercial Rows (Torgovye riady), on the east side of the Square, by crowning it with a flat cupola and adding to it a wide Doric portico with a low pediment. The imposing portico and the cupola over the arcades established the square's east-west axis oriented toward the large dome over the Senate building inside the Kremlin. Beauvais thus succeeded in obtaining not only the desired architectural effect for an important unit in the general scheme of the square, but also dramatized the essential relationship between the Red Square and the Kremlin.

Clearing the square of the unsightly buildings also opened to view the surrounding ancient monuments, especially St. Basil's. The reconstruction commission further issued an order that prohibited future buildings of more than one story near St. Basil's.

The old Commercial Rows, removed in the 1880's, were replaced a few years later by a pseudo-seventeenth-century sandstone building three stories high, intersected in each direction by three corridors with connecting bridges at each floor, 275 yards long, 95 yards wide, all under one glass roof—an engineering feat for Moscow of those days. The lower floor is now occupied by the government department store known as the GUM.

The Historical Museum, at the north end of the square, was erected between 1874 and 1883, during the period of academic infatuation with the old national forms in architecture. Many of its elements are reminiscent of the Kremlin towers—tent-shaped belfries and details associated with church architecture. Much of the decorative detail is reminiscent of seventeenth-century Moscow—brick corbels and recesses reproducing forms usually associated with wood carving.

The architect, V. O. Sherwood (1833–1897), aimed to invest his design of the Historical Museum with the spirit of national Russian art—one of the more successful attempts of this period. But the very complex grouping of the masses—the gloomy manner in which the towers, tents, and roof ridges are arranged—does not truly re-create the beauty of old Russian architecture.

South of the Historical Museum stands the monument to Minin and

Pozharskii by the sculptor I. P. Martos (1752–1835), erected in 1818 in commemoration of the liberation of Moscow from the Polish occupation forces in August, 1612. The heroic bronze figures of Minin-Sukhoruk and Prince Dmitrii Pozharskii, organizers and leaders of the army of liberation, stand on a granite pedestal decorated with reliefs depicting the valor, patriotism, and self-sacrifice of the Russian people in their struggle with the Polish interventionists during the Time of Troubles and interregnum of 1606–1613.

During the Bolshevik revolution of October, 1917, the Kremlin, the Red Square, and the adjoining streets were the scenes of bitter fighting between the adherents of the Provisional and Revolutionary governments—the Whites and the Reds. On October 26th (O.S.), the Kremlin was occupied and held for a brief time by the Reds; it was stormed and taken over by the Whites, who in turn were attacked and forced to surrender to the Reds on November 2, 1917 (O.S.). In the struggle, the Kremlin became the target not for bows, flaming torches, and arquebuses, but for machine guns, mortars, and heavy artillery from both sides. About five hundred people were killed, many more wounded, and considerable damage was done to the Kremlin walls, towers, and cathedrals.

The small Nikolai Palace, near the Saviour's Gates, which served as barracks for the White defending forces, was bombarded and plundered. The Beklemishev Tower, on the southeast corner, was partly destroyed. One of the cupolas of the Assumption Cathedral was pierced by a shell, which, fortunately, did little damage. The frescoes of the Annunciation Cathedral were badly scarred by gun fire. The corner of the Ivan Velikii Belfry was hit by a shell. The Chudov Monastery was hit many times, but only the brick window moldings and the roof cornices suffered extensive damage. The clock and chimes of the Saviour's Tower were smashed; the Trinity Gates were battered, and one of the lower towers lost its brick spire. No harm was done either the Church of St. Basil or the Grand Kremlin Palace, which contained all the treasures of Moscow and Petrograd in its cellar and the crown jewels in the adjoining Armory (Oruzheinaia Palata).

The Soviet authority soon transferred the governmental administrative machinery from Leningrad, whose exposed position was threatened by the White Army advancing from all directions, to Moscow in the heart of European Russia. In 1918 Moscow, after a lapse of two centuries, again resumed its role as the capital of Russia, and the Kremlin once more became the nerve center of the land.

On October 5, 1918, the principle of state preservation of monuments of art and antiquity was established by a decree of the Soviet government. A single state central organ was set up to take charge of museums and the preservation of monuments of art and antiquity, under the People's Commissariat for Education. A special Restoration Commission of archaeologists, architects, and painters began the reconstruction of the walls, towers, and churches of the Kremlin to restore them to their medieval appearance.

The original appearance of the Church of St. Basil—marred by successive alterations and excrescences—was restored. Of great interest was the discovery and restoration of an arcade of galleries around the base.

The narrow gates of the Chapel of the Iberian Virgin (Iverskaia Chasovnia) were removed, to be replaced by a wide, unimpeded approach to the Red Square.

The restoration within the Kremlin has been particularly successful. The questionable alterations and additions made during the previous attempts to "improve" the Kremlin have been removed. The elimination of various wings, screens, and clumsy adaptations proved to be of great advantage to the original structures, often resulting in surprising discoveries. The passageways under the Church of the Twelve Apostles (Tserkov' Dvenadtsati Apostolov), built in 1656, were thus discovered. The galleries concealing the portals of the Church of the Consecration of the Priests (Tserkov' Riz-Polozheniia), 1484–1486, were removed, and its windows were restored to their original form. The metal-and-glass hood at the entrance of the Archangel Cathedral was taken down, revealing the stone carving on the Renaissance portals. The interior arrangement of the former Patriarchal Palace (Patriarshaia Palata), 1650, which had been completely distorted in the nineteenth century to provide a series of apartments, was restored. Many garish decorations and hangings in the cathedrals were taken down, revealing the original appearance.

The interior of the main body of the Uspenskii Cathedral has been restored to its original glory. Coatings of lime and cement were removed, revealing the works of great fourteenth- and fifteenth-century painters—Theophanos the Greek, Andrei Rublev, and the Moscow icon painter Feodosii (son of Dionosii). These paintings were painstakingly restored after having been hidden for centuries under layers of paint and plaster.[7]

Near the Kremlin wall, between the Nicholas and Saviour's towers, are the Brothers' Graves (Bratskie Mogili) containing the bodies of Soviet heroes.[8] In front of the Brothers' Graves stands the Lenin Mausoleum, opposite the Kremlin Senate Tower. The mausoleum, originally built of wood from the design of A. V. Shchusev[9] as a temporary shelter for the sarcophagus containing the embalmed body of Lenin, was later rede-

103

THE RED SQUARE

104

THE HISTORICAL MUSEUM

105

THE CHURCH OF ST. JOHN THE PRECURSOR

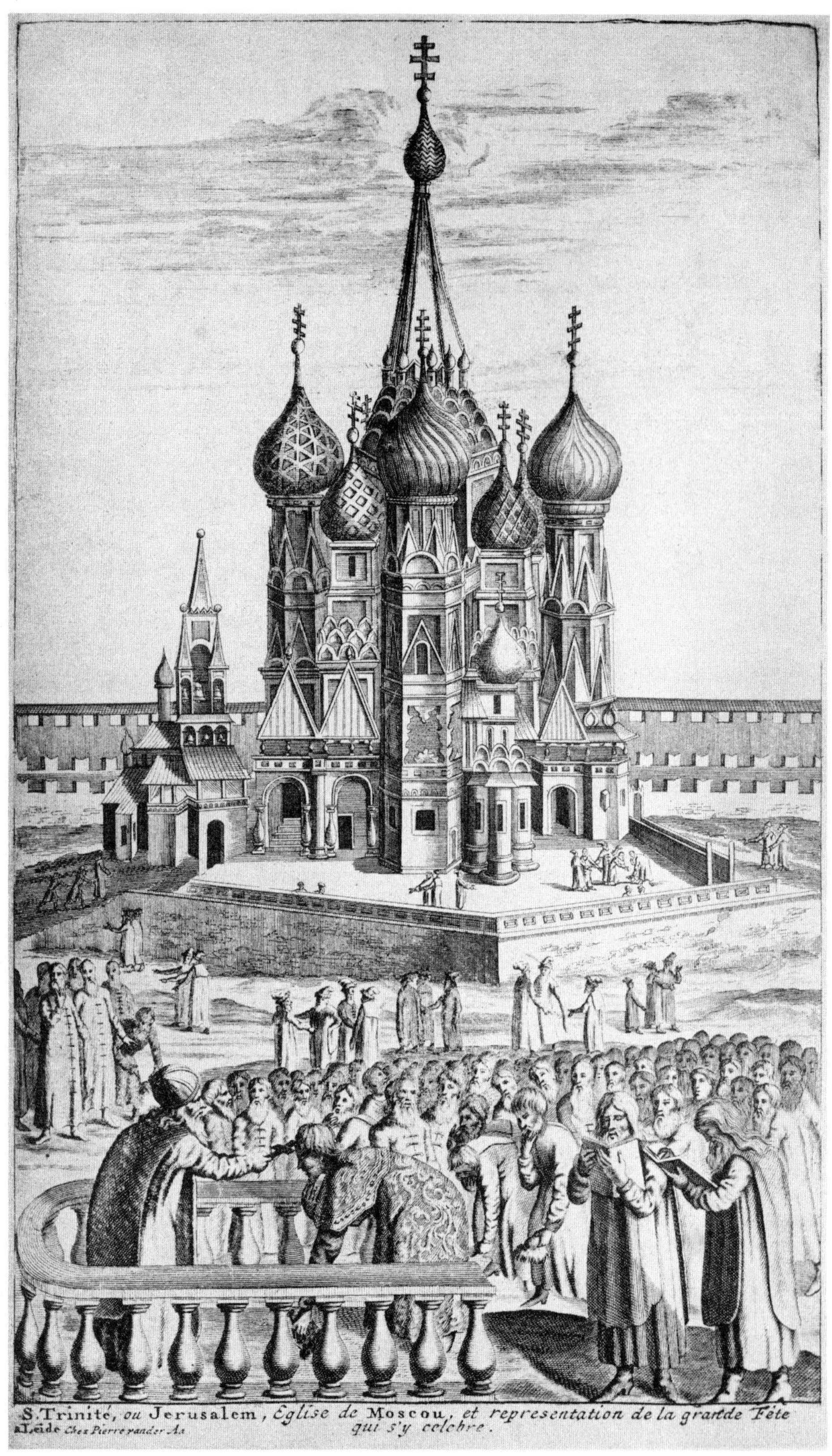

S.Trinité, ou Jerusalem, Eglise de Moscou, et representation de la grande Fête qui s'y celebre.
a Leide Chez Pierre vander Aa

106

THE CHURCH OF ST. BASIL THE BLESSED

107

THE CHURCH OF ST. BASIL THE BLESSED

108

STAIRWAY IN THE CHURCH
OF ST. BASIL THE BLESSED

109

CIRCULAR DRUM AND CUPOLA ON THE CHURCH OF ST. BASIL THE BLESSED

110

OCTAGONAL TENT ROOF AND CUPOLA ON THE CHURCH OF ST. BASIL THE BLESSED

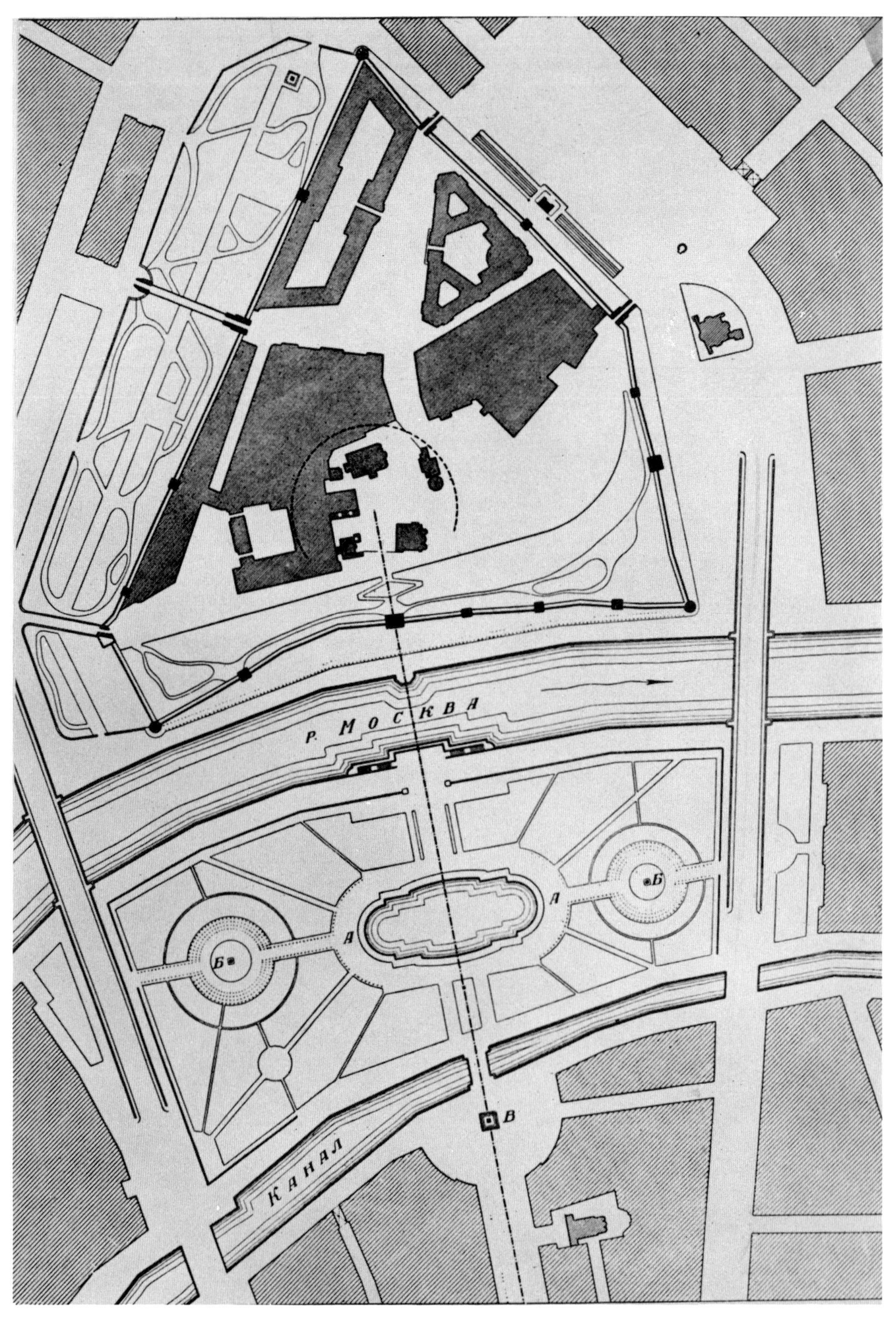

111

PROPOSED PARK ACROSS THE MOSKVA RIVER FROM THE KREMLIN

signed and rebuilt by the same architect as a permanent structure. In the general scheme of reconstruction it was envisioned as the main theme in the composition of the new Red Square. Relatively small in scale, the mausoleum is organically integrated with the mass of the Kremlin and with the heart of Moscow's busiest, most modern section.

The design is restrained, the general silhouette being suggestive of an ancient burial mound of a tribal chief.

The base of the mausoleum is slightly above the level of the square, and is enclosed within a low parapet. The main body of the structure, of highly polished red Ukrainian granite and black-and-gray labradorite flecked with iridescent blue, is surmounted by a twenty-six-foot monolith of red Carelian porphry. The parapet and the rows of tribunes, which run parallel to the Kremlin wall, are of a grayish-white, semi-polished granite. Architecturally the mausoleum is highly successful—simple, serene, and powerful. Rectangular, low, flat-roofed with set-backs, it has the dignity of the mastabas of ancient Egypt as well as the austere beauty of any truly functional architecture. Although the structure harmonizes with the medieval walls and towers of the Kremlin, it does not clash with the modern structures of present-day Moscow—rather it is a link binding the past and the present. Just as the architectural forms of St. Basil's evoke the aesthetics of medieval Russia, so do the simple lines of the Lenin Mausoleum suggest the aesthetics of the early phases of the Bolshevik revolution.

ABBREVIATED REFERENCES USED IN CATALOG OF ILLUSTRATIONS

Barshchevskii — Barshchevskii, I. F., *Russkiia drevnosti* (*Russian Antiquities*).

Bartenev — Bartenev, S., *Moskovskii Kreml'* (*The Moscow Kremlin*).

Grabar' — Grabar', I. (ed.), *Istoriia russkago iskusstva (History of Russian Art).*

Gradostroitelstvo — Bunin, A. V., and M. G. Kruglova, *Arkhitekturnaia Kompozitsia Gorodov (Architectural Composition of Cities).*

Moskva — *Moskva v eia proshlom i nastoiashchem (Moscow, Past and Present).*

Olearius — Olearius, A., *The voyages and travels of the ambassadors from the Duke of Holstein to the great Duke of Muscovy, and the King of Persia, 1633–1639.*

Rzianin — Rzianin, M. I., *Pamiatniki russkogo zodchestva* (*Monuments of Russian Architecture*).

Simakov — Simakov, N., *Russkii ornament v starinnykh obraztsakh khudozhestvenno-promyshlennago proizvodstava (Russian Ornament in Ancient Objects of Industrial Art).*

Snegirev — Snegirev, I. M., *Uspenskii Sobor v Moskve* (*Uspenskii Cathedral in Moscow*).

Solntsev — Solntsev, F. G., Delineator. *Drevnosti rossiiskago gosudarstva* (*Antiquities of the Russian Empire*).

Vel'tman — Vel'tman, A., *Opisanie Novago Imperatorskago Dvortsa v Kremle Moskovskom* (*Description of the New Imperial Palace in the Moscow Kremlin*).

Viollet Le Duc — Viollet Le Duc, E., *L'Art russe; Ses origines, ses elements constitutifs, son apogée, son avenir.*

CATALOG OF ILLUSTRATIONS

End paper. Plan of Moscow in 1610, known as the Sigismund Plan. The drawing, by I. P. Abelin-Gottfrid, was dedicated to King Sigismund III of Poland. Engraving by L. Kilian. (From Bartenev, vol. i, plate 44.)

Plate 1 (frontispiece). The iconostasis in the Cathedral of the Assumption (Uspenskii Sobor). The iconostasis is a high wall of burnished vermeil, with five rows of icons set in richly ornamented encasements of embossed metal that leave visible only the faces and hands of the saints. The top row – the Forefathers' (*Praotecheskii iarus*) – symbolizes the Church of the Old Testament: the Lord of Sabaoth, seated upon a throne, with Christ and the Dove in the midst of the twelve patriarchs. (The length of the image of the Lord, including the "glory," is 15 feet, 11 inches; the breadth 8 feet, 7 inches.) The second row – the Prophets' (*Prorocheskii iarus*) – symbolizes the Church from Moses to Jesus Christ: the Mother of God holding Emmanuel upon her lap, flanked by David and Solomon and the Prophets. The third row – the Festivals' (*Prazdnichnii iarus*) – depicts the Church festivals: the Birth of the Virgin, the Presentation in the Temple, Baptism, Raising of Lazarus, Entry into Jerusalem, Transfiguration, Crucifixion, Descent from the Cross, Entombment, Ascension, the Descent of the Holy Spirit, and the Dormition. The fourth row—Prayer or Intercession (*Deisusnyi poias*) – is given to the Deesis: the Saviour flanked by the Mother of God and St. John the Baptist, the Archangels Michael and Gabriel, St. Peter, St. Paul, and the other Apostles. In the bottom row are the icons of the locally revered festivals and saints (*mestnyia ikony*) and the Royal Doors with the Annunciation and the Four Evangelists on the door leaves. To the left of the Royal Doors is the icon of Our Lady of Vladimir (*Vladimirskaia ikona Bogomateri*)—claimed by tradition to have been painted by St. Luke – which was brought in the twelfth century from Constantinople to Kiev, then from Kiev to Vladimir, and later transferred to the Cathedral of the Assumption in the Moscow Kremlin. This icon is set in a fabulously rich shrine (*kiot*) and encased in a frame of pure gold adorned with precious stones. Next follow the icons of Our Lord, adored by Varlaam Khutynskii (brought from Novgorod in 1476), and of Our Lady of Smolensk. To the right of the Royal Doors is the icon of Our Most Merciful Lord (also brought from Novgorod), and next to it is the icon of the Dormition or Repose of the Most Holy Mother of God *(Ikona Uspeniia Presviatyia Bogoroditsy)*—the dedication feast of the cathedral. This icon is traditionally attributed to the Metropolitan Peter and is a good example of the thirteenth- and fourteenth-century Russian icon painting. (From Solntsev, pt. vi, plate 15.)

Plate 2. Plan of the Kremlin in the reign of Boris Godunov (1598–1605). (From Bartenev, vol. i, plate 33.)

Plate 3. The Kremlin and adjoining Kitai Gorod (to the right, in the very center of the ringed-in city) in the middle of the seventeenth century. From a drawing by S. K. Bogoiavlenskii, edited by I. A. Golubtsov. (From *Istoriia Moskvy.*)

Plate 4. The Kremlin of Grand Princes Ivan III and Vasilii III about 1533. Schematic plan by I. A. Golubtsov, based on data drawn mainly from Ivan Zabelin's *History of Moscow,* part i, and the reconstructed schematic plan in S. P. Bartenev's *The Moscow Kremlin, Past and Present.* (From *Istoriia Moskvy.*)

Plate 5. The Kremlin during the reigns of Tsars Aleksei Mikhailovich and Feodor Alekseevich. Schematic plan by I. A. Golubtsov, based on data drawn mainly from Ivan Zabelin's *History of Moscow,* part i, and S. P. Bartenev's *The Moscow Kremlin, Past and Present.* (From *Istoriia Moskvy.*)

Plate 6. The Kremlin from the Moskvoretskii Bridge. (From Rzianin, plate 1.)

Plate 7. Model of the seventeenth-century Kremlin. Executed, from a drawing by Bondarenko, at the Moscow Zemstvo Woodworking School.

Plate 8. Dmitrii Ivanovich Donskoi, Grand Prince of Vladimir, Moscow, and All Russia (1363–1389). From the *Tituliarnik.* (From Bartenev, vol. ii, fig. 89.)

Plate 9. Ivan IV—the Terrible (1533–1584). From the *Tituliarnik.* (From Bartenev, vol. ii, fig. 199.)

Plate 10. Ivan III, Grand Prince of All Russia (1462–1505), was the builder of the masonry Kremlin. Like his grandson Ivan IV, Ivan III was known as the "Terrible" (Grozny). Sketch by Greek artist from *La Cosmographie universelle* (1575), by André Thevet. (From Bartenev, vol. ii.)

Plate 11. The Saviour's Tower (Spasskaia Bashnia), main elevation. Base designed by Pietro Antonio Solario (1491); superstructure, by Christopher Halloway (1625). (From Bartenev, vol. i, fig. 116.)

Plate 12. The Armory Tower (Oruzheinaia Bashnia), view from the south. On the right is the Armory Museum. (Oruzheinaia Palata). (From Bartenev, vol. i, fig. 316.)

Plate 13. The Forest (Borovitskaia) Tower, about 1900. (From Bartenev, vol. i, fig. 200.)

Plate 14. The Trinity (Troitskaia) Tower, Kutaf'ia Tower, and Troitskii Bridge before their restoration in 1900. (From Bartenev, vol, i, fig. 167.)

Plate 15. The Water-Pumping (Vodovzvodnaia) Tower. The Grand Kremlin Palace is at the left; and the Annunciation (Blagoveshchenskaia), Secret (Tainitskaia), and Nameless (Bezymiannaia), towers are at the right. (From Bartenev, vol. i, fig. 249.)

Plate 16. The Beklemishev (Beklemishevskaia) Tower, west view from the wall ramparts. Base by Marco Ruffo in 1487; superstructure added in the seventeenth century. (From Bartenev, vol. i, fig. 237.)

Plate 17. Kremlin wall sections and plan of wall segment. (From Bartenev, vol. i, figs. 81–87.)

a. Between Alarm and Konstantin towers
b. Between Peter and Second Nameless towers
c. Between First and Second Nameless towers
d. Between First Nameless and Secret towers
e. Between Secret and Annunciation towers (twice the scale)
f. Between Annunciation and Water-Pumping towers (twice the scale)
g. Plan of wall between Armory and Forest towers

Plate 18. Kremlin wall sections. (From Bartenev, vol. i, figs. 88–96.)

a. Between Water-Pumping and Forest towers
b. Between Armory and Forest towers
c. Between Commandant and Armory towers
d. Between Trinity and Commandant towers
e. Between Trinity and Commandant towers at another point
f. Between Trinity and Corner Arsenal towers
g. Between Corner Arsenal and Middle Arsenal towers
h. Between Nicholas and Corner Arsenal towers
i. Between Nicholas and Saviour's towers

Plate 19. Elevation (*a*) and section (*b*) of the Saviour's Tower. (From Bartenev, vol. i, figs. 119, 120.)

Plate 20. Floor plans of the Saviour's Tower. (From Bartenev, vol. i, figs. 121–130.)

a. First floor
b. Second floor
c. Third floor
d. Fourth floor
e. Fifth floor
f. Sixth floor
g. Seventh floor
h. Eighth floor
i. Ninth floor
j. Tenth floor

Plate 21. Decorative details of the Saviour's Tower. (From Bartenev, vol. i, figs. 133, 134.)

a. Sixth floor, front elevation
b. Sixth floor, side elevation

Plate 22. Elevation (*a*) and section (*b*) of the Nicholas tower. (From Bartenev, vol. i, figs. 186, 187.)

Plate 23. Plans of the Nicholas Tower. (From Bartenev, vol. i, figs. 188–193.)

a. Section of the annex tower
b. First floor
c. Second floor
d. Third floor
e. Fourth floor
f. Fifth floor

Plate 24. Floor plans of the Forest Tower. (From Bartenev, vol. i, figs. 204–212.)

a. Basement
b. First floor
c. Second floor
d. Third floor
e. Fourth floor
f. Fifth floor
g. Sixth floor
h. Seventh floor
i. Eighth floor

Plate 25. Elevation (*a*) and section (*b*) of the Trinity Tower. According to tradition, a prison was situated under the gateway of this tower in the sixteenth century. In 1895–1896, during some repair work necessitated by a pavement cave-in, there came to light a two-story underground vaulted structure that contained a number of dungeons and black holes. (Bartenev, vol. i, figs. 169, 170.)

Plate 26. Floor plans of the Trinity Tower. (From Bartenev, vol. i, figs. 171–174.)

a. Lower basement
b. Upper basement
c. First floor
d. Second floor

Plate 27. Elevation (*a*) and section (*b*) of the Corner Arsenal Tower. (From Bartenev, vol. i, figs. 260, 261.)

Plate 28. Elevation (*a*) and section (*b*) of the Water-Pumping Tower. (From Bartenev, vol. i. figs. 251, 252.)

Plate 29. The Cathedral of the Assumption (Uspenskii Sobor). Designed by Aristotle Fieravanti, 1475–1479. This edifice, the largest cathedral in the Kremlin, is a well-proportioned cubic mass of unequal sides — 126 feet long, 83 feet wide, and 140 feet high — surmounted by a large cupola that is flanked on all four sides by smaller cupolas. (From Snegirev.)

Plate 30. Interior of the Cathedral of the Assumption. (From Snegirev.)

Plate 31. The seventeenth - century Seat of the Patriarch, of carved stone, in the Cathedral of the Assumption. (From Snegirev.)

Plate 32. The Repository of the Robe of Our Lord in the Cathedral of the Assumption. This reliquary stands in the southwest corner of the Cathedral of the Assumption, among the sarcophagi of the patriarchs. The repository was erected by order of Patriarch Philaret in 1625 to house the Robe of Christ sent to Moscow by the Shah Abbas of Persia. According to an ancient tradition, the Robe was brought into Georgia by one of the Roman soldiers stationed at the foot of the Cross and was preserved for many centuries in the Cathedral of Mtschet. The structure, of chiseled gilded bronze, decorated with kokoshniki running around the base of its roof, is ten feet, six inches square by twenty-four feet high. According to Oruzheinaia Palata records, it was built by Dmitri Sverchkov. (From Solntsev, pt. vi, plate 19.)

Plate 33. The Throne (*Tsarkoe mesto*) of Ivan the Terrible in the Cathedral of the Assumption. Front and side elevations. From Solntsev, pt. ii, plate 67.)

Plate 34. Details of carved panels on the Throne of Ivan the Terrible. (from Solntsev, pt. ii, plate 71.)

Plate 35. The Church of the Saviour in the Forest (Spas na Boru), 1330. This miniature church, in the courtyard of the Grand Kremlin Palace, is the oldest building in Moscow. It represents the Russia of the appanage period, whereas the Cathedral of the Assumption, a short distance away, represents Russia of the grand princely period. (From Vel'tman.)

Plate 36. The Cathedral of the Annunciation (Blagoveshchenskii Sobor). Designed by Pskov architects, 1482–1490. (From *Moskva.*)

Plate 37. The Cathedral of the Archangel Michael (Arkhangel'skii Sobor). Designed by Alevisio the Milanese, 1494. (From *Moskva; Sobory, Monastyri i Tserkvi.*)

Plate 38. The Cathedral of Our Saviour behind the Golden Grille (Verkhospasskii Sobor za Zolotoi Reshotkoi.) At the left is the Palace of Facets (Granovitaia Palata). This highly decorated, small cathedral, built in 1678–1681, was originally the private chapel of the tsars. It is at the east end of the fourth story of the Terem Palace (Teremnoi Dvorets), and is reached by a double stairway with a gilded grille—hence the latter part of the name. Because the design of this church was planned as an ornamental feature of the Terem Palace, the builders lavished most of their attention on the upper part—particularly on the eleven cupolas. The cornice and cupola drums are decorated with colored tiles designed by the seventeenth-century master craftsman Elder Ippolit. (From Grabar', vol. ii, p. 260.)

Plate 39. The Church of the Twelve Apostles (Tserkov' Dvunadesiati Apostolov), 1656. This church, on the second floor of the former residence of the metropolitans and patriarchs, was built by Patriarch Nikon in 1656 and renovated in 1723 and again in the reign of Nicholas I. It contains an icon of the Apostles Peter and Paul dating from the twelfth century. (From *Moskva; Sobory, Monastyri i Tserkvi.)*

Plate 40. The Belfry of Ivan the Great (Ivan Velikii). (From Rzianin, plate 39.)

Plate 41. The Terem Palace. Designed by Bazhen Ogurtsov and collaborators, 1635–1637. (From Rzianin, plate 44.)

Plate 42. The Red Stairway, with the Palace of Facets at the right. (From *Moskva; Sobory, Monastyri i Tserkvi.)*

Plate 43. Interior of the Palace of Facets. Designed by Marco Ruffo and Pietro Solario, 1487–1491. (From Rzianin, plate 33.)

Plate 44. Chamber in the Terem Palace. (From Vel'tman.)

Plate 45. The Golden Tsaritsa Chamber (Zolotaia Tsaritsyna Palata) in the Terem Palace. (From Solntsev, pt. vi, plate 1.)

Plate 46. Bedroom in the Terem Palace. (From Barshchevskii, plate 147.)

Plate 47. Private chapel of the tsar in the Terem Palace. (From Barshchevskii, plate 127.)

Plate 48. Stairway with double arch in the Terem Palace. Bazhen Ogurtsov and collaborators, architects. (From Rzianin, plate 45.)

Plate 49. Window in the Terem Palace facing the Armory Museum (Oruzheinaia Palata). (From Solntsev, pt. vi, plate 6.)

Plate 50. Window in the Terem Palace facing the Cathedral of Our Saviour behind the Golden Grille. (From Solntsev, pt. vi, plate 4.)

Plate 51. Window in the Terem Palace facing the Armory Museum. (From Solntsev, pt. vi., plate 7.)

The windows in the Terem Palace are of various forms and are remarkable for their ornamentation as well as for the meticulous quality of workmanship; they differ from one another in design of their arches, architraves, entablatures, kokoshniki, and sills. One of them—double-arched at the entrance stairway to the terem apartments—has a hanging keystone and a full, highly ornamental entablature (Plate 50). The others—also double-arched and with rounded, carved, hanging keystones dividing the windows into two sections—have a broken pediment with a pedestal in the center supporting a carved medallion (Plates 49, 51). The ornamentation of one window consists of griffins and dragons, double-headed eagles, pigeons, and birds of paradise with crowns and necklaces; on others the ornamentation consists of foliage, flowers, and arabesques. The carving on the window architraves, as well as that on the doors, is in high relief.

Plate 52. Exterior door in the upper chamber of the Terem Palace facing the Cathedral of Our Saviour behind the Golden Grille. (From Solntsev, pt. vi, plate 3.)

Plate 53. Window, with carved stone ornament, in the Palace of Facets. (From Grabar', vol. ii, p. 265.)

Plate 54. Door architrave in the tsar's study, Terem Palace. (From Barshchevskii, plate 128.)

Plate 55. The Grand Kremlin Palace, southwest elevation. Designed, 1848, by: K. A. Thon, architect; Rikhter, Chichagov, and Gerasimov, associates; N. Cherkasov, delineator. (From Vel'tman.)

Plate 56. The Hall of St. Vladimir (Vladimirskaia Zala) in the Grand Kremlin Palace. This room is dedicated to the Order of St. Vladimir, founded by Catherine II in 1782. Octagonal in plan, the hall measures fifty-eight feet across, sixty-three feet from the floor to the circular lantern in the cupola. The walls are faced with a reddish marble (the color of the Order of St. Vladimir); the richly ornamented dome rests on the mezzanine arcade. Notable features are the enormous bronze chandelier that weighs 8,640 pounds, the four multibranched candelabra, and the star-patterned parquetry of the floor. From a drawing by N. Cherkasov. (From Vel'tman.)

Plate 57. The Hall of St. George (Georgievskaia Zala) in the Grand Kremlin Palace. This hall, once the site of the ancient Middle Golden Palace, is dedicated to the military Order of St. George, founded by Catherine the Great in 1769.

The white-and-gold walls, columns, and vaulted ceiling are almost entirely covered by ornamentation designed by Chichagov. Eighteen alabaster twisted columns, flanking the wall niches, serve as pedestals for alegorical "victories" symbolizing the important conquests and annexations in Russian history—beginning with the conquest of Perm' in 1472, and ending with the annexation of Armenia in 1828. At one end of the hall is a group in silver, designed by Verkhovtsev, representing the two Cossack leaders (atamans): Iermak, the conqueror of Siberia, and Platov the hero of the war of 1812. The color scheme of the furnishings is black and yellow, the colors of the Order of St. George. From a drawing by Cherkasov. (From Vel'tman.)

Plate 58. The Hall of St. Andrew (Andreevskaia Zala) in the Grand Kremlin Palace. This hall is dedicated to the Order of St. Andrew, founded by Peter the Great in 1698. Before the Bolshevik revolution it was the imperial throne room and scene of coronations. Now the Central Executive Committee of the Soviet Union meets here. From a drawing by Sakharov. (From Vel'tman.)

Plate 59. The Image of Our Lady, said to have belonged to Patriarch Ioasaph, in the Cathedral of the Archangel Michael. The image is painted on a lime panel. In the solemnity of expression, manner of highlighting (*ozhivki*), and symbolic representation it shows some relation to the Byzantine prototypes. Yet the modeling of the face, the precise, delicate drawing, and the fluent blending of the pigments reveal that it is a product of a new age in Russian icon painting. The face is somewhat oval and modeled with hardly any suggestion of bone structure. The nose is thin and slightly prominent, the hands supple and refined. The soft flesh coloring, tone, and quality identify the painting as belonging in sentiment to the work of Rublev (*circa* 1370–1430) or one of his closest followers. The composition reflects a new kind of rhythm; the angularity and rigidity of the Greek painters are gone, and the style is distinguished by an aristocratic subtlety, a soft poetic quality informed by a new spiritual significance. The embellishment of the gold encasement in filigree and enamel is remarkable for its artistry and richness. The crown or the halo (*venchik*) is of gold and cloisonné. To it are attached a collar (*grivna*) in the form of a crescent and three pendants (*tsaty*), all heavily encrusted with precious stones, mostly uncut. The image of the Saviour is embellished in the same way. On the golden medallions around the pearl-bordered frame are niello engravings of the saints whose name days correspond with the Christian names of the owner and the members of his family. Tradition claims that this icon was presented by Patriarch Ioasaph I to Tsar Michael Feodorovich. (From Solntsev, pt. i, plate 2.)

Plate 60. The panagia of Patriarch Philaret in the Patriarchal Vestry. This panagia is an elliptical medallion. The gold frame, set with precious stones and two rows of pearls, contains a four-ply agate on which the image of the Virgin is carved. The back has an engraved representation of the Epiphany. At the top is a large amethyst. The workmanship is by craftsmen from the patriarch's shops. (From Solntsev, pt. i, plate 111.)

Plate 61. The Tabernacle called "Jerusalem" in the Cathedral of the Assumption. Of silver gilt embellished with niello, the tabernacle is one foot seven inches square by two feet, ten inches high; it weighs about forty-five pounds. It is built in the form of a five-cupola church surrounded by embossed, high-relief figures of the Twelve Apostles. On the sloping walls of the superstructure are the figures of four prophets among winged beasts. The Slavonic inscription on the inside of the door indicates that the tabernacle was built at the order of Ivan the Terrible for the Cathedral of the Assumption to commemorate the conquest of Tver'. The style of the decorations and of the inscription suggests Moscow workmanship. (From Solntsev, pt. i, plate 60.)

Plate 62. Gold censer in the sacristy of the Cathedral of the Archangel Michael. This censer *(kadilo),* rich in gold and precious stones, weighs nearly four pounds. The cup and lid are in the form of a single-cupola church, its drum having grilled windows. The lower part, which holds a pan for charcoal, is engraved and nielloed with figures of saints and scriptural subjects representing the Archangel Michael at the head of the Church and the celestial hierarchy; leading the latter are St. Theodore Stratelates and the martyr St. Irene, namesakes of Tsar Feodor and Tsaritsa Irina. The eight-lobed foot is entirely covered with niello tracery and decorative inscriptions of interlaced Slavonic letters. The whole is enriched with cut and uncut emeralds and amethysts in variously shaped settings. The thumbpiece (*erdanka*) is of pure gold ornamented in niello and lavishly studded with precious stones. Although the censer is officially listed as a gift of Tsar Feodor Alekseevich (1676–1682), the inscription engraved in niello on the bottom indicates that it was made, by order of Tsaritsa and Grand Princess Irina in 1598, as a memorial to Tsar Feodor Ivanovich. (From Solntsev, pt. i, plate 38.)

Plate 63. The armlets of Patriarch Nikon in the Patriarchal Vestry (Patriarshaia Riznitsa). (From *Mir Iskusstva,* 1904, no. 10.)

Plate 64. The crown of Patriarch Nikon in the Patriarchal Vestry. (From *Mir Iskusstva,* 1904, no. 10.)

Plate 65. Pectoral cross of Tsar Mikhail Feodorovich in the Oruzheinaia Palata. According to the Oruzheinaia Palata inventory of 1835, the cross is made of gold, enriched with precious stones and ornamented with foliate motifs of varicolored enamels. In the center are ten emeralds surrounded by diamonds. An image of St. Peter is on the reverse side of the cross, which weighs about seven ounces. (From Solntsev, pt. ii, plate 45.)

Plate 66. Silver panagia with applied gilt ornament in the Patriarchal Vestry. (From Simakov, plate 23.)

Plate 67. Front cover of the Mstislav Gospels in the sacristy of the Cathedral of the Archangel Michael. Written and illuminated on parchment about 1103, this book derives its name from its first owner, Prince Mstislav Vladimirovich of Novgorod. The scribe is identified by Russian historians as Aleksei Lazarev, the son of a Novgorod priest. According to tradition, the prince sent the finished manuscript to Tsargrad (Constantinople), celebrated then for its jeweled and enameled metals, to be bound and embellished with enameled gold covers. The book remained for several centuries in the Church of the Annunciation at Novgorod. In 1551, by order of Ivan Grozny, its cover was renovated and the book removed to the Cathedral of the Archangel Michael in the Moscow Kremlin. The present enamel decorations (the images of the saints) on its silver-gilt filigree cover are the products of different periods varying in styles and techniques. (From *Mir Iskusstva,* 1904, no. 10, p. 235.)

Plate 68. Cover of the Book of the Gospels, gift of Natal'ia Kirillovna, in the Cathedral of the Assumption. This book was printed in Moscow in 1689. Size, binding, and ornamentation distinguish it as one of the outstanding examples of book design. It is thirty-five inches high, nineteen and one-fourth inches wide, and weighs about seventy-four pounds. The illuminations, chapter heads, and page borders are remarkable for their beauty and brilliancy of color. The book is probably the collective work of native and foreign icon painters, illuminators, and jewelers who worked in the Oruzheinaia Palata. The covers of the book—front and back—exceed, in magnificence of workmanship and wealth of precious metals and stones, the splendor of the book itself. Both covers are of gold. The front is ornamented with figures of crowns, flowers, and foliate designs executed in diamonds, emeralds, amethysts, and enamel. Among them are seven large emeralds on which are carved the images of the Pantocrator, the Virgin, the Precursor, and the four Evangelists. The entire surface of the front cover is so lavishly studded with gems that they seem to form one blazing mass. The back cover contains images of various saints in painted enamel on a gold background. The book was made at the time of the young Tsar Peter I's first sea voyage to Arkhangel'sk; there is reason to think that the book was planned by the tsar's mother as a votive offering to the Virgin in gratitude for his safe return. (From Solntsev, pt. i, plate 62.)

Plate 69. Cover of the Book of the Gospels, gift of Boyarin B. M. Morozov, 1669, Patriarchal Vestry. The Gospels appear in Slavonic on parchment, two columns on a page, according to fifteenth-century regulations. The front cover is of gold embellished with filigree patterns and colored enamel plaques. In the center are representations of the Resurrection of Christ and of the Evangelists. Above, below, and on the sides are the Twelve Apostles and the archangels. In the corners are Saints Basil the Great, Gregorius the Theologian, John the Golden-Mouthed, Nicholas, and four cherubims. (From *Mir Iskusstva,* 1904, no. 10, p. 216.)

Plate 70. Saccos of Metropolitan Dionisii in the Patriarchal Vestry. The saccos (sakkos) is similar to the Western dalmatic in that it is slit up the sides and has short sleeves. Originally worn only by the patriarch, it is now common to all bishops. The saccos of Metropolitan Dionisii was made during the reign of Ivan IV, and was altered in the seventeenth century. (From *Mir Iskusstva,* 1904, no. 10, p. 209.)

Plate 71. Details of the ornamentation on the saccos of Metropolitan Dionisii. (From *Mir Iskusstva,* 1904, no. 10, p. 209.)

Plate 72. Details of tau on pastoral staff of Patriarch Nikon, in the Patriarchal Vestry. Green and dark blue champlevé enamel, 1652. (From *Mir Iskusstva,* 1904, no. 10, p. 226.)

Plate 73. Details of tau on pastoral staff of Patriarch Philaret, in the Patriarchal Vestry, 1619. (From *Mir Iskusstva,* 1904, no. 10, p. 226.)

Plate 74. Carved wood altar crosses in the Oruzheinaia Palata. The crosses are made of cypress wood. On the branches, extending from the foot to the arms, are carved images of the prophets; on the body of the cross are scenes representing the twelve holy days; at the extreme ends, left and right, are the Apostles and their symbols. The branchlike ornamental motifs suggest the Tree of Life, whose branches shelter and protect all who come under their shade. The initials on the side are probably those of the artist, who was very likely Brother Sviatogorts of Mount Athos. (From Solntsev, pt. i, plate 34.)

Plate 75. Greenish-gray jasper chalice, from the twelfth century, in the Patriarchal Vestry. (From *Mir Iskusstva,* 1904, no. 10, p. 234.)

Plate 76. Seventeenth-century costumes of the tsar and his attendants. The painting, by Solntsev, shows Tsar Aleksei Mikhailovich (1629–1676) in full regalia. With him are Boyarin Lev Naryshkin and two bodyguards dressed in seventeenth-century uniforms of their branch of service and rank. The picture is based on supposedly authentic portraits of the tsar and descriptions of him by foreign writers and eyewitnesses. The tsar is shown with the imperial insignia: crown (*shapka*), royal collar (*barmy*), scepter, and orb. The robe is of heavy silk embellished with precious stones and pearls. The two attendants, right and left—known in seventeenth-century Russia respectively as *strelets* (harquebusier) and *ognenik* (from *ogon'* meaning "fire" or "flame," suggested by his flaming red uniform)—are interesting as illustrations of the uniforms, accouterments, and weapons of the tsar's bodyguards. (From Solntsev, pt. iv, plate 7.)

Plate 77. Ancient embroidered regalia collars *(barmy)*. These peculiarly shaped regalia collars or capes *(barmy)* are traditional emblems of imperial authority worn, during the coronation investiture and other solemn occasions, by the Russian tsars and emperors. Together with the golden bonnet or Cap of Monomakh (*Shapka Monomakha*), they are said to be fashioned in the style of the ancient Byzantine imperial regalia. The inventory of the "Large Treasury" *(Bol'shaia Kazna)* of 1642 describes the *barmy* illustrated here as embroidered in spun gold on dark-violet satin. The borders between the figures are of strung pearls. (From Solntsev, pt. ii, plate 31.)

Plate 78. The Orb of Monomakh. The orb, surmounted by a cross, is the symbol of the sanctified rule of religion over the earth. In the age of Augustus Caesar the idea of imperial might was symbolically represented by a figure of a victory on top of a globe. With the establishment of Christianity in Constantinople, the symbol of world rule became the Cross overshadowing the universe. The 1642 inventory of the Treasury of Tsar Mikhail Feodorovich says that the orb is "Frankish" work (*Friazheskoe delo*) — that is, made in the Italian or French style. The "apple" or the globe (*Iabloko Velikoderzhavnoe*) of this symbol of power is of chased gold embellished with enamel and precious stones. It is studded with fifty-eight diamonds, eighty-nine amethysts, twenty-three sapphires, fifty emeralds, and thirty-seven pearls set in enameled gold frames. In the four triangular sectors of the globe are depicted: the annointment of David by Samuel; the victory of David over Goliath; David's victorious return from the fight; the banishment of David by King Saul. (From Solntsev, pt. ii, plate 20.)

Plate 79. The Crown of St. Vladimir, or the Cap of Monomakh (*Shapka Monomakha*), in the Oruzheinaia Palata. This crown always has been the symbol of power in Russia. Its significance, and the implied heavy burden upon the head of its wearer, was best epitomized by Pushkin in *Boris Godunov* — *"Tiazhela ty shapka Monomakh"* ("Heavy art thou, Cap of Monomakh"). The exact origin of the crown is debatable, but tradition claims that it was sent as a gift by the Byzantine Emperor Alexius Comnenus to Grand Prince Vladimir in 1116. It is the oldest of the imperial caps, and all the Russian emperors were crowned with it. Aside from the historical, sentimental, and intrinsic values attached to it, it is a work of exquisite taste and craftsmanship. On a foundation of eight triangular gold filigree panels, forming the body of the crown, are incrusted pearls and other jewels of great value, arranged with admirable understanding of the art of ornamentation. The 1696 inventory of the treasury says: "The Tsar's cap, called Monomakh, is of gold filigree work. It is surmounted by a plain gold cross having four pearls at the extremities. On the base of the cross [the dome or the "apple"] are three large stones — a topaz, a sapphire, and a ruby. Between them are three large pearls, all in gold settings. Upon the crown itself are four emeralds, four rubies set in gold, and twenty-five pearls of Ormuz in gold settings. The cap is bordered with sable fur and lined with red satin." (From Bartenev, vol. ii, pp. 52–53.)

Plate 80. The ivory chair of Grand Prince Ivan III in the Oruzheinaia Palata. Tradition claims that this chair, with many other gifts, was brought from Byzantium by Princess Zoe Paleologue on the occasion of her marriage to Grand Prince Ivan III in 1472. The original ivory panel carvings contained a set of scenes depicting various episodes from the mythological story of the adventures of Orpheus. However, the years and vandalism have taken their toll, and a number of those panels have disappeared. In their place new panels were inserted, sometime during the early part of the eighteenth century, depicting battle scenes with warriors in German costumes and arms. On the back of the chair is a figure of the double-headed eagle flanked by a lion and a unicorn. On the lower front panels are mythological figures of Leda, Saturn devouring a child, and cupids mounted on dolphins. (From Solntsev, pt. ii, plate 84.)

Plate 81. Details of the ivory chair of Grand Prince Ivan III in the Oruzheinaia Palata. (From Solntsev, pt. ii, plate 85.)

Plate 82. The throne of Tsar Aleksei Mikhailovich in the Oruzheinaia Palata. This throne, lavishly covered with gold ornament and jewels of beautiful workmanship, is embellished on its front, sides, and rear with carved ivory panels containing figures of animals, birds, and flowers. The ivory carvings, of undoubtedly Eastern origin, are in light relief against a tinted background. The metal ornaments, as well as the miniature paintings that decorate the vertical and horizontal members of the chair, are of Russian workmanship; they harmonize beautifully with the foreign elements. The Oruzheinaia Palata inventory of 1676, in a detailed listing of the gems on the various parts, describes the chair as studded with 876 diamonds of various sizes and 1,223 amethysts in addition to rubies, turquoises, and three strands of pearls running around an inscription in Latin, which reads in part: "Potentissimo et Invictissimo Moscovitarum Imperatori Alexio. . . ." (From Solntsev, pt. ii, plate 63.)

Plate 83. Details of the carved panels on the throne of Tsar Aleksei Mikhailovich in the Oruzheinaia Palata. (From Viollet le Duc, plate xix.)

Plate 84. Tsar's boots. It was the fashion, in sixteenth-century Russia, for the wealthy and the prominent to embroider their boots and embellish the seams, toes, and heels with pearls or occasionally with precious stones. During the reign of Tsar Mikhail Feodorovich (1613–1645) men and women wore high-heeled boots ornamented with Morocco or some other colored leather or velvet. Wealthy people had them decorated with gold and silver inserts, open work, and braiding. (From Solntsev, pt. iv, plate 27.)

Plate 85. Tsar's gloves. (From Solntsev, pt. iv, plate 25.)

Plate 86. Buttons, clasps, plaques, and other ornaments of the tsar's costumes. The decoration of the tsar's clothes, in addition to laces and embroidery in gold and silver, consisted of sets of buttons, buckles, clasps, plaques, and other ornaments. Some of the finest of Russian jewelers' work was bestowed upon these, especially when made for the ceremonial robes. The illustrated pendants, clasps, fasteners, and buttons are from the caftan of Tsar Peter I. (From Solntsev, pt. ii, plate 56.)

Plate 87. The helmet of Grand Prince Nevskii in the Oruzheinaia Palata. This helmet, or Cap of Jericho (*Shapka Ierikhonskaia*), is said to have belonged to Grand Prince Alexander Nevskii (1246–1263), celebrated for his victories over the Swedish and German knights (the subject of Prokofiev's cantata). Of Oriental workmanship, the helmet has an Arabic inscription from the Koran: "Help from God, victory is drawing nigh. . . ." According to the Oruzheinaia Palata inventory of 1687, the ornamentation, the embellishment in precious stones, and the enamel image of the Archangel Michael above the nose protector were made by Davydov and Ivan Markov, Russian craftsmen employed at the Oruzheinaia Palata during the reign of Tsar Mikhail Feodorovich (1613–1645). The helmet is of wrought iron, richly damascened in gold. Its name (the Cap of Jericho) and its shape suggest the possibility that it was made in Palestine for some Christian knight, probably during the Crusades. (From Solntsev, pt. iii, plate 6.)

Plate 88. The saber of Grand Prince Vladimir Monomakh. (From Solntsev, pt. iii, plate 87.)

Plate 89. Seventeenth-century gunpowder flask in the Oruzheinaia Palata. This gunpowder flask (or priming horn) is of chased silver and is three and one-half inches in diameter. According to the inscription running round the edge between the two plaques, it belonged to Chamberlain (*Stolnik*) A. I. Nesterov, the assistant to Boyarin Khitrovo, superintendent of the Oruzheinaia Palata. Both sides of the flask are decorated with symbolic scenes: on one side is St. George striking a dragon; on the other, a combat between an eagle and a dragon. Around these is a border of foliate design interspersed with birds and beasts, all on a matted ground. This flask is probably the work of the craftsmen of the Oruzheinaia Palata, who frequently used these symbolic motifs (borrowed from Byzantium) for the decoration of the tsar's arms. (From *Khudozhestvennyia sokrovishcha Rossii,* 1902, p. 220.)

Plate 90. The tsar's quiver (*kolchan*). This quiver is of the same character and workmanship as the scepter and orb. Like a number of other extant magnificent bow-and-arrow cases, this seventeenth-century quiver recalls the ancient Scythian form. They are all made of various precious materials and elaborately decorated with enamel and enriched with jewels. The work is ascribed to Ivan Iuriev. (From Solntsev, pt. iii, plate 124.)

Plate 91. Silver food-serving dish in the Oruzheinaia Palata. This tureenlike serving dish, known in seventeenth-century Russia as *kroshnia,* is of embossed silver. The Oruzheinaia Palata inventory of 1663 describes it as having two gilded handles, its body embellished with embossed foliate designs, and on its lid, nestled among embossed flowers and leaves, eight gilded nut-shaped ornaments and five "apples." The lid is furnished with two ornamental hasps and locking devices. The latter were evidently for insuring that the food would not be poisoned while on its way from the kitchen to the dining room, where it was formally unlocked and tasted by the chief steward before being served to the tsar. This dish weighs twelve pounds, eight ounces. (From Solntsev, pt. v, plate 40.)

Plate 92. The teapot of Tsaritsa Evdokia Feodorovna in the Oruzheinaia Palata. This teapot, known in seventeenth-century Russia as a *voronok,* is from the silver-plate service of Tsaritsa Evdokia Feodorovna (the nun Elena). The pot is decorated with embossed gilded flowers on a silver field. On the medallions are figures of double-headed eagles with three crowns. The teapot weighs three pounds, three ounces. (From Solntsev, pt. v, plate 39.)

Plate 93. Pitcher and washbasin presented by Tsaritsa Natal'ia Kirillovna to her grandson Tsarevich Aleksei Petrovich, in the Oruzheinaia Palata. The Oruzheinaia Palata inventory describes the pitcher as made of gold embellished with green enamel and solidly encrusted with diamonds, emeralds, and rubies (754 gems). The vessels are Eastern in character, but the craftsmanship is Muscovian. They were made in the private shops of Tsaritsa Natal'ia Kirillovna. The pitcher weighs more than three pounds. Vessels of this type were used for hand washing on ceremonial occasions: in church before communion, and in the palace on receiving foreign non-Christian ambassadors. According to Olearius, only ambassadors of Christian lands were permitted to touch the tsar's hand. (From Solntsev, pt. v, plate 44.)

Plate 94. The gold plate of Tsar Aleksei Mikhailovich in the Oruzheinaia Palata. This is fairly representative of the artistry and skill attained in the shops of the Oruzheinaia Palata in the seventeenth century. It is fully equal to the art of the East. The borders of the plate are decorated with a band of flowers and foliate designs in green, blue, white, and azure enamels. The edges are scalloped and studded with sixteen rubies. In the center, surrounded by eight roses on a green star-spangled field, is the Russian imperial seal—the double-headed eagle with three crowns. The inscription reads: "Tsar, Sovereign and Grand Prince Aleksei Mikhailovich, Autocrat of all Great, Little and White Russia." The plate weighs slightly less than fourteen ounces. (From Solntsev, pt. v, plate 41.)

Plate 95. Silver-gilt goblet (*hanaper*) in the Oruzheinaia Palata. According to the Oruzheinaia Palata inventory, each of the convex facets of the goblet is embellished with amethysts and diamonds. The goblet weighs approximately one pound, twelve ounces. (From Solntsev, pt. v, plate 25.)

Plate 96. The memorial silver-gilt *bratina* and silver incense burner of Tsar Mikhail Feodorovich in the Oruzheinaia Palata. The *bratina* is embellished with engraved nielloed ornaments. Around the lip, interspersed among the foliate designs, are nielloed inscriptions indicating that the *bratina* was made by order of Tsar Mikhail Feodorovich to be placed on the bier of Tsarevich Ioann Ioannovich. The incense burner is of open-work design. Its three legs are in the form of miniature whales; there is also a figure of a whale on the lid. (From Solntsev, pt. v, plate 7.)

Plate 97. The goblet of Tsar Mikhail Feodorovich. The inventory lists this goblet under the name of *stopa.* Octagonal in shape, the goblet is made of gold and embellished with enamel and precious stones: amethysts, sapphires, rubies, and diamonds. The owner's name is inscribed in gold on black enamel. It weighs slightly more than one pound, twelve ounces. (From Solntsev, pt. v, plate 21.)

Plate 98. The silver *bratina* of Peter Tretiakov in the Oruzheinaia Palata. The *bratina* of *Dumnyi Diak* (Councilor) Peter Tretiakov was presented to Tsar Mikhail Feodorovich in 1618 by the councilor's wife. The surface of the bowl and cover is embossed with foliage and flower designs. On the four plaques attached to the body of the *bratina* are heraldic figures of a lion, unicorn, dolphins, young men, and birds. Inside the *bratina,* on an open-work silver-gilt plaque, is a figure of a man. Around the plaque's edge runs a Slavonic inscription: "Man, who looketh at me, dost thou perchance desire to swallow me? Look into the bottom of this *bratina* and thou shalt discover its secret." Around the lip runs a rather extensive inscription, which, freely translated, says: "Know thou, man, as arms are necessary to a warrior in battle and rain in time of drought, as drink to the thirsty, and as a true friend in time of misfortune, so moderation, understanding and good fellowship are beneficial to all those who would partake of the sweetness of this cup. . . . The *bratina* of Peter Alekseevich Tretiakov." The *bratina* weighs about one pound, twelve ounces, and is eleven and one-half inches high. (From Solntsev, pt. v, plate 9.)

Plate 99. Silver-gilt tankard embellished with enamel. The ornament is of open work. On the sides of the tankard, on silver medallions, are scenes in varicolored enamels depicting the Annunciation, the Nativity, and the Adoration. On the lid is a scene depicting the Baptism of Our Lord. The tankard weighs two pounds, three ounces. According to the inventory of the Oruzheinaia Palata, there are no data as to when and where it was made, nor is there any indication as to the donor or recipient. (From Solntsev, pt. v, plate 30.)

Plate 100. Silver-gilt tankard embellished with enamel and precious stones. Oxhorn mounted in gold and studded with precious stones. Both in the Oruzheinaia Palata. The tankard, for about half its height, is octagonal. The foliate designs in green and blue enamels (*finift'*) are outlined in filigree work (*skan'*). According to the description in the inventory of the Oruzheinaia Palata, the gems set on green strips under the upper band are small rubies, sapphires, and emeralds. On each of the eight facets below are larger rubies, sapphires, and emeralds in gold settings. The handle is in the form of a coiled snake. On the top of the lid is a cast figure of a monkey. The tankard weighs about one pound, three ounces. In ancient Russia, oxhorns, instead of goblets and *bratiny,* were often used for drinking and toasting. The Russian chronicles, *byliny*, and fairy tales mention the gifts and use of these horns on a number of occasions. The illustrated horn is mounted in gold and embellished with many amethysts, rubies, and turquoise. (From Solntsev, pt. v, plate 38.)

Plate 101. Flask (*Suleiia Turskaia*) in the Oruzheinaia Palata. According to the Oruzheinaia Palata inventories of 1663 and 1676, this flask, known in ancient Russia as a *suleiia,* is of drawn gold wire and embellished with jasper, amethysts, and emeralds. The spout is of solid gold, and the stopper is of crystal. It was presented in 1653 to Tsar Aleksei Mikhailovich by Tsarevich Seid Burkhan Araslanovich of the Kasimov Tartar khanate. (From Solntsev, pt. v, plate 38.)

Plate 102. Sixteenth-century porcelain flagon of Tsarevich Ivan Ivanovich. The flagon (*suleiia*) is of Chinese porcelain; its top section is embellished with silver gilt and fastened to the body with a finely wrought chain. Around the neck runs an inscription in Slavonic: "Suleiia of Tsarevich, Prince Ivan Ivanovich." (From Solntsev, pt. v, plate 36.)

Plate 103. The Red Square. (From Rzianin, plate 3.)

Plate 104. The Historical Museum. Designed by V. O. Sherwood. (From *Moskva.*)

Plate 105. The Church of St. John the Precursor at Diakovo near Moscow, 1529. (From Martynov.)

Plate 106. Cathedral of the Intercession (Pokrovskii Sobor), later known as the Church of St. Basil the Blessed. In the foreground is the Proclamation Platform (Lobnoe Mesto). Designed by Barma and Posnik, 1555–1560. (From Olearius.)

Plate 107. The Church of St. Basil the Blessed. (From *Moskva; Sobory, Monastyri i Tserkvi.*)

Plate 108. Stairway in the Church of St. Basil the Blessed. (From Rzianin, plate 38.)

Plate 109. Circular drum and cupola supported on kokoshniki, Church of St. Basil the Blessed. (From Viollet le Duc, plate xi.)

Plate 110. Octagonal tower tent roof and cupola supported on kokoshniki, Church of St. Basil the Blessed. (From Viollet le Duc, plate xii.)

Plate 111. Proposed park across the Moskva River from the Kremlin. Designed by Bunin and Kruglova. (From *Gradostroitelstvo.*)

Figure 1. Plan of the Kremlin walls and towers, 1911. Clockwise from the top of the plan, the towers are in order: Corner Arsenal (top), Nicholas, Senate, Saviour's, Tsar, Alarm, Konstantin, Beklemishev, Peter, Second Nameless, First Nameless, Secret, Annunciation, Water-Pumping, Forest, Armory, Commandant, Kutaf'ia, Trinity, Middle Arsenal. (From Bartenev, vol. i, plate 80.)

Figure 2. Plans and section of the Cathedral of the Assumption (Uspenskii Sobor). (From Rzianin, p. 47.)

Figure 3. Plan of the Cathedral of the Archangel Michael. (From Rzianin, fig. 28.)

Figure 4. Plan and section of the Cathedral of the Annunciation. (From Rzianin, fig. 27.)

Figure 5. Bazhenov's proposed plan for the Grand Kremlin Palace, 1768–1773. (From Rzianin, p. 116.)

Figure 6. Plan of the Senate Building. (From Rzianin, p. 120.)

Figure 7. Plan of the lower floor of the Grand Kremlin Palace. (From Vel'tman.)

Figure 8. Plan of the upper floor of the Grand Kremlin Palace. (From Vel'tman.)

A. Red Stairway
B. Holy Vestibule
C. Palace of Facets
D. Hall of St. Vladimir
E. Antechamber
F. Grand Stairway
G. Hall of St. George
J. Hall of St. Alexander Nevskii
K. Hall of St. Andrew
N. Guard Room
O. Hall of St. Catherine

P. State Drawing Room
Q. State Bedroom
U. Winter Garden
A′. Golden Tsaritsa Chamber
B′. Church of St. Catherine the Martyr
C′. Church of Investiture
D′. Old Terem Chambers
E′. Church of the Saviour in the Forest

Figure 9. Plan of the Church of St. John the Precursor. (From Rzianin, fig. 30.)

Figure 10. Plan and section of the Church of St. Basil the Blessed. (From Rzianin, p. 54)

APPENDIX

IMPORTANT EVENTS IN THE HISTORY OF THE KREMLIN

1147
Moscow first mentioned.

1156
Prince Iurii Dolgorukii builds a stockade around the settlement.

1223
Battle of the Kalka. The Tartars defeat the Russian princes and establish their rule over Russia.

1237–1240
Conquest of Russia by Batu; destruction of Kiev, burning of Moscow, and beginning of the Tartar domination of Russia.

1240–1242
Victories of the Novgorodians under Alexander Nevskii over the Swedish and German knights.

circa 1272
Daniil, son of Alexander Nevskii, receives the small principality of Moscow as his appanage (*udel*), thus becoming the progenitor of the Moscow princely dynasty.

1299
Metropolitan Maksim transfers the see from Kiev to Vladimir.

1303–1325
Iurii Danilovich, second prince of Moscow.

1305–1326
Peter, Metropolitan of Russia (the first to reside in Moscow, 1309).

1326
The metropolitan see officially transferred from Vladimir to Moscow; cornerstone laid for the first masonry structure of the Cathedral of the Assumption.

1325–1341
Ivan Kalita, great prince of Vladimir (1325–1328), third prince of Moscow (1328–1341).

1330
Construction of the Church of the Saviour in the Forest.

1354–1378
St. Aleksei, Metropolitan of Russia.

1362–1389
Dmitrii Donskoi (of the Don), great prince of Vladimir and Moscow.

1365
The great conflagration that "made ashes out of Moscow."

1367
Construction of the first masonry walls and towers around the Kremlin, at the instigation of the Metropolitan Aleksei.

1380
Battle of Kulikovo. Victory by Dmitrii, resulting in growing unity among the several Russian principalities. Awakening of the creative powers of the Russian nation and progress of art.

1382
Destruction of Moscow by the Tartar Khan Tokhtamysh.

1390–1430
Period of artistic activity of the icon painter Rublev.

1439
Council of Florence.

1446
Church of Russia declared autocephalous.

1452
Fall of Constantinople.

1462–1505
Ivan III.

1471
Novgorod begins its last decisive struggle with Moscow. Defeat of the Novgorodian army.

1472
Ivan III marries the Byzantine Princess Zoë Paleologue, adopts the Byzantine coat-of-arms — the double-headed eagle.

1474
First mission under Simeon Tolbuzin dispatched by Ivan III to Venice with instructions to hire architects, engineers, and craftsmen.

1475–1478
Construction of the Cathedral of the Assumption by Fieravanti.

1478–1510
Novgorod, Tver', Pskov, and Riazan' principalities annexed to Moscow; Tartar suzerainty discarded; successful wars of "liberation" with Lithuania and Livonia. Unification of Russian lands and centralization of the Russian state with Moscow as its capital.

1484–1493
Missions sent abroad for the purpose of obtaining foreign artistic and technical help.

1485
Construction of the Cathedral of the Annunciation by Pskov builders.

1485–1516
Reconstruction of the masonry walls and watchtowers of the Moscow Kremlin.

1487–1491
Construction of the Palace of Facets.

1502
Dissolution of the Golden Horde; end of the Tartar domination.

1505–1509
Construction of the Cathedral of the Archangel Michael by Alevisio Novyi.

1505–1533
Vasilii III.

1508
Construction of the first section of the Terem Palace.

1508–1510
Construction of a moat along the east wall of the Kremlin.

1511
Establishment of the office of armorer.

1526–1533
Herberstein, envoy of Charles V, in Moscow.

1529–1560
Construction of the churches of Diakovo, Ostrovo, and Kolomenskoe, and the Cathedral of St. Basil the Blessed, ushering in a new era in Russian architecture.

1530
Birth of Ivan IV (the terrible).

1533–1584
Reign of Ivan IV.

1534–1538
Construction of walls around Kitai-Gorod, during the regency of Grand Princess Elena Glinskaia, mother of Ivan IV.

1546
Ivan IV proclaims his majority.

1547
The great Moscow fire; Ivan IV assumes the title of tsar; Novgorod and Pskov icon painters ordered to Moscow.

1551
The Hundred-Chapters Ecclesiastical Council convenes.

1552
Conquest of Kazan'.

1553
First arrival of a British merchant ship under the command of Captain Chancellor at Arkhangelsk. Establishment of the Muscovy Company.

1556
Conquest of Astrakhan', the last Tartar stronghold on the lower Volga.

1560–1570
The Illuminated Nikonian Compilation, the Imperial Book (*Tsarstvennaia Kniga*). The Book of Degrees of the Imperial Genealogy propounding the concept of Moscow as the Third Rome, and emphasizing the legend of the transfer of imperial insignia and dignity from Byzantium to Kiev and thence to Moscow.

1563
Establishment of a printing press in Moscow.

1565
Beginning of the Reign of Terror. Establishment of the *oprichnina*.

1565
Construction, in the center of the Kremlin, of a two-story masonry building for the foreign office.

1566
The first Zemskii Sobor (Consultative Land Assembly) convenes in Moscow.

1570
Destruction of Great Novgorod and Tver'. Intensification of the Terror.

1571
Sacking of Moscow by the Crimean Tartars.

1576
Cessation of mass terror.

1582
Tsar Ivan IV kills his eldest son Ivan in a fit of rage.

1584
The Cossack leader Iermak overthrows khanate of Siberia.

1584–1598
Tsar Feodor, the last of the Rurik Dynasty; Boris Godunov, "Lord-Protector."

1588
The visit of the Constantinople Patriarch Jeremiah.

1589
See of Moscow raised to patriarchal rank.

1598
Boris Godunov elected tsar by the Zemskii Sobor.

1601–1603
Famine in Moscow; erection of the Belfry of Ivan Velikii (Ivan the Great).

1604–1613
Time of Troubles.

1605
Death of Tsar Boris and accession of the Pretender False Dmitrii.

1606
The Pretender is murdered.

1606–1610
Reign of Vasilii Ivanovich Shuiskii.

1610–1612
Polish occupation of Moscow.

1610–1613
Interregnum.

1613
Mikhail Feodorovich Romanov elected tsar by the Zemskii Sobor.

1620–1642
Period of artistic activity of the icon painter Prokofii Chirin.

1624
Initiation of building decorative superstructures over the Kremlin towers.

1634–1638
First and second visit of Olearius of Holstein to Moscow.

1645–1676
Tsar Aleksei Mikhailovich.

1645–1686
Period of artistic activity of the icon painter Semion Ushakov.

1651–1679
Construction of the Amusement Palace (Poteshnyi Dvorets).

1654
Reforms of the church service books and rites by Nikon, leading to the great schism.

1654–1680
Oruzheinaia Palata under management of Khitrovo.

1662
"Copper" revolt in Moscow.

1666
Patriarch Nikon deposed.

1676–1682
Tsar Feodor Alekseevich.

1682
Founding of the Slavonic-Greek-Latin Ecclesiastical Academy.

1682
Mutiny of the *strel'tsy;* murder of Matveev.

1682
Accession of Peter the Great.

1682–1689
Ivan V and Peter nominal tsars. Regency of Tsarevna Sophia.

1689
Attempted *coup d'etat* by Sophia against Peter. Sophia immured in convent.

1698
The last mutiny of the *strel'tsy;* their wholesale executions on the Red Square and abolition of their formations.

1705
Construction of the first floor of the Arsenal Building in the Kremlin.

1713
Transfer of the capital from Moscow to St. Petersburg.

1721
Abolition of the patriarchate and institution of the Holy Synod.

1721
Peter I adopts title of emperor.

1725
Death of Peter I.

1736
Addition of second floor to the Arsenal.

1741–1761
Empress Elizabeth.

1762–1796
Catherine II.

1767–1774
Projected reconstruction of the Kremlin by Catherine II.

1776–1789
Construction of the Senate Building.

1801–1825
Alexander I.

1812
Napoleon in the Kremlin; walls and several towers damaged by fire and explosions.

1814
Reconstruction of the Red Square.

1825–1855
Nikolai I.

1833–1838
Construction of the Cathedral of the Redeemer.

1839–1848
Construction of the Grand Kremlin Palace.

1874–1883
Construction of the Historical Museum, Red Square.

1889–1893
Construction of the Upper Commercial Arcades, Red Square.

1917
Bolshevik revolution; the Kremlin occupied by Red forces.

1918
Moscow again becomes capital of Russia.

1925–1930
Construction of the Lenin Mausoleum.

THE MOSCOW PRINCES AND TSARS

Daniil Aleksandrovich (son of Alexander Nevskii)	1272–1303
Iurii Danilovich	1303–1325
Ivan Danilovich Kalita (Grand Prince of Vladimir)	1328–1341
Semion (the Proud)	1341–1353
Ivan II	1353–1359
Dmitrii Donskoi	1362–1389
Vasilii I	1389–1425
Vasilii II (the Dark)	1425–1462
Ivan III	1462–1505
Vasilii III	1505–1533
Ivan IV (the Terrible)	1533–1584
Feodor	1584–1598
Boris Godunov	1598–1605
Dmitrii the False	1605–1606
Vasilii Ivanovich Shuiskii	1606–1610
Interregnum	1610–1613
THE HOUSE OF ROMANOV	
Mikhail Feodorovich	1613–1645
Aleksei Mikhailovich	1645–1676
Feodor Alekseevich	1676–1682
Ivan V Alekseevich (co-ruler with Peter I)	1682–1696
Sophia (regent)	1682–1689
Peter I	1682–1725

THE METROPOLITANS OF MOSCOW AND ALL RUSSIA

St. Peter	d. 1326
St. Feognost	1328–1353
St. Aleksii (builder of the first masonry walls of the Kremlin)	1354–1378
St. Kiprian	1380–1385
Pimen	1385–1390
St. Kiprian (for the second time)	1390–1407
St. Photii	1408–1431
Isidor (deposed because of his agreement, at the Council of Florence, to a union with Rome)	1437–1441
St. Iona (first metropolitan installed independently of the Constantinople patriarch)	1449–1461
Feodosii	1461–1464
Philipp I	1465–1473
Gerontii	1473–1489
Zosima (banished to the Trinity Monastery)	1491–1494
Simon	1496–1511
Varlaam	1511–1522
Daniil	1522–1539
Ioasaph	1539–1543
Makarii (compiler of the *Cheti-Minyei)*	1543–1564
Afanasii	1545–1566
St. Philipp II	1566–1569
Kirill	1570–1577
Antonii	1577–1580
Dionisii	1581–1586

THE PATRIARCHS OF ALL RUSSIA

Iov (deposed by the False Dmitrii)	1589–1605
St. Iermogen	1606–1612
Philaret (Feodor Nikitich Romanov, Father of Tsar Mikhail)	1619–1633
Ioasaph I	1634–1642
Iosif	1642–1652
Nikon	1652–1658
Ioasaph II	1667–1672
Pitirim	1672–1673
Ioakim	1674–1690
Adrian	1690–1700

KREMLIN TOWERS

Tower	Height (feet)	Floors	Perimeter of base (feet)	Height of sub-structure (feet)	Height of super-structure (feet)
Saviour's *(Spasskaia)*	238	10	203	98	140
Tsar *(Tsarskaia)*	56	2	59	11	45
Alarm *(Nabatnaia)*	119	5	112	56	63
Konstantin *(Konstantinovskaia)*	119	5	189	45	73
Beklemishev *(Beklemishevskaia)*	168	6	94	80	88
Peter *(Petrovskaia)*	88	4	135	44	44
2nd Nameless *(Vtoraia Bezymiannaia)*	100	4	119	42	58
1st Nameless *(Pervaia Bezymiannaia)*	112	4	168	42	70
Secret *(Tainitskaia)*	130	2	238	32	98
Annunciation *(Blagoveshchenskaia)*	98	4	133	39	59
Water-Pumping *(Vodovzvodnaia)*	199	5	126	94	105
Forest *(Borovitskaia)*	196	10	175	70	126
Armory *(Oruzheinaia)*	101	4	98	49	52
Commandant *(Komendantskaia)*	126	5	136	70	56
Trinity *(Troitskaia)*	227	9	245	101	126
Middle Arsenal *(Sredniaia-Arsenal'naia)*	129	5	91	70	59
Corner Arsenal *(Uglovaia-Arsenal'naia)*	203	5	168	105	98
Nicholas *(Nikol'skaia)*	217	5	203	63	154
Senate *(Senatskaia)*	119	4	112	59	59
Kutaf'ia *(Kutaf'ia)*	63				

NOTES

I. INTRODUCTION

[1]*Strel'tsy* (fusiliers, musketeers) were militia units who lived with their families in special quarters in Moscow and engaged in handicrafts and petty trade. Founded by Ivan the Terrible, these units constituted the most efficient part of the army until the importing of foreign military specialists was begun under Tsar Mikhail Romanov. The most serious revolts of the *strel'tsy* occurred in 1682 and 1698, and led to their abolition by Peter I in 1699.

[2]*Prikaz* (command, order) was a central administrative-juridical office of the Muscovite state that governed certain regions or supervised other special activities. The various offices were established in the last decades of the fifteenth century; they were replaced by the collegia of Peter the Great.

II. SITE, PLAN, AND CONSTRUCTION FEATURES

[1]M. P. Fabritsius, *Kreml' v Moskve,* p. 15. See also V. L. Snegirev. *Moskovskoe Zodchestvo,* p. 71.

III. HISTORICAL BACKGROUND

[1]*Bylina* (that which has occurred) was a narrative poem, popular from the tenth to the nineteenth century, about historical events and outstanding personalities. The *byliny* were anonymous, having been handed down by oral tradition from one narrator *(skazitel')* to another. Several representative collections exist in English translation, notably N. Kershaw Chadwick's *Russian Heroic Poetry.*

[2]N. Nikol'skii, *Po Moskve (Up and Down Moscow),* p. 9.

[3]Ivan Zabelin, *Istoriia goroda Moskvy (History of the City of Moscow),* pt. i,

pp. 36–38; also Gudzy, *History of Early Russian Literature,* pp. 470–473.

[4]*Udel*—appanage. According to Russian custom, an inheritance was equally divided among the surviving sons. Hence, each son of a prince received a *udel,* a portion of his father's territory with full sovereign rights. This practice was especially widespread from the twelfth to the fifteenth century; consequently this has been called the "appanage period" *(Udel'naia Rus),* the Russia of small domains, in contrast to the Russia of the grand principalities *(Velikokniazheskaia Rus).*

[5]The Rusisan word *gorod* (and its older form, *grad*) meant "fencing"—hence, the erection of fortifications around an estate.

[6]The surname Kalita (moneybag) was given to Ivan because of the bag he always wore attached to his belt, and also because of his frugality and his habit of haggling over small pieces of land.

[7]The derivation of the word *Kreml'* has long been the subject of debate. The historian Karamzin maintains that the word is derived from *kremen',* which means "flint"—hence a flintlike rock fortress that is difficult to penetrate. The lexicographers Stroev, Dahl', and Grot say that *Kreml'* is derived from the old Russian word *krom* (fortress). Modern authorities trace the derivation to the north Russian *krem* (large structural timber). See V. L. Snegirev. *Moskovskoe Zodchestvo,* p. 29.

[8]*Detinets*—archaic Russian word meaning "inner fortress."

[9]Horde *(orda)* was the camp of a Tartar tribe; the word is used figuratively as the name of the Mongol government. The capital of the Great Horde was Karakorum; that of the subsidiary Golden Horde *(Zolotaia Orda)* was Sarai on the Volga.

[10]The Russian for Consolidator of Russia is *Sobiratel' Zemli Russkoi. Sobiratel'* means literally "collector," but it has been variously translated as "coagulator," "organizer," "gatherer," "consolidator of the land of Russia."

[11]Peter—primate of Russia, first metropolitan, and tutelary saint of Moscow.

[12]Ioann (Ivan) Lestvichnik (John Climacus of Sinai) died in A.D. 563. He was known for his work *The Ladder* (or *Climax*). Boris Godunov erected the Ivan Velikii Belfry on the site of the Lestvichnik church.

[13]The remnants of these walls were discovered during the excavations made for the construction of the Grand Kremlin Palace (1838–1848).

[14]The battle of Kulikovo (the field of woodcocks), also known as the "Mamai Massacre" *(Mamaevo poboishche),* is regarded by Russian historians as having broken the power of the Tartar domination.

[15]Ivan Zabelin, *Istoriia goroda Moskvy,* p. 89.

[16]*Ibid.*

[17]Theophanos, a Greek artist, the Russian counterpart of El Greco, was a resident of Moscow for many years about 1400, and decorated many of the Moscow churches with frescoes. Some of the work on the iconostasis in the Cathedral of the Annunciation is also attributed to him. He is considered by some authorities to have been the first painter of secular subjects in Russia.

[18]Andrei Rublev *(ca.* 1360–1430) was the most famous of Russian icon painters and creator of religious types with a new expression in them, informing religious art with a new spiritual significance. He was a monk of the Spaso-Andronikov (Androniev) Monastery (on the Iauza River, West Moscow); earlier he had been a lay brother in the Troitsko-Sergievskaia Lavra (Monastery of the Trinity) at Zagorsk, near Moscow, where he was a student of icon painting. He (together with Theophanos the Greek), painted many of the icons in the Cathedral of the Annunciation at Moscow and (together with Daniil Chernyi, his "brother in fasting") the icons in the Cathedral of the Assumption at Vladimir.

[19]Kitai Gorod, the busiest, most crowded, and richest section of the city, derived its name from the woven baskets (*kit* or *kita*) that, filled with earth, were used like fascines to reinforce the wall built by the Friazin Petrok Malyi. Kitai Gorod has been at times erroneously translated as "Chinatown," *kitai* being the modern Russian word for "China."

[20]The Council of Florence was a council of the Orthodox and Catholic clergy at Florence in 1439 that proclaimed a union of the Eastern and Western churches. The union left the Orthodox Church in possession of its ritual but obliged them to recognize the Catholic doctrines and the primacy of the pope.

[21]*Stepennaia Kniga (Book of Degrees of the Imperial Genealogy)* extolls and glorifies to the utmost the historic past and the present of Muscovite Rus, primarily by praising and glorifying the rulers as having acted in full accord with the Church. It lists the ecclesiastical and civil events of Russian history from a purely religious point of view, and is arranged by the reigns of the grand princes. The beginning of this book is attributed to Metropolitan St. Kiprian, who is said to have brought it to the thirteenth degree (his own times). The Metropolitan Makarii continued the work to the seventeenth degree (from Grand Prince Vladimir to Ivan IV), and later to the eighteenth degree (to the reign of Aleksei Mikhailovich).

IV. THE ITALIAN KREMLIN

[1]The boyars were members of the highest social and political class until Peter the Great established the Table of Ranks in 1722.

[2]The Russian chroniclers seem to be of the opinion that Fieravanti was called Aristotle because of his many accomplishments in art and science (see *Russ. Biog. Slovar*, vol. 21, p. 141). The *Encyclopedia Italiana* (vol. xv, pp. 237–238) gives his name as Aristotele Fieravanti della Alberti (1415–1486).

[3]At the end of the fifteenth century, a ruble was worth 100 late nineteenth-century rubles (Kliuchevskii, as cited in *Istorii Moskvy*, p. 94).

[4]*Friazin* (Frank) was a generic name by which all Latins of the Mediterranean basin were designated. Their works were called *Friazheskiia dela* (Frankish works).

[5]The size of these still extant bricks is 31 x 14 x 18 centimeters.

[6]The tower was called Tainitskaia (secret tower) because it contained a secret spring, a source of water in case of prolonged sieges.

[7]The Beklemishevskaia derives its name from the neighboring estate of the boyar Ivan Beklemishev, who was noted for his sharp tongue. His head was cut off by order of Grand Prince Vasilii III (1505–1533) for "being overly smart." The estate and tower were turned into a prison. Near the tower, behind the wall, were the dungeons and torture chambers where "confessions" were obtained. The bodies of those tortured to death were left lying along the moat on the east side of the Kremlin.

[8]The Vodovzvodnaia (water-pumping) was formerly known as Sviblova. In 1633 the English builder Christopher Halloway (see note 11) built a stone reservoir and a water distribution system for the well within the tower. The tower was also equipped with a clock and an alarm bell.

[9]*Pozhar* (fire, conflagration) became the name for an empty space that was bare of all buildings as a result of fire.

[10]V. L. Snegirev, *Moskovskoe Zodchestvo (Moscow Architecture)*, p. 67.

[11]Christopher Halloway arrived in Russia in 1621 and entered the service of the tsar at a salary of 60 rubles a year, with a daily allowance for food (6 *altyns* and 4 *den'gi*) and a weekly allowance of one wagonload of wood.

[12]The Kolymazhnaia Tower, one of the best examples of Russian seventeenth-century national masonry architecture, was taken down in 1801 by

order of the Kremlin Superintendent General Valuev, who wanted to "clean up and improve the Kremlin."

[13] Pickard's engraving, *ca.* 1715; Quarenghi's watercolor, 1786; Tishbein's, Alekseev's, Hilferding's, Egotov's, and other drawings and paintings.

V. TOWERS AND GATES

[1] At present only four towers function as entrance gates; the Tainitskaia has been eliminated.

[2] *Bashnia* is a word of Tartar origin, *bash* meaning "head" or "top" and, by extension, "tower."

[3] V. I. Bazhenov (1737–1799), one of Catherine II's favorite architects, is noted for his project for the construction of a palace in the Kremlin (see chapter vii). Matvei Feodorovich Kazakov (1738–1813) was the architect of many outstanding buildings, including the Senate Building in the Kremlin and the Golitsyn Hospital and the Petrovskii Palace in Moscow. He is often considered the cofounder, with Bazhenov, of the Moscow classic school of architecture.

[4] During the eighteenth century the chimes played the German folk song *Ach, du lieber Augustin;* later, the Russian hymn *Kol' Slaven* and the *March of the Preobrazhenskii Regiment;* after the revolution, the *Internationale;* recently, the *Soviet Hymn.*

[5] Lobnoe Mesto was a circular stone tribune on the Red Square, near St. Basil's, from which the tsars proclaimed their edicts. Death sentences were also announced from it; executions were carried out near the Kremlin wall.

[6] St. Nicholas the Miracle Worker (*Nikolai Chudotvorets)* is often considered the guardian saint of Russia; his image has always received the greatest reverence from the people. According to legend, the image, its protective glass, and the lantern were undamaged by the repeated explosions ordered by Napoleon in 1812, which destroyed most of the tower.

[7] Karl Ivanovich Rossi (1775–1849) was the son of an Italian ballerina and an unknown father. He was brought to Russia at the age of ten, and educated in Russia and Italy. Rossi was the last of the great Russian classic architects; his professional activities extended beyond the reign of Alexander I, and he designed many of the vast ensembles of St. Petersburg.

[8] A prison is thought to have been under the gateway in the sixteenth century. Pavement repairs in 1895–1896 brought to light a two-story underground vaulted structure the basement of which contained a number of dungeons.

[9] Kutaf'ia (awkward) was so nicknamed because of its huge, sprawling bulk.

[10] On non-Russian seventeenth-century maps these gates are identified as Porta Magnae Sylvae.

[11] Sumbeka Tower was named after a Tartar queen.

[12] *Khoromy* was the name for an ancient Russian nobleman's mansion or palace.

[13] The stars, measuring 10 feet from point to point, have taken the place of the old imperial arms. They were installed in commemoration of the twentieth anniversary of the Bolshevik October Revolution.

[14] *Shatior* is a tentlike roof, usually octagonal, somewhat akin to a pyramid. This architectural feature had been in great favor with the Russian medieval builders; having had its beginning in wood architecture, it was adopted and brilliantly translated into stone by the Russian architects of the sixteenth century.

VI. CATHEDRALS, CHURCHES, AND MONASTERIES

[1] *Sobor,* commonly translated as "cathedral" (A. V.), literally means "bringing together." Hence the word can mean: a synod or great council of Church or State; a service conducted by several priests; a collegiate church, and so the

principal churches of towns and monasteries but not a bishop's seat—e.g., the five sobors in the Kremlin at Moscow, the small Spas na Boru (Our Saviour in the Forest), the great Uspenskii Sobor (Assumption or Dormition), Blagoveshchenskii (Annunciation), Arkhangel'skii (Archangel Michael), and Voznesenskii (Ascension). (See S. A. Penrhyn, *Lectures on the History of the Eastern Church.*)

[2] Icon (from the Greek *eikon,* meaning "picture" or "image") was originally used for both murals and easel paintings. The Russian religious picture is called *ikona* or *obraz,* signifying primarily a likeness (*podobie*) but not a realistic portrait; it is usually painted on lime or cypress wood with tempera colors.

[3] The archives of the city of Milan contain a letter, written by Fieravanti on February 22, 1476, to the Duke of Milan, describing the former's travels in northern Russia. (See Ettore lo Gatto, *Gli artisti italiani in Russia,* vol. i, p. 20.)

[4] *Kiot, kioty* (niche, frame, or cupboard in which icons are housed) usually has a pediment at the top and is glazed in front. It may either be a shrine by itself or it may form part of a triptych, often with appropriate religious scenes painted upon the doors.

[5] The iconstasis is the screen or partition separating the sanctuary from the nave in Orthodox churches. It serves as a stand and frame for many icons, which are arranged in a traditionally prescribed manner. Before the fifteenth century the iconostasis was usually a simple, low railing, but it became in time an important and elaborate architectural element that was rich in ornament and contained several rows of icons. There are usually three doors, with the Royal Doors (Tsarskiia Vrata), always decorated with the icons of the Annunciation and the four Evangelists, in the center. In the center of the iconostasis, above the Royal Doors, a row of panels contains icons. The central panel represents Christ the Pantocrator or Christ the Almighty *(Vsederzhitel');* on His right is the Mother of God, and on His left is St. John the Baptist—both in the attitude of intercession. On the adjoining panels at the right and left are the Archangel Michael with St. Peter, and the Archangel Gabriel with St. Paul, respectively, in the same attitude. This entire ensemble is called *de'esis* (prayer, intercession). Above, a row of icons represents the twelve great festivals of the Church. Still higher are representations of the Prophets paying homage to the Mother of God. At the very top are the patriarchs of the Church with the Lord God of Sabaoth in the center.

[6] I. M. Snegirev, *Uspenskii Sobor v Moskve.*

[7] *Acathyst, akafist* is a special form of prayer in the Orthodox Church to glorify Christ, the Virgin Mary, or any of the saints.

[8] One of Napoleon's cavalry troops was stabled in the cathedral during the French occupation of Moscow. The French removed five tons of silver and five hundred pounds of gold from this cathedral alone. Fortunately, the Cossacks recovered most of this booty, and in gratitude presented to the cathedral a silver chandelier with forty-six branches that weighed nine hundred pounds.

[9] Vladimir Monomakh, Grand Prince of Kiev (1113–1125), was the last outstanding ruler of Kiev. He was the father of Iurii Dolgorukii, and has been idealized in Russian chronicles as a prince of great wisdom and many virtues.

[10] Time of Troubles (*Smutnoe vremia*), sometimes designated as the Epoch of Disorder, is the name given to the tragic events that took place in Russia beginning with the murder in 1591 of Tsarevich Dmitrii, son of Ivan IV. The famine of 1601–1603 was followed by the struggle between the supporters of the contender to the throne, the False Dmitrii, and the followers of Boris Godunov. The civil war was further complicated by Polish and Swedish intervention, and ended by the establishment of the Romanov Dynasty in 1613.

[11] Kokoshnik is a false zakomara (see

note 12) having no vaulting. Originally a structural feature—a series of corbelled round, or pointed arches arranged in receding tiers for the purpose of supporting the elements of the superstructure—it later developed into a purely decorative feature used as ornament for all kinds of articles.

[12]Zakomara is the parapet over the extrados of the vaulting, conforming in outline to the type and number of vaults, and thus dividing the parapet into several arched sections.

[13]Philaret (Filaret) was Patriarch of Moscow from 1619 to 1633. He was the oldest son of Nikita Romanov (progenitor of the Romanov Dynasty), and was the protegé, later rival, of Boris Godunov, who forced him to take the tonsure. Philaret was the father of Mikhail, the first tsar of the Romanov Dynasty.

[14]Boris Godunov (1598–1605), of Tartar origin, was the brother-in-law of Tsar Feodor and regent during his reign (1584–1598). He was accused of having caused the murder of Dmitrii, Ivan IV's younger son, at Uglich.

[15]The inscription, translated literatim, reads: "By the grace of the Holy Trinity and by the order of the Tsar and Grand Prince, Boris Feodorovich, Autocrat of all Russia, and his orthodox son, Feodor Borisovich, Tsarevich of all Russia, this temple [*khram*] was finished and gilded in the second year of their reign."

[16]The four largest bells of the Ivan Velikii Belfry are: the Uspenskii or Holiday, weighing 4,000 *pud;* the Reut or Revun (one that makes a roaring noise), weighing 2,000 *pud;* the Sunday; and the Weekday. (The Russian *pud* is equivalent to 36 pounds avoirdupois.)

[17]According to Coxe, the bell's height is 21′ 4½″, its largest diameter 22′ 4¾″, its greatest thickness 23 inches. (*Travels,* Vol. ii, p. 7.) Fabritsius gives its height as 19 feet.

[18]Maxim the Greek, theologian and philologist (1480–1556) born in Albania, was educated in Italy, where he was closely associated with prominent humanists of the Renaissance. At the invitation of Grand Prince Vasilii he came to Moscow in 1518 as translator and editor. He translated a number of ecclesiastical books and undertook the work of correcting the Russian theological books. As a result of becoming involved in the ecclesiastical and political disputes that were raging at this time, Maxim was condemned to imprisonment in the Volokolam Monastery (1525–1551).

[19]Grigorii (Grishka) Otrepiev was a monk attached to the Romanov household who fled to Poland. He is frequently identified with the first False Dmitrii.

[20]Hermogen (St. Iermogen) was Patriarch of Moscow (1606–1612) and author of proclamations appealing for an uprising against the Poles.

VII. PALACES

[1]*Terem,* an upper-floor apartment traditionally reserved for the women of the family, is usually at the top story of the *khoromy.* It is provided with an arcaded open balcony, sometimes with a small observation tower. The word *teremok* (little *terem*) came to signify a dwelling unit built in the style of the ancient *terem.*

[2]*Palata* (mansion) is usually a storied masonry structure containing many chambers and halls; by extension, a bureau in charge of production.

[3]"In foreign historical literature the meaning of this appellation has been utterly distorted by its translation as 'Ivan der Schreckliche,' 'Iwan der Grausame,' 'Jean le Terrible,' or 'Ivan the Terrible,' thus emphasizing the accusation that Ivan IV was inhuman. In the sixteenth century, however, the term 'Grozny' had a majestic and patriotic ring. This appellation had been previously applied to Ivan III." R. Wipper (translated by J. Fineberg), *Ivan Grozny,* p. 28.

[4]The Josephite doctrine, promulgated by Joseph Volotsky (Ivan Sanin, 1440–1515), abbot of the Volokolamsk Monastery, advocated the sanctification of autocracy and the preservation of all the privileges and landed possessions of the

Church. The abbot taught that "the Tsar was similar to humans only by nature, but by the authority of his rank similar to God; he derived his authority directly from God, and his judgment could not be overruled by that of any prelate."

[5]It is said that Ivan IV, who inherited a fine library from his grandfather, Ivan III, augmented this collection by many rare Greek, Hebrew, and Latin volumes that he procured through his agents in the capitals of Western Europe. There is some evidence that he commissioned the German scholar Vesterman (Vetterman) to translate some of the works into Russian. This collection and its whereabouts have been the subject for speculation by many bibliographers. In 1891, searches were conducted throughout the subterranean passages of the Kremlin, but no trace was found. (See Bartenev, *Kremlin,* vol. ii.)

[6]The khanate of Kazan' was a Tartar principality of the middle Volga founded in the fifteenth century when the Golden Horde was dissolving; it was conquered by Ivan the Terrible (1552), as was also the khanate of Astrakhan' (1556).

[7]Richard Chancellor was commander of one of three vessels under Sir Hugh Willoughby sent by Edward VI of England to find a northeastern passage (1553). Willoughby was frozen to death in the Arctic, but Chancellor made his way to Moscow, thus discovering the trade route around Norway. In 1555 Chancellor was sent to Russia again, this time as envoy of Mary and Philip; he was drowned off the coast of Scotland on the return voyage (1556).

[8]The first printing press was established in Moscow under the direction of Deacon Ivan Fedorov and Peter Mstislavets, who published a fine edition of *The Apostles* in 1564 with beautiful chapter heads and illuminations. The printing establishment was burned by mobs incited by some envious high officials and ignorant clergymen, and the printers had to flee for their lives to Lithuania.

[9]*Grand Cheti Minyei (Lives of the Saints)* were instructing and eulogistic discourses intended for daily reading. Makarii completed this grandiose twelve-volume collection in 1552. It covers about 1,300 lives, and contains about 27,000 pages. The largest of the three existing copies was destined for the Uspenskii Cathedral in the Kremlin. The second copy is in the library of the St. Petersburg (Leningrad) Religious Academy.

[10]Silvester, a Novgorod priest who was brought to Moscow in 1547 by the Metropolitan Makarii, was archpriest and dean of the Blagoveshchenskii Cathedral. He was the mentor of Ivan IV, over whom he exercised considerable influence. His political career was cut short in 1553 because of his opposition to the Livonian War undertaken by the Tsar. He was imprisoned in the Solovetskii Monastery, where he died about 1566.

[11]*Domostroi* (house orderer) came to mean "a guide for living." The word also was used for a book aimed to regiment behavior to the smallest detail, providing a religious, moral, and practical life pattern for the family under the guidance of the master of the house—the father and husband. It determined the usages and customs of the land for generations and was instrumental in excluding women from public life, relegating them to separate quarters in the house, the *terem.* (See note 1.)

[12]Prince A. M. Kurbskii (died 1583) was a descendant of the House of Rurik, associated with Silvester and Adashev in the elected council during the reform period in the reign of Ivan IV. He was commander-in-chief of the Muscovite armies in the Livonian War. His desertion to Lithuania was followed almost immediately by the establishment of the *oprichnina* (a portion of the state domains allotted by Ivan to himself, to be governed by a strictly separate administration). Kurbskii was the author of *The History of the Grand Prince of Moscow,* written during the 1560's and 1570's in

Lithuania, which provoked the famous epistolary duel between Kurbskii and Ivan IV.

[13]These descriptions, as well as those of Anthony Jenkison, Ambassador Jeremy Bowes, and Horsey and Rose, are given in the voluminous *Principal Navigations of Richard Hakluyt.*

[14]P. Miliukov, *Outlines of Russian Culture,* pt. iii, p. 38.

[15]For Ushakov's detailed description (1672) of the frescoes, see Bartenev, *Kreml',* vol. ii, pp. 183–193; also Grabar'-Muratov, vol. vi, p. 320. The original manuscript was deposited in the Imperial Public Library, Petersburg, in 1867.

[16]R. Wipper, *Ivan Grozny,* p. 60.

[17]Viskovaty, Ivan IV's state secretary, brought up the matter of the "heretical" novelties in icon painting before the Ecclesiastical Council of a Hundred Chapters *(Stoglav sobor)* of 1554. The issue was debated at length and caused much bitterness, but the Metropolitan Makarii succeeded in proving to Viskovaty that his misgivings were groundless, causing him to withdraw his accusations. For the "Affair Viskovaty," see N. V. Pokrovskii, *Pamiatniki Khristianskoi ikonographii i iskusstva (Monuments of Christian Iconography and Art),* pp. 335 ff.; also Ivan Zabelin, *Domashnii byt russkikh tsarei,* pt. i, p. 149.

[18]Bartenev, *op. cit.,* vol. ii, p. 234.

[19]Artamon Matveev, the son of a deacon, was adviser to Tsar Aleksei. He was one of the best-educated men of his day, a lover of music and literature. His Scottish wife entertained at her home some of the more progressive Russian noblemen, the tsar himself often appearing at her musicals. When the Ukrainian War began, Tsar Aleksei made Matveev minister of Ukrainian affairs and guardian of the Sovereign Seal.

[20]The Orthodox Church forbids the placing of altars over living quarters, much less over a theater.

[21]Bartolomeo Rastrelli (1700–1771), the son of an Italian-French emigré, was one of the great architects and founders of the baroque school in Russia.

[22]A new plan of Moscow was devised and approved by Catherine II in 1775. The most important measures, taken in accordance with this plan, were the removal of the walls and towers of Belyi-Gorod (White City), located immediately west and north of the Kremlin, and the creation of the Tver'skaia Ploshchad' (Square) and Boulevard.

[23]Grigorii Orlov was one of the leaders in the *coup d'etat* that deposed Emperor Peter III and put the latter's wife Catherine on the throne. A notorious, unhibited playboy and rake, Orlov became the empress' lover and rose to a position of great influence and power during the first half of Catherine's reign.

[24]For a more detailed description of the project and the life and work of Bazhenov, see V. Snegirev, *Arkhitektor V. I. Bazhenov,* pp. 56–80; see also Grabar', vol. iii.

[25]Edward Daniel Clarke, *Travels in Europe, Asia and Africa,* part i; Russia Tartary and Turkey, pp. 128–129.

[26]The model is now in the Museum of the Academy of Architecture, Moscow.

[27]Count Uvarov was Minister of Public Instruction during the reign of Nicholas I.

[28]The Decembrists were a secret revolutionary society of young liberal officers who advocated political and social reforms, by peaceful means if possible, by force if necessary. Their unsuccessful *coup d'etat* took place on the 26th of December, 1825, hence the name "Decembrists."

[29]Konstantin Andreevich Thon (Ton) (1794–1881) was an architect educated in the St. Petersburg Academy of Fine Arts. He began his professional career as a neoclassicist, but later became the leader of the movement back to the "Byzantine-Russian" style and official interpreter of the "national" style.

[30]The Church of Christ the Saviour *(Khram Khrista Spasitel'ia),* designed in the Russian-Byzantine style by Thon and built in 1838 near the Kremlin, was taken down in the 1930's to make room for the proposed Palace of the Soviets.

The sculptures and the carved decorative details of the church were dismantled and put into a museum.

[31]During the costly war with Poland, it was decided to mint copper coins at the same face value as the usual silver ones. This led to a tremendous rise in the cost of living and brought about the uprising, during which some seven thousand persons were killed.

VIII. ART TREASURES

[1]*Oruzheinaia, Oruzhnichia*—from *oruzhie,* "arms or weapons"; *palata*—"chamber" or "hall." Hence the Hall of Arms, and by extension the Bureau of Arms Manufacture.

[2]Viollet le Duc, *L'art russe,* p. 88.

[3]Archdeacon Paul of Aleppo accompanied Patriarch Macarius of Antioch on his visit to Russia during the reign of Aleksei Mikhailovich, arriving in Moscow in 1654. He left a detailed journal. (See *The Travels of Macarius in the 17th Century;* see also Kondakov, *The Russian Icon,* pp. 189–191.)

[4]Jacques Margeret's description of the tsar's treasury is quoted by Alfred Maskell in *Russian Art,* pp. 119–120 from Margeret's book *Estat de l'empire de Russie.*

[5]*Kazennyi*—from *kazna,* signifying "treasure." *Dvor*—literally "yard" and, by extension, "office," "bureau"; hence "office in charge of the state treasure."

[6]S. Stroganov was a scion of the great Stroganov family of merchant princes that accumulated much wealth in the sixteenth century by exploiting the region of the Kama River and the northern Urals. The family contributed greatly to the conquest of Siberia (1584) and established itself in Perm in 1740. The early Stroganovs were keen patrons of art and collected around them a number of painters. Their name is associated with that of the seventeenth-century school of icon painting.

[7]Hakluyt, *Principal Navigations,* vol. ii, pp. 229, 230.

[8]In medieval Russia the word *diak* meant "functionary," "secretary." The word *diak* is of the same origin as the English "deacon." *Dumnyi diak* meant executive secretary of the Boyar's Council.

[9]Patriarch Nikon was born Nikita of peasant origin. He began his clerical career as a parish priest, took the orders, and assumed the name of Nikon. He was named metropolitan of Novgorod in 1648, elevated by Tsar Aleksei Mikhailovich to the patriarchate in 1652. His correction of the holy books and religious texts brounght about the great schism *(raskol).*

[10]Icon painters have from early times divided their work into the drawing of the face *(lichnoe* from *lik* or *litso,* "face") and the preliminary drawing that comes before the face *(dolichnoe),* that is, the backgrounds and figures. The helper or pupil *(dolichnik)* painted the preliminary part, and left the face and the finishing for the master face painter *(lichnik).* This was done even in detailed and many-figured icons but especially in icons with one figure. Later the work was even further divided: the master designer *(znamenshchik)* outlined the composition; a helper covered the panel with gesso *(levkas,* a layer of gypsum and glue); a senior artist painted the face *(lik);* a junior artist filled in the vestments and background *(dolichnoe);* another junior did the gilding or silvering; and still another junior painted the ornament *(travy).*

[11]Archpriest Avvakum (Habakkuk), the leader of the Old Believer opposition, was a talented and prolific writer produced by the schism. For a most interesting sketch of the life and works of this remarkable man, see N. K. Gudzy, *History of Early Russian Literature,* pp. 378–396; also *The Life of Archpriest Avvakum by Himself.*

[12]*Parsunnoe*—from *persona,* "person," *pis'mo*—literally "letter," "writing," but used here in the sense of "painting." Hence *parsunnoe pis'mo* means "portrait painting."

[13]V. K. Trutovskii, director of the Oruzheinaia Palata at the beginning of the twentieth century, in "Boyarin i oruzhnichii Bogdan Matveevich Khitrovo i Moskovskaia Oruzheinaia Palata," ("Boyarin and Armorer B. M. Khitrovo and the Oruzheinaia Palata"). *Starye Gody,* July, 1909, p. 366.

[14]A. I. Nesterov was assistant (in 1660) to Khitrovo, superintendent of the Oruzheinaia Palata.

[15]*Sirin,* a legendary bird of paradise with the head of a man, is one of the oldest decorative motifs in Russian art.

[16]Sigmund von Herberstein was ambassador from Germany to the court of the Grand Prince Vasilii Ivanovich in 1517 and again in 1526. (See his travel notes *Rerum Moscoviticarum Commentarii,* vol. i, pp. 95–96, 105–106; vol.ii, pp. 131–132.)

[17]Bartenev, vol. ii, p. 324.

[18]Trutovskii, *Starye Gody,* July, 1909, p. 348.

IX. THE RED SQUARE

[1]L. Kovalev, ed., *Moskva,* p. 150.

[2]For a description of corporal punishment and public executions in medieval Moscow, see V. V. Nechaev, "Street Life in Moscow of the XVI-XVII Centuries," *Moskva,* vol. iii, pp. 66–68.

[3]The Stoglav Council (Stoglav sobor) was convened by Ivan IV to bring before a council of the clergy a list of all the various abuses visible in Church and State and to ask their coöperation in reforming them. The decisions of the council were divided into a hundred chapters *(stoglav),* hence its name. (See also note 17, chap. vii.)

[4]On Palm Sunday, before the communion service, a holy procession, from the Cathedral of the Assumption in the Kremlin, depicted the entrance of Jesus into Jerusalem, in which the patriarch rode upon an ass to St. Basil's and thence to the Lobnoe Mesto. In this procession —headed by children singing hosanna, followed by white-robed priests carrying church banners, processional crosses, and icons, by boyars waving palm branches—the patriarch's mount was humbly led by the magnificently attired tsar.

[5]Barma and Posnik (Postnik) Iakovlev. Barma was evidently the senior architect because he is mentioned in seventeenth-century chronicles as working with a group of collaborators or "comrades" *(s tovarishchi).*

[6]V. A. Nikol'skii, *Staraia Moskva (Old Moscow),* p. 53.

[7]I. Grabar', *Protection of Cultural Monuments in the USSR.*

[8]Among them are Sverdlov, Frunze, Krasin, Dzerzhinsky, Maxim Gorki, and the American poet John Reed. Urns containing the ashes of some of the Bolshevik leaders are housed in special niches in the Kremlin wall.

[9]Aleksei Viktorovich Shchusev (1872–1949) was a graduate of the Russian Academy of Fine Arts. He was awarded a traveling fellowship and studied at the Atelier Julien, Paris. A member of the Russian Archaeological Society, a student and admirer of Russian national architecture, Shchusev was one of the most gifted and prolific of his profession —a happy combination of the learned archaeologist, practical builder, and sensitive artist. He designed the Kazan' Railway Station in Moscow, the Marx-Engels-Lenin Institute at Tbilisi, the Academy of Science in Moscow. In 1941 he was awarded the Stalin Prize First Class and named Laureate of the Stalin Prize in architecture.

BIBLIOGRAPHY

ARCHITECTURE

Ainalov. Dmitrii Vlas'evich, *Geschichte der russischen Monumentalkunst.* Berlin, 1932–1933.

Akademiia khudozhestv, Petrograd, *Monuments de l'art ancien russe.* St. Petersburg, 1908–1912.

Alpatov, Mikhail, *Geschichte der altrussichen Kunst.* Augsburg, *circa* 1932.

Bartenev, S. P., *Moskovskii Kreml' v starinu i teper' (The Moscow Kremlin, Past and Present).* St. Petersburg, 1912–1918.

Vol. I: *Historical Outline of Its Fortifications, Walls, and Towers.*

Vol. II: *The Court of the First Grand Princes and Tsars of the House of Rurik.*

——, *Bols'hoi Kremlevskii Dvorets (The Grand Kremlin Palace).* Moscow, 1909.

Bernshtein, E., *Moskovskii Kreml' v XVII veke (The Moscow Kremlin in the Seventeenth Century).* Moscow, 1947.

Cross, Samuel Hazzard, *Mediaeval Russian Churches.* Cambridge, Mass., 1949.

Lectures, sponsored by the Mediaeval Academy of America, delivered at the Fogg Museum, Harvard University, in 1933.

Fabritsius, M. P., *Kreml' v Moskve, Ocherki i kartiny proshlago i nastoiashchago (The Kremlin in Moscow, Descriptive Sketches and Pictures of the Past and Present).* Vol. I, Moscow, 1883.

Good source of nontechnical data on Kremlin architecture, art, and history. Pen and ink drawings by Vishnevskii, Svetoslavskii, and others; photographs by Panov.

Grabar', Igor (ed.), *Istoriia russkago iskusstva (History of Russian Art).* Moscow, 1910.
Vol. I: *Pre-Petrine epoch.*
Vol. II: *Pre-Petrine epoch, Moscow and Ukraine.*

Ivanov, V. N., P. N. Maksimov, and S. A. Toropov, *Sokrovishcha russkoi arkhitektury* (Treasures of Russian Architecture). Moscow, 1950.

Leger, Louis Paul Marie, *Moscou.* Paris, 1910.

Lo Gatto, Ettore, *Gli artisti italiani in Russia.* Rome, 1934–1943.

Lukomskii (Loukomski), Georgii K., *L'Architecture religieuse russe du XIe siècle au XVIIe siècle.* Paris, 1929.

——, *Le Kreml de Moscou.* Paris, 1928 (?).

Moskva, Sobory, monastyri i tserkvi (Moscow, Cathedrals, Monasteries, and Churches). Moscow, *circa* 1880.
Collection of plates.

Moskva v eia proshlom i nastoiashchem (Moscow, Past and Present). Moscow, 1910–1917.
Extensive collection of articles and historical essays on the Kremlin and Moscow from the earliest times to the twentieth century. The authors: historians, political scientists, economists, and art critics.

Novitskii, A., *Istoriia russkago iskusstva, s drevneishikh vremen (A History of Russian Art from Antiquity to the Last Part of the Nineteenth Century).* Moscow, 1903.

Okunev, N. L., *Pamiatniki russkago iskusstva Moskovskoi epokhi (Monuments of Russian Art of the Moscow Epoch).* St. Petersburg, 1913.
Collection of plates of cathedrals and palaces in Moscow and suburbs.

Pavlinov, Andrei Mikhailovich, *Istoriia russkoi arkhitektury . . . (History of Russian Architecture . . .).* Moscow, 1894.

Perchik, L., *Bolshevistskii plan rekonstruktsii Moskvy (The Bolshevist Plan for the Reconstruction of Moscow).* Moscow, 1935.

Réau, Louis, *L'Art russe.* Paris, 1921, 1922.
Vol. I: *L'Art russee des origines a Pierre le Grand.*
Vol. II: *L'Art russe de Pierre le Grand a nos jours.*

Rikhter, F. F., *Pamiatniki drevniago russkago zodchestva (Monuments of Ancient Russian Architecture).* Moscow, 1850.

Rzianin, M. I., *Arkhitekturnye ansambli Moskvy i Podmoskov'ia XIV-XIX veka (Architectural Ensembles of Moscow and Its Suburbs from the Fourteenth to the Nineteenth Century).* Moscow, 1950.

——, *Pamiatniki russkogo zodchestva (Monuments of Russian Architecture).* Moscow, 1950.

Shamuriny, Iu. and Z., *Moskva v eiia starine (Old Moscow); Kul'turnyia sokrovishcha Rossii (Cultural Treasures of Russia).* Moscow, 1915.

Snegirev, I. M., *Uspenskii Sobor v Moskve (Uspenskii Cathedral in Moscow).* Moscow, 1856.

Snegirev, V. L., *Arkhitektor V. I. Bazhenov; Ocherk zhizni i tvorchestva (Architect Bazhenov; An Outline of His Life and Works).* Moscow, 1937.

——, *Moskovskoe zodchestvo (Moscow Architecture).* Moscow, 1948.
Covers the period from the fourteenth to the nineteenth century.

Starye Gody (Yesteryears). St. Petersburg, 1907–1917. (A monthly review.)

Suslov, V. V., *Pamiatniki drevniago russkago zodchestva (Monuments of Ancient Russian Architecture).* St. Petersburg, 1897.
Five portfolios of photographs and measured drawings, many in colors.

——, *Tserkov' Vasiliia Blazhennago v Moskve (The Church of Basil the Blessed in Moscow).* St. Petersburg, 1912.

Vel'tman, A., *Dostopamiatnosti Moskovskago Kremlia (Memorable Fea-*

tures of the Moscow Kremlin). Moscow, 1843.

——, *Opisanie Novago Imperatorskago Dvortsa (Description of the New Imperial Palace).* Moscow, 1851.

——, *Description du nouveau palais imperial du Kreml' de Moscou.* Moscow, 1851.

Viollet le Duc, E., *L'Art russe, Ses origines, ses elements constitutifs, son apogee, son avenir.* Paris, 1877.

Voyce, Arthur, *Russian Architecture; Trends in Nationalism and Modernism.* New York, 1948.

Zabelin, Ivan, *Cherty samobytnosti v drevne-russkom zodtchestve (Traits of Originality in Ancient Russian Architecture).* Moscow, 1900.

——, *Istoriia goroda Moskvy (A History of the City of Moscow).* Vol. I, Moscow, 1905.

DECORATIVE ART

Adelung F., *Risunki k puteshestviiu po Rossii barona Meierberga (Drawings Made During the Travels of Baron Mayerberg in Russia).* St. Petersburg, 1903.

Ainalov, D. V., *Istoriia drevne-russkago iskusstva (History of Ancient Russian Art).* St. Petersburg, 1915.

Barshchevskii, I. F., *Russkiia drevnosti (Russian Antiquities).* St. Petersburg, *circa* 1910.

Butovskii, *Istoriia russkago ornamenta (History of Russian Ornament from the Tenth to the Sixteenth Century).* Paris, 1873.

Conway, Martin, *Art Treasures in Soviet Russia.* London, 1925.

Georgievskii, W., "Ikony Ioanna Groznago ("The Icons of Ivan the Terrible"), *Starye Gody,* 1910, vol. 4, no. 11.

Kondakov, N. P., *Russkaia ikona (The Russian Icon).* Prague, 1933.

Lukomskii (Loukomski), G. K., *L'Art décoratif russe.* Paris, 1928.

Maskell, Alfred, *Russian Art and Art Objects in Russia. A Handbook.* London, 1884.

Minns, Ellis, H., *The Russian Icon.* Oxford, 1927. (A shortened translation of N. P. Kondakov's *Russkaia ikona).*

Mir Iskusstva (The World of Art). St. Petersburg, 1899–1904. (A monthly review).

Nekrasov, A., *Ocherki dekorativnogo iskusstva drevnei Rusi (Outlines of Decorative Art of Ancient Russia).* Moscow, 1924.

Novitskii, A., *Istoriia russkago iskusstva s drevneishikh vremen (A History of Russian Art from the Earliest Times to the Last Part of the Nineteenth Century).* Moscow, 1903.

Pokrovskii, N., *Zametki o pamiatnikakh pskovskoi tserkovnoi stariny (Notes on Monuments of Pskovian Ecclesiastical Antiquity).* Moscow, 1914.

Polonskaia, N. D., *Istoriko-Kul'turnyi Atlas po russkoi Istorii s obiasnitel'nym tekstom (A Historical-Cultural Atlas of Russian History with Explanatory Text).* Kiev, 1913.

Prokhorov, V., *Materialy po istorii russkikh odezhd i obstanovki zhizni narodnoi (Materials on the History of Russian Costume and Environmental Articles in the Life of the People).* St. Petersburg, 1881–1885.

Réau, Louis, *L'Art russe.* Paris, 1921, 1922.

Vol. I: *L'Art russee des origines a Pierre le Grand.*

Vol. II: *L'Art russe de Pierre le Grand a nos jours.*

Simakov, N., *Russkii ornament v starinnykh obraztsakh khudozhestvenno-promyshlennago proizvodstva (Russian Ornament in Ancient Objects of Industrial Art).* St. Petersburg, 1882.

Solntsev, F. G. [illustrator], *Drevnosti rossiiskago gosudarstva (Antiquities of the Rusisan Empire).* Moscow, 1849–1853.

More than five hundred plates in color. Edited by Sergei Stroganov,

Mikhail Zagoskin, Ivan Snegirev, and Alexander Vel'tman.
Tserkovno-istoricheskie pamiatniki i vklady doma Romanovykh Moskovskago perioda (Ecclesiastical-Historical Monuments and Contributions of the House of Romanov during the Moscow Period). Moscow, 1890 (?).
Vel'tman, A., *Moskovskaia oruzheinaia palata (The Moscow [Kremlin] Armory).* Moscow, 1860.
Viollet le Duc, E., *L'Art russe, Ses origines, ses elements constitutifs, son apogee, son avenir.* Paris, 1877.

CHURCH AND RELIGION

Fedotov, G. P., *The Russian Religious Mind.* Cambridge, Mass., 1946.
Golubinskii, E., *Istoriia russkoi tserkvi (History of the Russian Church).* Moscow, 1881.
Stanley, Arthur Penrhyn, *Lectures on the History of the Eastern Church.* New York, 1884.

HISTORY

Grekov, B. D., (ed.), *Istoriia SSSR (History of the USSR).* Moscow, 1947.
Kliuchevskii, V., *Kurs russkoi istorii (A Course in Russian History).* Moscow, 1923.
Likhachev, D. S., *Kul'tura Rusi epokhi obrazovaniia russkogo natsional'nogo gosudarstva (The Culture of Rus of the Epoch of the Formation of the Russian National State).* Moscow, 1946.
Miliukov, Paul, *Ocherki po istorii russkoi kul'tury (Essays in the History of Russian Culture).* Paris, 1930–1937.
Mirsky, D. S., *Russia, a Social History.* New York, 1930.
Pokrovsky, M. N., *History of Russia; From the Earliest Times to the Rise of Commercial Capitalism.* New York, 1931.
Rambaud, A., *History of Russia.* Boston, 1888 (?).
Solov'ev, S. M., *Istoriia Rossii s drevneishikh vremen (A History of Russia from Earliest Times).* Moscow, 1851–1853.
Waliszewski, K., *Le Berceau d'une dynastie, les premiers Romanov, 1613–1682.* Paris, 1909.
Zabelin, Ivan, *Domashnii byt russkikh tsarei (Home Life of the Russian Tsars).* Pt. II, Moscow, 1915.

INDEX

MOSCOVIA VRBS METRO
Moscva seu Moscouia urbs, Russiæ albæ seu magni Ducatus Moscouiæ metropolis, ob amplitudinem etiam à Botero quatuor maximus Europæ urbibus accensita, Constantinopolique, Lutetiæ, Vlyssiponæ, quarta addita; in quatuor partes diuiditur. Primæ, eique intimæ Kitaigorod, secundæ Bielgorod nomen, utrique suo peculiari muro circumdatæ, tertiæ Skorodum, quarta Strelecka Sloboda: aggere omnes, seu Palancka, è lignis et terra congesto atque repleto, perpulchris cum turribus, circumcinctæ. Tribus integris horis ab expedito equite circuiri uix potest. In meditullio ferè urbis, inter Moscuam et Negelinam fluuios, magni Ducis arx sita est Czargoroda nuncupata, perampla magnaque. In qua templa XVIII. e cæmento et lapide exstructa, totidem turribus, tectis inauratis, insignia, adspectu gratissima. Templa uero urbis partim è latere, partim lignea magno numero domus ligneæ omnes. Nemini enim è cæmento aut lapide ædificare, fas, nisi quòd Proceribus aliquot, et primarijs mercatoribus in atrijs suis licet certum quoddam Conclaue seu receptaculum exstruere, laterttio opere fornicato, paruum atque humile, in quod incendio grassante, charissima quæque sibi et pretiosissima congerant atque recondant. Angli etiam Hollandi et ex Hanseaticis urbibus mercatores quique præcipui merces suas ibi deponunt, distrahendis ibidem pannis, mercimonijs sericis, et aromatibus grauí admodum negotiatores. Incolæ ad negotiationes propensissimi, sed perquam fraudulenti, aliquanto etiam politiores seu ciuiliores sunt alijs huius terræ habitatoribus.
Quarta pars urbis uersus Austrum vocata Strelecka Sloboda
14
MOSQVA
13
Inuen. F. P. A. cæl. L. Kilian. A. Inpend. utriusque.
cum S.C.M. priuilegio.